Raising the Bottom Line

LONGMAN SERIES IN PUBLIC COMMUNICATION

Series Editor: **Ray Eldon Hiebert**

RAISING THE BOTTOM LINE

Business Leadership in a Changing Society

Carlton E. Spitzer

Longman

New York & London

RAISING THE BOTTOM LINE
Business Leadership in a Changing Society

Longman Inc., 19 West 44th Street, New York, NY 10036
Associated companies, branches, and representatives
throughout the world.

Development Editor: Gordon T.R. Anderson
Editorial and Design Supervisor: Frances Althaus
Manufacturing and Production Supervisor: Anne Musso

Library of Congress Cataloging in Publication Data

Spitzer, Carlton E.
  Raising the bottom line.

  (Longman series in public communication)
  Includes index.
  1. Industry — Social aspects — United States.
I. Title.   II. Series.
HD60.5.U5S64   658.4'08   81-14308
ISBN 0-582-28241-1   AACR2

Manufactured in the United States of America

9 8 7 6 5 4 3 2 1

To the Spitzer family, near and far, especially ...
Margaret Carney Spitzer
and
Robert Franklin Spitzer

Contents

Foreword

You have to admire Carl Spitzer's courage. He has been through the wars on the corporate social responsibility movement, and he still comes back asking for more. A masochist, some cynics might conclude. In his quest to find moral creatures among the corporate behemoths, he gets little sustenance from business leaders ("Our social responsibility is to make a profit and provide jobs"), the media ("Are you kidding? Those guys are in it for the bucks"), or the academicians. The latter bunch, for the most part, particularly resists suggestions that corporate social responsibility is worthy of serious attention.

Their resistance breaks into two camps. One is the Milton Friedman line of the defense discussed in Chapter 2. This simply says that social concerns are of no concern to the managers of a company; their job is to run the business well — and not make social decisions. The second school is more important in terms of the objections it raises. This camp is made up of economists, sociologists, and political scientists, many of whom are critics of the capitalist system and who might be expected to favor reforms in the corporate world. However, when they cast their Ph.D.-clouded eyes on efforts to make companies more socially responsible, they usually end up saying it's a waste of time, akin to the influence of a flea on the back of a rhino. As a matter of fact, Edward S. Herman says that programs to apply constraints on corporate behavior, even if adopted, "would be the equivalent of second-order fleas [flea on the flea] on the back of a rhino."

Herman is professor of finance at one of the nation's leading business schools, the Wharton School at the University of Pennsylvania, and he made this characterization in his book, *Corporate Control, Corporate Power* (Cambridge University Press, 1981). Herman comes down in the end to agreeing with the brilliant English essayist William Hazlitt, who wrote in 1824:

> Corporate bodies are more corrupt and profligate than individuals, because they have more power to do mischief, and are less amenable to disgrace or punishment. They feel neither shame, remorse, gratitude, nor good-will.

Herman concludes then, after looking at modern efforts to tame the corporation, that it's not possible — short of mobilizing great power against business interests. He says (and would certainly say after reading Carl Spitzer's book): "It is easy to conjure up proposals for altering corporate power structures; it is quite another thing to get such proposals enacted in forms that retain any bite." And Herman's final, despairing advice for us is this:

> The hope for the future must be that a series of survivable small shocks or minor catastrophies will occur, leading to the emergence of new ideologies, values, and institutional arrangements that will strengthen the powers of small groups and nations to protect themselves and to cope with the lack of international authority. The autonomy and power of the business system, the weakness of government, and the resultant immobility of the whole are such, however, that a bleaker forecast is plausible.

Thank you very much, Professor Herman.

Carl Spitzer doesn't see things the same way Professor Herman does. He would like to see new ideologies, values, and institutional arrangements come to pass in the business world without having to go through some "survivable small shocks or minor catastrophies." As he points out in Chapter 1, the roots of modern corporate social responsibility sprang from the shocks of the 1960s. (Those shocks were, I guess, survivable — but who needs to look for more of them?) At the end of the 1960s, there appeared to be a realization, as Carl puts it, that "never again could business operate in a vacuum, separate and apart from the social aspirations and basic needs of the people." A lot of us felt that way at the time. I know because I was one of this crowd. Social responsibility, we felt, was about to come into its own — in the business world.

In 1968, I started a newsletter, *Business & Society*, that said in its first issue:

> The winds of change are now blowing vigorously through American society. So vigorously are they blowing that the entire posture of U.S. business is undergoing a radical transformation. The new watchword

in American business is "social responsibility." Corporate leaders today preach this gospel the way their predecessors preached "free enterprise." It's quite clear, in fact, that "free enterprise" no longer serves as the slogan of American business. Corporate goals have changed.

That's the way we saw it then. We were a little optimistic, some might say even naive. In any case, the early 1970s brought Richard M. Nixon and the Watergate caper, which flushed out stories of big corporations whose sense of social responsibility was so dim that they willingly flouted the law to pay bribes and make other undercover payments to curry favor with politicians here and abroad. I wrote my newsletter for six years before giving it up because the audience was so small (850 subscribers) that it made no economic sense to continue its publication. Its work survives in a quarterly publication, *Business and Society Review*, to which I contribute.

My newsletter was not the only casualty of this period. In 1969, *Business Week,* the flagship magazine of McGraw-Hill, launched an annual competition honoring companies for their social actions. The business response to this competition was so feeble that it lasted only a year. "It was not so easy to be a good business citizen and earn a dividend in 1970 as it had been in 1969," said *Business Week's* publisher, confirming the view of left-wing critics that when times get tough economically, the first thing business throws out is its social commitment.

Still, Carl Spitzer hung in there, working on various fronts, in different cities, in good times and bad, always confronting business people not with moral preachments but with practical recommendations for social actions they could take that would improve the communities in which they worked and lived. He never gave up hope — and this book is his latest testament to a sunny optimism that Carl Spitzer, for one, believes they can be social leaders.

Ideology is not something Carl Spitzer gets hung up on. He's pragmatic. He refuses to be frustrated. He looks for the good that people and companies and institutions can do. Managers in business usually turn away when they hear the word "ethics" mentioned. Carl Spitzer manages the difficult art of impregnating concrete programs of action with ethical content. I recently saw Bill Moyers interview Dame Rebecca West on television. Moyers, at the end of the interview, asked Rebecca West if she could characterize the turmoil of our times. She replied instantly: "A desperate search for pattern."

Raising the Bottom Line is Carl Spitzer's contribution to our search for a pattern.

Milton Moskowitz
July 1981

Preface

Businessmen are raising the bottom line to achieve social as well as economic goals; to engage fully in the external affairs of the communities in which they invest, employ, and sell.

Raising the bottom line is not a public affairs program. It is no longer a response to outside pressure. It is, rather, the meshing of social and economic planning in America.

The neglect of fermenting social needs by both business and government created an undercurrent that erupted in the domestic riots of the sixties. That violence was the catalyst for raising the bottom line.

Government enacted virtually thousands of regulations in the sixties and seventies because that is what government does under attack when private initiatives are wanting. Since the late sixties, business leaders have come to realize that the change in society is permanent and constructive. They have exercised leadership, demonstrated public accountability, and the regulations are coming down.

But our problems are far from being solved.

Racism is there, beneath the surface most of the time but emerging occasionally in all its ugliness with cross burnings and cruelties.

Inflation haunts us; the average citizen is hard-pressed to meet daily expenses, much less purchase a home or put money away.

Unemployment is up, and crime rates are up. Investment is down.

Minority citizens are hardest hit: minority-owned businesses receive less than 1 percent of gross business receipts in America; minority unemployment in urban centers is as high as 40 percent, even higher among minority youth.

Black-on-black crime is alarming: the leading cause of death for a black male under twenty-five years of age is murder.

The United States of America must cling together to preserve its freedoms, to constantly address its long-term domestic problems, and to strive for harmony among nations, even as it maintains a strong national defense.

To do all these things, it must regard the bottom line in a new light.

Traditionally, the bottom line has required a single-minded devotion to profits. Profits enable the company to invest, employ, pay taxes, and satisfy shareowners. Profits pay bonuses and support the United Way.

Business profits have also contributed to the social progress of the nation. But business has been a modest philanthropist, not a full participant in relating social and economic goals to assure the preservation of the private enterprise system and the nation as a whole.

The bottom line remains; profits are the essential ingredient in raising the bottom line to accommodate the profound and permanent changes in our society. Business is not asked to forsake its own goals in raising the bottom line, but rather to identify its legitimate aspirations within the context of broad national objectives.

All of this is happening. This book is not so much an appeal as a report on the leadership business executives are exercising to raise the bottom line.

The book describes activity since the riots of the sixties. It reflects on the shortcomings as well as the achievements of business. Through interviews, case studies, and personal observations, some of the men and women who have struggled to raise the bottom line during the past fifteen years have helped the author set forth a limited version of what occurred, what was done, and what is being done to strengthen business-government relations in order to preserve and improve our way of life.

It is a personal account, reflecting the imperfections and struggles and hard decisions of people in a free society.

Many people in industry are searching for ways to raise the bottom line to meet public expectations. They seek to create a "Neutral Zone" in which they can make progress with government officials toward the solution of controversial issues. They are determined to harmonize relationships between business and government at every level and to redefine the role of business in society. Working with other private institutions and nonprofit organizations, they also hope to renew the diminishing spirit of independence and innovation that has characterized the Republic for more than 200 years.

A number of fellow searchers have shared their experiences and files and speculated with me about what might have been and what may yet unfold. I am grateful for their interest and critical assistance.

For their wise counsel and extraordinary insights, I am especially thankful to Donald C. MacNaughton, Augustine R. Marusi, Luther H. Hodges, Jr., Arthur H. White, Daniel Yankelovich, Thomas K. Hamall, James T. McCrory, Raymond Simon, Dan H. Fenn, Jr., Milton Moskowitz, Charles Seib, James Langton, and John W. Gardner.

For arranging interviews, and offering helpful suggestions and encouragement, I owe special thanks to Richard C. Spitzer, Lee Goodman, and Walter Coyne.

For taking on extra burdens in the office and at home to permit me to work on this book, I express my deepest appreciation to Joan and Amy Spitzer, Susan Hodge and Kathryn Alim. Deborah Bongiorno read drafts and offered valuable suggestions.

For their time and interest in sitting for interviews, responding to lengthy correspondence, and providing essential background information, I am indebted to Clifford Anderson, Donald Anderson, A.R. Angelos, Richard Armstrong, Denise Baken, Judy Jones Barker, Walter Barlow, Don Bates, Clarence Bishop, Sherwood Boehlert, Floyd Bragg, Morton Calvert, Major Clark III, Joseph Colmen, Robert Colodzin, Virginia Doscher, William Duke, Walter D. Eichner, Jose Antonio Font, Paul S. Forbes, Glen Ford, Herbert Fowler, Peter Gamble, Earl G. Graves, Jur-1 Hall, the late Ellis Haller, Samuel Halperin, John E. Hansan, Anthony Hatch, Jamie Heard, Anne L. Howard, Isabelle Hyde, James Joseph, Stanley G. Karson, Alan Katzenstein, the late Walter King, E.B. "Burt" Knauft, Lee Lawrence, Morton Lebow, Franklin Lett, F. Peter Libassi, Norman V. Lourie, William Marcussen, Frederic Markowitz, Louis Martin, Richard "Max" McCarthy, Harry McCoy, John A. McDermott, James McLean, Kim McQuaid, John Meagher, Martha H. Mitchell, Parren Mitchell, John Naisbitt, Richard R. Neblett, Leo Northart, Horace Ogden, Helen O'Rourke, Alan Pinado, Elsa Porter, Bernard Posner, the late Dion Rahill, Margaret Z. Richardson, William A. Ridpath, Alan Clement Spitzer, Edward Sprague, Richard Swantek, the late Hobart Taylor, Jr., Edward Tormay, Carol Townsend, Anne Wexler, Franklin H. Williams, Joseph Williams, Thomas Williams, Fritz Witti, Adam Yarmolinsky, and Paul Ylvisaker.

Most especially, I thank Gordon T.R. Anderson and Ray E. Hiebert for inviting me to write this book and for their wise and helpful counsel throughout.

Finally, I thank my father, Rudolph Spitzer, for his unfailing support and example.

Carlton E. Spitzer

PART ONE

Public
Accountability

WEBSTER'S NEW WORLD DICTIONARY

bottom line 1. the bottom line of the earnings report of a company on which a net profit per share of stock is shown   **2.** [Colloq.] profits or losses, as of a business   **3.** [Slang]   *a)* the basic or most important factor, consideration, meaning, etc.   *b)* the final or ultimate statement, decision, etc. — **bot'tom-line' adj.**

THE FINAL OR ULTIMATE STATEMENT

"I didn't agree with Friedman. I didn't see how a large corporation such as Atlantic Richfield Company, employing nearly 30,000 people and affecting the lives of hundreds of thousands more, could isolate itself from the social changes that were affecting our country so deeply. We had seen the country torn apart in the sixties over foreign and domestic issues, particularly Vietnam and civil rights. And I felt that my company had to be involved, had to intervene usefully where it could — without, of course, ignoring the need to make a profit, the sine qua non of our existence."

THORNTON F. BRADSHAW
JUNE 9, 1976

Chapter One

Searching for the "Neutral Zone"

The eighties began as the sixties had ended. Riots erupted in American cities. A black leader was shot down from ambush and left for dead.

Violent and white-collar crime were on the rise.

Unemployment, especially among minority youth, had reached epidemic numbers.

Inflation and declining markets for basic products, such as automobiles and houses, put the nation in an economic spin.

Students marched against proposed draft registration.

Industry railed against too much government intrusion in the marketplace.

Government hit out at industry for its poor performance in protecting the environment, safeguarding workers, and applying profits to socially oriented needs.

The oil companies took advertisements to explain their abundant riches and their efforts to find new sources of energy.

The nation, tired of big government and disenchanted with big business, began to seek local remedies through popular vote.

The goals of the sixties had become the demands of the early seventies and, as Daniel Yankelovich would say, the perceived entitlements of citizens, even before the end of the decade.

Citizens believed the government owed them health care, enough to eat, a place to live, and a decent job because they were residents of the greatest nation on Earth.

3

The changes in public attitude equaled the rapid pace of technological advances. Yet, man's basic problems remained the same: disharmony, racism, strife.

The sixties had ended as the eighties had begun: an incumbent President struggling under the weight of negative opinion polls, fighting attacks from within his own party; racial tensions in urban centers bubbling near the surface; and violence, death, and looting in the streets of many cities.

Vernon Jordan, the leader of the National Urban League, was shot in the back from ambush outside a Fort Wayne, Indiana, motel. He recovered.

On April 4, 1968, the Reverend Martin Luther King, Jr., was shot from ambush on a motel balcony in Memphis. He died almost instantly from a powerful rifle bullet that smashed his jaw and throat. And within a few weeks of King's murder, on June 5, Senator Robert Kennedy, brother of the assassinated President, John F. Kennedy, would be the victim of a handgun assault in a Los Angeles hotel while campaigning for the presidency. He died the following morning. The nation, already torn by domestic riots, a divisive war in Vietnam, faced a wild and violent Democratic political convention in Chicago.

It seemed to most observers that the splintering of America had occurred suddenly, almost without warning. People were preoccupied with their own lives and cares: jobs, raising kids, caring for older parents, making enough money, staying well.

When the buildings went up in smoke in Watts, Newark, Detroit, Cleveland, New York, Washington, Hartford, Plainfield, and other teeming racial hotbeds, the average citizen read his newspaper in disbelief and watched his television screen with growing horror and mounting anger.

How dare these people strike at America from within!

It would take many months for citizens to realize that the America that had erupted was not the America most of them lived in.

Westchester citizens, commuting to and from Manhattan, had glimpsed that 'other' world for years, of course, when the commuter trains stopped every morning and every afternoon at the 125th Street station in Harlem. One could peer over the *New York Times* or *Wall Street Journal* and see the other side of America living in dilapidated buildings; wash strung on lines across alleys; black and Puerto Rican kids playing in filth.

But the trains hurried on to Grand Central Station where the commuters dispersed to their plush offices along Park and Madison avenues, to the new buildings on Third Avenue, to the Avenue of the Americas and Rockefeller Center, and south to Wall Street.

Wall Street and 125th Street are not in the same country.

So great a tear in the fabric of American society did not develop quickly. The first punctures were invisible. Questions raised by blacks. Hopes expressed. Anger converted slowly to action. Blacks and other minorities talking together. Frustrations churning. People wanting to be equal and free. The ferment was brooding there is the bland Eisenhower years; in the all-white brotherhood dinners staged by civic leaders who gave their money and their hearts to the building of hospitals and parks and marinas, and whose walls were filled with awards and citations, and who always made certain that the rabbi was one of those who spoke on Brotherhood Day, along with the Catholic priest and the Protestant minister, but who did not ask why blacks were not present at the vast majority of brotherhood dinners at the time.

The good citizens who arranged the affairs unconsciously accepted the notion that racial distinctions in American society were acceptable. Later, the famed Kerner Commission was to articulate, "Two nations, one white, one black." It was no surprise to blacks.

Indifference was the norm. In upstate New York at the end of the fifties, hard-working representatives of local industries planned an industrial exposition to herald the "Soaring Sixties." Products of the future as well as the past were put on display. Employment needs were projected for the next decade.

There was not a black in attendance or a single black business represented in the week-long show. Nor did anyone even raise a question about their exclusion.

The nation was not so much callous as unseeing and compartmentalized. Most people were isolated from minority citizens. They did not see, did not know, did not speak with minority citizens.

Entertainers and sports heroes were the exceptions, people agreed. It had required a long and painful effort for blacks and other minorities to earn a place in the theater and in the sports arenas. But what did their success on the stage and in athletics have to do with minorities working in offices, or in the shops, or minorities running businesses or holding public office?

The rips and punctures in society were even more apparent in the sixties. Still, most people did not look up over their *Times* at the 125th Street station. Warnings were written and spoken but little heeded.

Unhappy people were always complaining, leaders sighed. Why didn't they stay in school and get an education? We all know about the welfare cheats. Get a job!

Look at our schools, minority leaders pleaded. Give us decent jobs, they said. Give us a fair chance.

Articles appeared in esoteric journals. James Langton at the Bank of America and Prof. Raymond Mack of Northwestern University delivered remarkably accurate analyses of future trouble if society did not recognize the clear warning signs. Black leaders, by then more vocal and strident, were not seen as men to be negotiated with, but as radicals to be put in their place.

The Vietnam war escalated and compounded tensions. Students fled to Canada. Other young men went to war either filled with patriotism or troubled about America's involvement. Other citizens marched on college campuses and in city streets, including the streets of the nation's Capital, and railed against the involvement of the United States. Then the riots sent the nation reeling.

And yet, in the turmoil, the signs of America's survival were evident. Formal organizations, such as the National Urban Coalition and the National Alliance of Businessmen, mobilized the power of business and government behind job training programs and housing renovations. Minorities were elected to the boards of directors of some of the largest corporations.

There was a determination to rectify long-standing injustices and an understanding — at least among most observers — that never again could business operate in a vacuum, separate and apart from the social aspirations and basic needs of the people.

Business and government officials began to assimilate the notion that the adversarial relationship that had characterized exchanges between the public and private sectors for generations must somehow be modified if the nation was to preserve its essential unity.

The questions hotly debated in the Congress, in boardrooms, and among still angry and absolutely determined black leaders centered on the means of pulling the nation together without destroying its pluralism or restricting its freedoms.

At the start, businessmen were persuaded to do "the right thing." They did not immediately see, even after the riots, that they were moving in a permanent new direction. They were not simply being asked to take on a new philanthropic role, or respond to a passing crisis, or temporarily improve relationships with government snoops and demanding black leaders, but to face up to the consequences of national neglect and blatant indifference of which they were a part.

It was John W. Gardner, in his role as secretary of Health, Education, and Welfare, who cautioned the nation to find solutions, not villains. "There are no villains, only victims," he would say to his colleagues and repeat in his speeches and essays.

Gardner, perhaps more than any other leader of his time, saw that the strength of America, its pluralism, was also its weakness.

The splintering of America by special interest groups had begun, fed by the political processes the nation's founders had assured. But special interests had proliferated wildly and grown in such strength in municipalities, counties, states, and on the national scene that a well-organized single-issue group could spell the difference between victory and defeat for candidates in many local and congressional campaigns.

Fear of losing, rather than personal conviction, often dictated the actions of elected officials.

"I can't help my constituents if I'm not elected," they would shrug, "so I must do and say whatever is necessary to win. Then I shall vote my convictions."

Nonsense, of course. The premise is void of any conviction.

But the pressures on elected officials were powerful, if not truly novel.

Single-issue groups continued to multiply, carry petitions door to door, and develop blocks of voters — 5000 or more — pledged to vote a candidate or an incumbent in or out of office on the basis of his or her stance on a single issue: for or against gun control; for or against consumer-protection legislation; for or against nuclear energy; for or against the location of a dump site for industrial wastes; for or against smoking in public places.

The popular swing to the local political process placed questions before the electorate at grass roots that were previously never asked at that level.

John Naisbitt, publisher of the *Trend Report*, called the shift a move towards "direct democracy" and pointed out that in the late seventies, communities voted on such issues as funding abortions, building terminals for oil tankers, and erecting nuclear power plants. "Local citizens will be voting on a great range of new things in the eighties, at times leap-frogging the old political process," Naisbitt said.

Naisbitt believes there must be a clear delineation of which issues should — must — be dealt with at the national, state, and local levels.

America is fragmented into some 83,000 separate units of government, many having their own powers of taxation. The units are prey to single-issue politics and local decision-making groups who seek not only to influence decisions on local issues but also on broad subjects such as trade with South Africa.

Change has come so rapidly, and with such staggering consequences, that the nation has not yet learned how to cope or plan. Some kind of a "Neutral Zone" must be discovered or invented to give us time to consider, to relate, to sort out the trade-offs, to articulate national and local priorities in a democratic but nonthreatening atmosphere.

The focus must be on the survival and strengthening of the nation and the rejuvenation of its people. The secondary issue — protecting the proprietary rights of groups and individuals — must be given full attention, within the context of broad national and international issues in which all citizens and organizations have a stake.

Nothing must be permitted to disturb our freedom to disagree, to pursue one's own course, to rebel and speak out. But neither can we permit the splintering of America to continue. Our central purpose must be identified through discussion and planning in the Neutral Zone, where we might prevent chaos and the further polarization of powerful special interest groups.

What is the Neutral Zone?

It is in the mind. It is the willingness of people having differing interests to come together to draw a montage on the wall; to identify gaps and misconceptions; to compromise in order to gain consensus toward the achievement of larger purposes in which all people have a stake. The nation is in urgent need of brokers and matchmakers willing to bring adversaries together on common ground. The Neutral Zone is not fashioned by laws and regulations. It is not dependent on mandates from impersonal authorities, but rather seeks the resolution of differences among conferees, through dialogue.

Since the perception of the common good is in the mind of the beholder, what is to prevent the Neutral Zone from becoming another forum for debate and more invective, a means for polarizing preconceived opinion and increasing adversarial posturing?

The Neutral Zone need not fall into that trap.

The structure of the Neutral Zone is of paramount importance. It must maximize freedom, assure nonattribution, and demand nothing in terms of official statements or decisions or actions. The Neutral Zone should promote constructive action through already existing official channels of communication between business and government.

One version of the Neutral Zone was conceived by accident in May 1964. Dan H. Fenn, Jr., and I brought together a dozen high-ranking business and government people for a private discussion of controversial issues in a small dining room at the Shoreham Hotel in Washington. The informal discussion continued until one in the morning.

We had a pleasant, frank, and sometimes exciting exchange of ideas. There was nothing startling about the nature of the meeting except that it was unusual for business and government people at the decision-making level to be able to speak candidly with their counterparts without fear of attribution.

No secrets were revealed. No confidential data were disclosed. These men simply posed hard questions about why business acted in this way and that and why government behaved as it did. Participants sincerely wanted to understand the environment in which their counterparts made decisions and to find some middle ground on which they might agree and thus begin to make progress toward the solutions of the problems they shared.

One of the participants in that first meeting was Glen Perry of the E.I. du Pont de Nemours & Company. He offered to host a second meeting in July.

I was representing the chemical industry at that time, and about to enter government. Dan H. Fenn, Jr. — who had served as President John F. Kennedy's recruiter in putting together the New Frontier team — had been appointed a U.S. tariff commissioner by the President in September 1963, only a few weeks before Kennedy's assassination in Dallas (on November 22, 1963).

Fenn and I met with Perry to discuss the ground rules for the July meeting — ground rules that were to be followed effectively at thirty-five such dinner meetings during the next seven years. We agreed that a cross-section of industry should be represented to avoid any suggestion of collusion or special pleading. We also agreed that Fenn and I would invite the guests from the executive and regulatory agencies of government, so that not even the host would know the names of his government guests until the very night of the dinner.

The second meeting, hosted by Perry, was held in the International Club, then located at Jefferson Place and 19th Street. Among the participants were Francis Keppel, U.S. commissioner of education, Ivan Nestigen, under secretary of Health, Education, and Welfare; Arthur Northwood of Shell Oil, Robert Semple, president of Wyandotte Chemicals, and Samuel Zagoria of the National Labor Relations Board.

What made these meetings special and productive?

First, no title was ever given the group. It remained neutral and unofficial. Starting with the third meeting in October 1964, hosted by Richard McCurdy, then president of Shell Oil, almost every dinner was hosted by a chief executive officer of a major company. Participants were the host's dinner guests, although, as I have explained, the government officials were actually invited by Fenn and me in accordance with the unwritten rules.

The nonattribution rule was applied from the start to encourage freewheeling discussion. Although well-known reporters attended on occasion and were free to report the substance of the discussion, they did not identify the location or host or quote participants by name.

I have advocated openness and candor in all dealings between business and government all my working life. So much grief and misunderstanding can be avoided when all the cards are placed face up on the table. But if we had not applied the nonattribution rule at these informal meetings between 1964 and 1970, we would not have created the desired Neutral Zone.

Business executives would have been cautious, noncommittal, or have simply stayed home. Government officials would have been uncomfortable. And the exchanges would have been as guarded and formal as testimony given at congressional hearings.

The whole idea was to relax guests, to stimulate useful but appropriate discussion of timely and often controversial issues.

No agenda was ever printed. The group was untitled during its seven years. We met in the Madison Hotel most often but also at the F Street, Metropolitan, and International clubs. A cadre of regulars soon formed: Alexander McFarlane, chairman of Corn Products Company (now CPC International); Louis Cabot of The Cabot Corporation; Richard McCurdy of Shell Oil; Robert Semple of Wyandotte Chemicals; A.R. "Gus" Marusi, chairman of Borden; and from government, John Macy, chairman of the Civil Service Commission [later to become the first president of the Corporation for Public Broadcasting]; Wilbur Cohen, under secretary, [and later, secretary] of Health, Education, and Welfare; Alan Boyd, who was promoted from under secretary of commerce to secretary of transportation during the period of the dinner meetings; J. Edward Day, postmaster general under Kennedy and a prominent Washington attorney; Samuel Zagoria of the National Labor Relations Board; Dr. James Goddard, commissioner of the Food and Drug Administration; the late Manuel Cohen, chairman of the Securities and Exchange Commission and Eugene Zuckert, former secretary of the Air Force.

David Packard of Hewlett-Packard Company; Douglass Cater, assistant to President Lyndon Johnson; Labor Secretary Willard Wirtz and Irving Shapiro of Du Pont also participated from time to time.

Glen Perry, Arthur Northwood, and Allen Chellas of *Newsweek* gave regular assistance in planning the meetings. Later, public affairs executive Howard Chase also helped.

Fenn and I asked ourselves why men of power — Irving Shapiro of du Pont and Augustine Marusi of Borden, for example — would find it useful, even exciting, to make a special trip to Washington to speak informally over dinner with decision makers in government. The meetings were strictly off the record. No decisions were made or called for; no specific actions were proposed.

Irving Shapiro told me, long after the meetings had concluded, that it was partly the element of surprise — not knowing in advance who would be there — and the nonthreatening environment. He noted that formal structures were already in place to lobby causes and debate issues (the Business Roundtable was formed after the meetings stopped), and while other discussion groups existed, they tended to focus on particular issues, bring in expert speakers, and become somewhat formalized.

"We come to the meetings to talk with friends about things that are troubling us. We think more intelligent action is taken through official channels as a result of these unofficial discussions," he said.

Indeed, there was evidence of subsequent action. Business executives who had shunned Washington came in to testify, sometimes on issues of public importance beyond the scope of their own self-interest.

Companies opened Washington offices, and their top executives agreed to serve on important advisory committees of the government. Mostly, the value of the meetings was apparent in the change of attitudes among both the business and government "regulars." The discussions became increasingly candid and helpful as time went along.

No guest was allowed to "make a speech" about any special problem or to plead for favor. If a new guest started to do so, he was politely cut off by the host, who served as chairman. While no agenda was printed, Fenn and I usually met with the host in advance to talk about the opening comment he might make when dinner was over and guests were sipping cordials and enjoying cigars.

Women and minorities participated, including FTC commissioner Mary Gardiner Jones, Elizabeth Hanford (now assistant to President Reagan and married to Senator Robert Dole, of Kansas), Dr. Andrew Brimmer, the late Dr. Berkeley Burrell, and the late Hobart Taylor, Jr., Esq.

At one of the early meetings, a business executive said he was offended by a committee of the Senate whose members had failed to show up to hear his testimony on behalf of an industry association. The one or two who did make an appearance seemed to be more interested in reading the newspaper than hearing the testimony, he complained. There was laughter and commiseration around the table, but Wilbur Cohen also heard a legitimate concern, and he responded in his good-natured way.

"Bob," and he paused to let the laughter die down and secure the full attention of the twenty-five men and women around the square table, "Bob, I share your concern. I have been testifying before the Congress for thirty years, and I have had the experience you describe. It can be embarrassing and disheartening. We want business executives to express their views to the Congress regularly. We want to do everything we can to encourage your participation. So please let me make a few suggestions. See the key people on the committee before you testify. They will welcome you, believe me. They want to know who you are and how you feel and what your main concerns are. If you do this, they will be present at the time you testify. Your visit will help them become better informed. And both you and they will be a lot more comfortable. More important, your testimony will count for more."

Cohen knew he was speaking to many of the business executives in the room, and to many more who would be told of his comments at private luncheons and in board rooms. He offered down-to-earth, practical advice — not the kind of advice business executives would commonly have heard from other sources in the sixties.

We stopped arranging the dinner meetings in 1970. Business interest remained high. But the Nixon cabinet and sub-cabinet people apparently thought the informal business-government dinner meetings were somehow a product of the Lyndon Baines Johnson White House. They were, in fact, private meetings, privately convened, privately financed (by the generosity of host companies), and without formal structure or influence of any kind. Nonetheless, they were perceived otherwise by the top-level Nixon people who declined our invitations.

In the mid-seventies, Robert Campbell and Allen Chellas of *Newsweek* hosted a dinner in New York to discuss the possibility of renewing the series. The new President, Jimmy Carter, was advocating openness between business and government. Perhaps the dinner discussions could be given new life. John Gardner, Wilbur Cohen, Augustine Marusi, and John Filer, chairman, Aetna Life & Casualty, were among the dinner guests at *Newsweek*.

Fenn and I described the earlier meetings, and some of the business executives agreed to talk with Michael Blumenthal, then secretary of the treasury and former chairman of Bendix Corporation. But nothing came of it.

Watergate had made people in both business and government wary of "innocent" contact. The whole climate had changed. The Neutral Zone for candid exchange that Fenn and I had established accidentally in the sixties had run its course. We would have to find other Neutral Zones, perhaps using entirely different configurations — or no configuration other than the willingness of thoughtful men and women to explore all sides of critical issues with the understanding that their own legitimate ambitions could not be realized if they ran counter to the public good and common need.

There is a moment in almost every transaction when people can find middle ground, protect their own proper interests, and join together, to some degree, in moving forward under a broader umbrella of concerns. But that moment goes by unrecognized if the mind set is wrong or the notion of mutual self-help has not occurred to the participants.

America desperately needs to create and nurture thousands of Neutral Zones that can bring together the special-interest groups (now so numerous they cancel each other out) and other divergent forces at the community and national level *before* the legal debates are drawn and the political battles are fought.

We might also use Neutral Zones to review those controversial, seemingly insolvable issues that drag on to the disservice of society: unemployment, racism, rising crime rates. We could do so more readily if we would accept John Gardner's advice given more that a dozen years ago: "Seek solutions, not villains."

Years ago I learned that the battle lines are set if attorneys participate in the *first* meeting. I do not wish to be misunderstood. Lawyers are absolutely essential in maintaining balance in our society, in resolving most of the difficult issues of our time, and in enacting laws to improve society. Lawyers and public affairs people have come to enjoy a rather special and mutually respectful relationship in recent years. Working together, they can defuse emerging issues and expedite the handling of sticky problems.

But the public presence of legal counsel in the early stages of any discussion is usually unwise and counterproductive. Many problems have no legal basis until one is applied. Most problems between neighbors, for example, could be settled without legal action. But neighbors often seek legal counsel at the slightest provocation because we have failed to create Neutral Zones in which neighbors might blow off steam, then let common sense and common decency prevail.

There is quite enough grief to go around. There are legal battles within legal battles to occupy generations of barristers. There is no lack of work for able attorneys. We do not need to create more work for them. We do need to solve more issues peacefully, as they emerge; to deal with basic problems in a commonsense manner; to concentrate on setting the facts right and then going forward with some degree of understanding, if not agreement.

By making pragmatic appraisals of everyday disputes, we might come to recognize our mutual responsibilities, work together where we can, to the degree we can, and fight only when fighting is unavoidable and we have exhausted all possibilities for compromise.

A young friend in Columbus, Ohio, once told me she wanted to become a lawyer because "pretty soon there will be a law for everything." It was a frightening thought then, and it is more frightening now upon reflection.

We have always cherished our freedoms in this great nation. Can we not see that the pursuit of narrow goals, without proper regard for the national purpose and the equal rights of others, is generating "a law for everything" mind set that will eventually take away the very thing we say we are willing to fight for: our basic freedom.

Creating Neutral Zones for consensus building is not a futile exercise. Organizations and individuals can master the art.

They can erase some of the mean-spirited, self-centered attention we all apply to narrow pursuits. We must not permit the recycling of problems of the sixties we once thought we had gotten under control.

When I first thought about this book, I wrote to a number of friends in business and government whose opinions I respect. One executive scrawled a note across the top of my letter and sent it back: "I don't need to stick my neck out [talking about social responsiveness]. We're back to bottom line here and justifiably so." This man had written eloquently in the early seventies about the need for corporations to take a broader view of their social influence. Now he was telling me that "bottom line" was no longer connected with societal needs. He knew better but had tired of the internal debate in his company. I could empathize with his position, but never condone it. The inescapable fact is that corporations are social institutions. They fail to recognize their social role at their own peril. No business can long suceed if the world crumbles around it and its markets evaporate. Protecting society is the best way of protecting the enterprise.

Every business decision has social implications: the location of new construction, disposal of old properties, removal of waste products, the allocation of investments and charitable contributions, the purchase of goods and services from minority-owned businesses, the surveillance of white-collar crime, the reduction of violent crime, and the integration of "corporate social responsibility" and "public accountability" philosophies and practices throughout the enterprise. As *Webster's* informs us, the bottom line is not simply an earnings report; it is the final or ultimate statement of who and what we are.

Chapter Two

Milton Friedman Says It's Hogwash

Do corporate officers have any responsibility other than to make money for their stockholders? The brilliant, award-winning economist and author Milton Friedman says absolutely not. In fact, the man says the whole idea of corporate social responsibility is hogwash.

"In the first place," says the feisty little genius, "the only entities who can have responsibility are individuals; a business cannot have responsibility. So the question is this: do corporate executives — provided they stay within the law — have responsibilities other than to make money for their stockholders? My answer is no, they do not."

Warming to his subject, Friedman continues, "Take the corporate executive who says, 'I have the responsibility over and above that of making profits.' If he feels he has such a responsibility, he is going to spend money in ways that are not in the interests of the stockholders. The crucial question is: what rights do executives have to spend their stockholders' money? If 'socially responsible' executives would stop and think, they would recognize that they are acting irresponsibly."

Most executives disagree with Friedman's theories simply because such ideas do not work in a society in which business's interests are so clearly and inextricably intertwined with those of government and private institutions.

The executive is not acting irresponsibly when he improves the company's reputation and thus increases its sales and investors. The executive is not acting irresponsibly when he maintains constructive relationships with government and avoids needless litigation.

15

Shortly before debating the late Eli Goldston in New York several years ago, the estimable Friedman dined with the remarkable Goldston and members of Goldston's family. Those of us who helped organize the conference on the "social involvement of business" and who would play supporting roles the following day, were also privileged to join the dignitaries at dinner.

Prof. Friedman was not only charming and agreeable but also in accord that industry's role in society was changing and that new strategies had to be developed. Later, standing before a large audience, the incisive and articulate columnist — later to be awarded the Nobel prize — tore into Goldston, promoting the rigid anti-involvement line that he had abandoned during the dinner discussion.

"The business of Business is business," said Friedman.

Did he purposely throw Goldston off guard at dinner? Or did he really believe that industry had to change but would not say so publicly? Only Friedman knew.

Those who heard him that evening gave the professor very high marks as a debater. His tactics were effective. He was assertive and commanding. I suppose if one were to award points for debate, he won. But he did not win the hearts and minds of his audience, although he surely earned their respect.

His insightful comments during dinner and his stereotyped performance behind the podium had suggested to some of us that evening that Friedman is a tactician and showman as well as an economist. He played his public role well. But some of us thought that public role was a disservice to industry and the nation. His observations at dinner made more sense, given the national trauma.

Friedman's public posture was shared by Richard M. Nixon, who once said, "Business should not pretend to be something it is not. Business is business, not philanthropy. Its actions should be justified essentially on business grounds, not on abstract ethical grounds. To try to do otherwise will only increase the credibility gap from which business already suffers.

"It is only through the profits that industry can buy new plants, the new equipment that will make our workers more productive and therefore more competitive in the world. . . . I am for more profits because I believe more profits mean more jobs."

Friedman and Nixon set up straw men. No reasonable person suggests that business should be something it is not or that business's role is that of a philanthropist. Very simply, industry is a vital part of society. It exercises tremendous economic and social power. It has an obligation to be accountable to the people. The objective should be to involve industry in the social life of the nation, in reasonable harmony with government and other private institutions.

Who would honestly advocate business's isolation, noninvolvement, and exclusive pursuit of narrow goals? Even investors scoff at Friedman's preachments. People invest across the board, in many companies and commodities. The health of the nation as a whole is of vital importance to shareowners. And the really major investments are made by banks and insurance companies.

Friedman's support is minimal on this subject. While it is true that no two industrialists would agree absolutely on either the scope of corporate social responsibility or corporate philanthropy, few would suggest that business should — if it could — remain aloof from the citizenry and community problems. The interdependence of business and society is self-evident.

Prof. Harlan C. Van Over of Indiana State University, who conducted a study of the attitudes of corporate chief executive officers in 1974, says, "profit maximization is a doctrine that is no longer consistent with the needs and desires of a dynamic society imbued with pluralism." Van Over concluded that executives are not in agreement with the classical doctrine of private property as it relates to the corporation and shareholder, that corporate charitable contributions and giving programs do not represent a misuse of ownership funds.

He also noted that corporate executives had not yet accepted the social ethic as a basic operating philosophy. (Nor have they done so in any great number to this day.) But 75 percent of respondents to Van Over's detailed study said their responsibility and accountability transcended shareholders' interests.

Eighty percent of the respondents also held the opinion that shareholders should not be permitted to vote on the percentage of earnings to be contributed to various social projects.

Interestingly, 81 percent of the respondents said they would publicize their firms as socially responsible enterprises if they thought that approach would increase profits. Not a nobly inspired sentiment, but a step forward.

The Committee for Economic Development (CED) issued a lengthy report of the social responsibilities of business corporations in June 1971, in which it said the diversified nature of business ownership altered the classically defined interest of the stockholder. The report stated that nearly all investors now hold equities in more than one company, and it added, "The stockholder's interest in the long run is best served by corporate policies which contribute to the development of the kind of society in which business can grow and prosper."

The CED report also pointed out that social improvement can be profitable and identified housing, manpower training, and urban development as areas strong enough to create profitable markets or markets that "can be made profitable by a combination of greater business initiative and more effective government incentives."

David Rockefeller has said, "Profit must remain the yardstick because it is the measure of our efficiency, but profit must be based more and more on calculations of social costs and benefits. We must accept the fact that economic growth is not an end in itself, but rather a means to a greater number of social as well as private ends."

The nation's foremost business writer, Peter F. Drucker, in his book *Managing in Turbulent Times* wrote, "It is no longer adequate to say: 'We will stick to doing what we know how to do and resist demands to concern ourself with anything else!" Drucker went on to say, "Today's post-industrial society is a pluralist one which has to demand from its institutions that they take responsibility beyond their own specific mission. . . . A manager has to think through the impacts of the decisions he makes." Drucker added, "Unless executives accept the responsibility of taking leadership in the common interest, they will become more and more powerless in the pluralist political environment, and will continue to be the losers in the politics of confrontation."

Writing in *Change* magazine in 1976, Donald MacNaughton, then the chairman of Prudential Life Insurance Company of America, said, "Profit is the key word in moving an enterprise forward. But there is general recognition today that maximizing profit at the expense of social and human values is a losing game. The much more difficult game of balancing profit with social and human values is our present concern."

Hogwash? It's doubtful that even the good professor Friedman believes it is.

Almost everyone would agree that the production and distribution of goods and services is the basic function of all societies, from the most primitive to the most complex. One of two systems is adopted: a free market concept or a government-dominated market. The first system demands innovation and self-discipline. The second system demands and rewards obedience.

In spite of its inefficiencies and imbalances, the free market has provided the greatest degree of wealth and human benefit. The free market has also provided the greatest degree of human freedom and personal options. What American business executives have now come to realize is that their involvement in social and political issues protects and preserves the free market system and maintains a healthy balance of power with big government.

Should business executives opt for isolation, government would set all the rules. Business leaders cannot be blind to the inadequacies of their own business practices or fail to act voluntarily to correct abuses in the marketplace if they wish to remain independent. Business initiatives in the public interest are the best insurance against unreasonable and unwanted government encroachment.

Friedman has abundant company when he talks about the basic purpose of business and business organizations: providing jobs and taxes, rewards for shareowners, and new products and services for mankind. But a popular misconception of business has persisted, probably dating back to the first struggling entrepreneurs: that business exists for its own ends; that its primary purpose is simply to provide a return to its owners.

Business has never been an end unto itself. It is a component of society, a means for improving the quality of life for all citizens. Business does not function in a vacuum. The people decide whether a business will succeed or fail.

As Donald MacNaughton told a Canadian audience in 1976, "Business is clearly not simply an economic institution, but a socioeconomic institution with a primary responsibility to society as a whole, and a secondary responsibility to stockholders and employees."

MacNaughton lamented the fact that "people know relatively little about their most fundamental value — the free enterprise system." The businessman is often derelict, he said, because "instead of clarifying public thought, the business executive tends to chastise the people for their lack of comprehension."

Stanley Goodman, chairman of the May Stores during the turbulent domestic crisis of the sixties, concluded that business is its own worst enemy: "Going all the way back to the 19th century, business has an almost unbroken record of opposing legislation that the public thinks is good." Goodman listed the Sherman Anti-Trust Act, the Federal Reserve Act, and the Federal Trade Commission Act, noting that business fought every one of them and lost. He also cited the Child Labor Act, the Fair Labor Standards Act, the Old Age and Survivors Insurance Benefits Act, the federal housing laws, the Marshall Plan for aid to Europe, the Federal Education Act, the poverty program and medicare. Business opposed every one. The legislation was passed. Business had to comply. Business lost the legislative battles. It also lost some of its credibility.

According to MacNaughton, the real tragedy is that while business was publicly opposing those proposals, it was also critical of the public because people didn't listen to its discourse on the virtues of the market system.

Irwin Miller, boss man at Cummins Engine at that time, put it this way: "We are making the mistake which most powerful groups in history have made. We are identifying the welfare of the whole society with that peculiar state of affairs which works best for us."

The impetus for the social actions of business over the past sixteen years has come from the public and government. The programs were devised by government and carried out largely by business. But without the impetus of laws and events, it is doubtful that any substantive involvement by business would have taken place. The starting point of corporate social responsibility is too sharply defined to explain any other reason.

Government stepped in with the Equal Employment Opportunity Act of 1964, and business moved to comply with it. Then came Watts — the riot of 1965 — followed by riots in Newark, Chicago, Detroit, and other cities. Out of that terrible trauma came the National Alliance of Businessmen, the National Urban Coalition, and the JOBS program.

"Business did a good job of responding to the valid demands of an unhappy society," A. R. "Gus" Marusi said. "Business has enormous resources and knows how to mobilize them when it wants to. But I am deeply concerned that as businessmen we have done too little to anticipate the needs of our society. I don't think we fully discharge our social responsibility by facing up to and solving problems as they arise. We have an obligation to see that they never come up in the first place."

Marusi believes that social programs must be made a permanent and integral part of corporate operations. He is convinced that social responsibility and viable business are compatible.

"Milt Moskowitz demonstrated this in an interesting way several years ago," Marusi recalled. "He put together a 14-company portfolio of firms that he considered socially responsible. Reviewing the portfolio after six months in his newsletter, *Business & Society,* he found that the 14 companies had an average price appreciation of more than seven percent — significantly better than the performance of the Dow Jones Industrials, the New York Stock Exchange Composite, and the Standard and Poor Industrials."

Moskowitz did not claim that only the virtuous make money. He did suggest that corporations which are committed to social responsibility will do better in the long run. Not because they are virtuous, but "because they have smarter managements."

After the riots and the development of business-sponsored activities, many companies began to spout rationales showing that they had always been socially responsive; that they had cared for the undereducated and poor before the riots; that they had enviable records for maintaining the health and safety of their workers. Here and there a company put a new twist on an action taken a half-century past to make it appear more nobly inspired than perhaps it really was.

General Foods noted that the chairman of the old Postum Cereal Company, C. W. Post, had, in 1906, demonstrated the social responsibility of business by placing advertisements in newspapers urging the passage of the first pure food and drug bill. Post stated in his ads that he had always printed on each package the contents of the product, as the proposed bill would require. Post was said to have expedited passage of that legislation.

Some of the stories, such as the vignette about Post, although interesting and true, were not exactly relevant to the sixties.

Other companies became unnecessarily defensive. They pointed to their records of good citizenship. They felt the people had turned against them, and they were both hurt and confused. It wasn't that the town park, the marina, and the new wing on the hospital were forgotten or unimportant. These contributions remained vital to community life. It was simply that life had changed. Information available to industry about societal expectations had been ignored. Race problems had surfaced. Emerging social problems pressed against the corporate body.

Many business executives said these problems were for government and the sociologists to solve. Business made clothes pins and computers and sold insurance. What did business have to do with social welfare and the delivery of health services?

How far should a food company go, for example, in trying to feed the hungry? A clothier in clothing the poor? A builder in renovating dilapidated housing? And even if the companies were willing to try, how could the tasks be accomplished? The answer: Business should develop a long-term partnership with government and integrate social responsibility into corporate life.

Why did it take riots in the streets to pull the nation together in a loose coalition to deal with such basic issues? It wasn't that business, industry, sociologists, and academicians didn't know. The problems had been fermenting for a long time.

People talked about the powder keg and the unease.

Prof. Raymond Mack of Northwestern University and James Langton of the Bank of America in San Francisco were making speeches in the early sixties, long before the riots, long before the student uprisings and the killings at Kent State.

There were noddings of agreement at seminars and commentary in esoteric magazines that something really ought to be done.

Walter Mondale said in the sixties, "It wasn't that we didn't know, we just didn't take heed."

Years later, columnist Meg Greenfield asked rhetorically, "How is it that we have all this information and never seem to know anything?" She was writing about Iran and Guyana. She might have been writing about race riots and environmental protection.

A certain amount of progress has been made. Some of business's severest critics are now its boosters . . . at least in select subject areas.

"We appreciate what industry is doing to revitalize urban centers and invest in minority business development," said Rep. Parren Mitchell of Baltimore, chairman of the House Small Business Committee, a former chairman of the Congressional Black Caucus and indefatigable advocate of minority business, "but we fear a recycling of the problems the nation endured in the sixties if there is a slackening of industry's resolve."

The legislator is uncertain of industry's commitment if laws and regulations are removed. Mitchell may soon find out. Many of the provisions for which he fought so hard may be rolled back by the Reagan administration. The problems the laws address are still unsolved. New pressures for their solution will surely be placed on industry.

One of the greatest challenges in the eighties is to transmit useful, understandable information to the citizenry. In a society of special-interest groups, jargon proliferates, creating unique languages within the English language. Communication becomes almost impossible among esoteric groups. The common bond of verbal and sign communication is lost. We must restore it, for people must comprehend before they can reason and share. Common language can reach hearts and minds, cut through red tape and artificial barriers, inspire a youngster to stay in school, shape a law, comfort the disadvantaged, rehabilitate a criminal, and bring about understanding among disparate groups. It is not only the translation of jargon that is needed but also the willingness to create Neutral Zones for the free exchange of ideas.

Chapter Three

Integrating Corporate
Social Responsibility

Next to kite flying on the mall, the favorite pastime in Washington is floating balloons.

These are not the pretty red and yellow balloons that hawkers display at the National Zoo, but "idea" balloons that test the attitudes of public, news media, and Capitol Hill on hundreds of different issues.

Sometimes the idea balloons are launched many miles from Washington in hopes they will be carried back to the Congress on a favorable media breeze. Sometimes the balloons are launched from 1600 Pennsylvania Avenue, and sometimes from the law firms that dominate the K Street corridor, Farragut Square, and Rosslyn, Virginia, across the Key Bridge.

Former commerce secretary Juanita Kreps lofted one such balloon several years ago from the pleasant campus of Duke University at Durham, North Carolina. Business executives said it was a hot air balloon and saw red, for lettered across the balloon were the words "Corporate Social Index." The government, said Kreps, was about to draw up a score card for business and tell the world which companies were being good and which companies were being naughty vis-à-vis their involvement in social issues.

The balloon was busted very quickly by irate business executives, led by the powerful Business Roundtable.

The proposed "index," described in detail in Chapter Four, was one of many well-intentioned efforts in the seventies to engage industry in social planning. It failed because the idea was imposed rather than shared. Industry was not invited to adopt voluntary procedures for public accountability. It was told that the Commerce Department wanted to play school marm and issue a report card. Thanks, but no thanks, said industry, annoyed that its private initiatives to address societal needs were largely ignored by the secretary.

Most of the balloons floating over Washington originate in the conference rooms of prestigious law firms; the balloons are sent aloft by special interests who want to know how far they may safely proceed in the pursuit of their own narrow interests before colliding with either the government or other powerful special interests.

Until recent times, with the exception of the Kreps launch, the balloons had precious little to do with integrating social and economic goals in America. They carried the myriad colors of special interests. But no fusing rainbows.

Lawyers aren't usually paid for harmonizing issues and avoiding controversy. They are paid for arguing a point of view. Washington is a city of wall-to-wall conference rooms filled with bright young lawyers — and patient old lawyers — pondering the details of specific pieces of legislation with single-minded lobbyists. They pinpoint whom to see, what to offer, what to ask for, what to avoid. The lawyers then gather their papers and move on to another conference room with another group of lobbyists to ponder yet another issue.

It is an unending game. The lawyers make a great deal of money. Everybody thinks he or she has won something — at least for the moment. But the game changes day by day. New issues emerge. Old issues are recycled. Battles won become battles that must be sustained lest disgruntled losers attempt to reverse hard-won victories.

With the proliferation of special-interest groups in the seventies, and the popularization of the "me first" and "I'm number one" syndrome, Washington law firms expanded, diversified, and multiplied.

But almost no one was talking about the integration of social and economic issues, taking corporate social responsibility seriously, considering public accountability as a continuing obligation of business, viewing the corporation as a social institution with responsibilities to the citizenry, or devising more enlightened ways to balance power between the public and private sectors through co-operative planning — and having *fewer* legal debates.

Of course not. The mystique of the Washington lawyer blends with the power mystique of the capital city: one must use potions and walk secret corridors to get things done. What would be gained by an appeal for business-government cooperation in solving the major issues of the day? Who would gain by the integration of corporate social responsibility into the day-to-day activities of the Fortune 500 companies and their Washington offices? Who? Everybody.

There would still be enough trouble to keep the lawyers fully occupied. But the tensions would be reduced. The adversarial posturing would be relaxed. Business and government might discover a sort of Neutral Zone in which they could explore, without legal constraint, the possible solutions to seemingly insoluble controversial issues.

Who would benefit? Industry would benefit. Minority groups and social service organizations would benefit. The nation would benefit.

The lawyers could still float their balloons, hold their meetings, prepare their testimonies, arrange their caucuses, trade their votes, offer and accept favors, jockey for power, and assure their clients of devoted service and unswerving loyalty. Lawyers could continue their tactics of keeping one bill from coming to the floor for a vote while making sure another bill is acted upon. The big paper war would continue. The protection of self-interest would prevail. The legal chess game would not be interrupted. Large fees would be invoiced and paid.

But overarching the game would be a new objective, born of the realization that special interests can continue only if the private enterprise system is strengthened. And the private enterprise system cannot be sustained, much less strengthened, unless business and government form a new compact. That compact requires the integration of corporate social responsibility as a permanent, integral component of corporate planning, marketing, and administration.

When consumer advocate Ralph Nader speaks, industry listens because it feels the heat of attack.

When columnist James J. Kilpatrick speaks, industry listens, ready to applaud.

But one of Kilpatrick's columns, entitled "Wake up, Businessmen!" must have drawn mixed reviews in board rooms across America. The crusty, conservative, syndicated writer chastised business for failing to rebuild consumer confidence in its products and in its integrity. Kilpatrick quoted a study of consumer attitudes conducted "under impeccable auspices" by Marketing Science Institute and Louis Harris and Associates, for Sentry Insurance.

Wrote Kilpatrick: "My friends in free enterprise can be maddening friends — bull-headed, bat-blind, insensitive, and inconsistent. They spend millions to buy the best public relations advice that money can buy, but reading this survey, one wonders how often they take it."

Kilpatrick then recited a familiar litany of consumer complaints against business, including the fact that half the respondents said they could not fathom product warranties and thought warranties were written "mainly for the protection of manufacturers."

He quoted from the report: "Most companies are so concerned about profits they don't care about quality."

Overall, Kilpatrick said, the survey added up to abysmal reading in boardrooms. "And perhaps the most striking conclusion is that businessmen are generally unaware of what is going on. The Harris interviewers questioned a sample of business executives. The executives, most of them, thought they were doing fine. They liked their products, their warranties and their service; they uniformly deplored regulation; they seemed not to understand that something is wrong."

Unless business can change these public attitudes for the better, as the authors of the survey point out, "the call for far-reaching changes in the management and regulation of business may become irresistible," Kilpatrick concluded.

That rare criticism from one of the nation's business boosters and card-carrying conservatives should have rattled industry's complacent foundations. It did at least raise some eyebrows.

The barbs had been coming for several years. Herblock, the famed political cartoonist, sketched two businessmen strolling the avenue as other men scurried away with suitcases in hand. The caption read, "The trouble is people today don't seem to have faith in our institutions." The labels on the disappearing suitcases were "FBI and CIA Illegal Activities," "Banking Deals," "Arms Industry Payoffs," "Kickbacks," "Corporate Slush Funds," "Aircraft Industry Bribes," "Medical Lab Bilking," and more.

Before the riots on American streets in the sixties, business had enjoyed a favorable reputation with the public. After the riots, the war in Vietnam, and the Watergate scandal, the public's regard for business plummeted to a new low — not that the public had always regarded business highly. Not at all. But in polls taken just prior to the riots, business rated way up there — a 76 percent favorable nod by the people.

It was a different matter down through the years. Even the giants of industry were caricatured — Henry Ford and Andrew Carnegie among them. Other business types were shown as hard-eyed, well-fed, extravagant wheelers and dealers. They were the manipulators; the robber barons. Sinclair Lewis gave the nation Babbitt; Upton Sinclair told the world about the glories of the meat-packing industry in the early days; and Theodore Dreiser recited the curious way financial giants had grown.

Countless movies and plays and comic strips have constantly reinforced the stereotype of the conniving business executive: heartless, uncaring, humorless.

Little wonder that presentations by trade association lawyers and company public relations people in defense of industry executives and their motives usually fell short. And occasional attacks upon the social welfare system and the health delivery services of the nation by executives on their yachts at Newport went down badly.

Business executives want to be loved like everyone else. Under fire, they reached out to organizations they had ignored, provided job training, supported minority colleges, invested in minority-owned companies, and began to preach the benefits of the private enterprise system to employees and the community.

The latter was a bit unfortunate. People understood profits better than industry imagined. They simply disagreed with the way profits were being utilized.

In days gone by, family-owned companies took the long view. They envisioned the day when junior or one of the grandsons would be managing the enterprise.

The new managers are sorely tempted to push for short-term profits and move up — or out. They seem poorly motivated to weigh the consequences of their decisions on society ten and twenty years hence.

Business executives have become much more sophisticated, of course. Later in this book, I shall talk about the Business Roundtable, the changes in the Chamber of Commerce of the United States, and the National Association of Manufacturers. But the business mind set about working with government, consumer groups, minority organizations, and the news media is still adversarial, defensive, and counterproductive.

If industry had met government and activist groups halfway or — better — if industry had taken initiatives early on, half the bothersome regulations of which industry bitterly complains would never have been written.

The true integration of social and economic planning will take time. The integration of corporate social responsibility into the fabric of business and commerce will require a total change of attitude on the part of management and a redefinition of the role of business in society.

Historically, businessmen, as a group, have been relatively ineffective spokesmen for business; they have failed to use words and approaches that captured the public interest. They have not tended to work from the perspective of society as a whole. Conversely, their messages have been filled with the demands of their own jobs and the goals of their enterprises.

Business executives responded to social revolt after the fact, after the streets were filled with smoke and looters and gunfire. Even in matters closer to the marketplace — consumer unrest and environmental protection — business executives were not conditioned to pay attention to developing criticism of their practices.

Businessmen tended to be taken by surprise.

Domestic trauma in the sixties taught business that it must design and heed early warning systems and make available informed and articulate spokespersons who can relate intelligently to individuals and groups who criticize business and the private enterprise system.

Chiefly, business learned that its spokespersons and principals must go out into the public arena if they want to be heard and respected. Contributions to the United Way and community projects would no longer suffice. Businesses must become a living part of the communities in which they conduct business — at the same time avoiding a dominant role that might suggest that business is taking too much control.

Even in the sixties, many companies ran their United Way campaigns on the principle that private money for social services would keep public money out of community affairs. In fact, federal and state monies were flowing into most communities at that time to help support a great number of services. Neither the public nor the private sector alone can meet public needs.

The legitimate objective is to develop a partnership between the public and private sectors. But it has taken many years for that concept to be widely recognized, and it is still not fully accepted.

Today, the trend is away from coordinated action. Not only have single-issue groups multiplied and strengthened, but the philosophy of "I'll get mine first and listen to you later" has taken hold. Further, the Reagan plan is to cut back on social and health services of all kinds and to leave the option to local communities as to the kind and degree of social services they wish to provide.

It is a very attractive notion to "get big government off our backs" and "make our own decisions." Its implementation will require the fusion of business into the social and educational life of every town. That idea is as repugnant to many people as the idea of having government send down all the signals from on high. People do not want business to replace government in the role of "father knows best."

In the eighties we are not considering the exchange of government largess for corporate benevolence; we are considering the necessity of facing problems on the local scene with local resources. The problems served by government funding will not disappear because federal dollars are withheld. On the contrary, the problems will be intensified, and the local businesses will be expected to respond by working with elected officials and civic leaders to design new strategies.

A MYTH DESTROYED

A myth circulating in the late sixties among corporate executives suggested that if the nation could mobilize sufficient money, manpower, and community resources, the violence would cease, racial wounds would heal, urban development would be a reality — and business could get back to business as usual. Inject enough management know-how; put enough dollars in the pot; assign enough young, bright, motivated executives to the community firing line during the crisis; spawn enough urban coalitions; inspire enough minority leaders to seek a better way of life through private enterprise; train enough hard-core workers; support enough minority-owned firms — and the nation would best those long-ignored societal problems and set them straight.

But there wasn't nearly enough of anything: not enough money, not enough men, not enough confidence, not enough commitment, and not enough realization that the nation faced a long-term evolution, not a short-term crisis.

Some observers believed, perhaps because they wanted to believe, that the crisis faded as the smell of smoke drifted away. By the early seventies, one might have thought them right. With the startling exception of support for welfare reform legislation by the National Association of Manufacturers, there was evidence that the zeal for social involvement had already diminished.

Rhetoric had cooled. The government was providing funds. A handful of major companies were deeply engaged in social programs, although most businesses were not. Why should they? The crisis had passed. Business had acted responsibly under stress, no question about that. And business could not provide funds and manpower indefinitely; surely everybody recognized that.

The National Association of Manufacturers quietly disbanded its Urban Affairs Committee, chaired by A. R. "Gus" Marusi, chairman and chief executive officer of Borden, Inc., despite his personal protest. The functions would be integrated with "normal" staff activity, Marusi was told. Many organizations cooled their ardor and reduced their expenditures for social involvement under the guise of "institutionalizing the extraordinary functions set up to deal with the crisis."

Some of the big companies began to integrate social planning, at least at the top. Minority affairs committees and corporate social responsibility task forces, composed of staff and board members, investigated a wide range of social issues impacting on the company, and on the communities in which the company did business. The reviews, for the most part, were focused inward rather than outward, but they were genuine and helpful.

James Langton of Bank of America; Milton Moskowitz, editor of a unique newsletter, *Business & Society*; Phillip Drotning of Standard Oil of Indiana; the late professor Ray Bauer of Harvard; and Thomas Roeser of Quaker Oats were among those academicians, writers, and corporate executives who feared that old wounds would fester if industry pulled back from the social arena. With the help of the Public Affairs Council, the Conference Board, and other business organizations, these men arranged seminars on corporate involvement and ways to measure its effectiveness.

There was general agreement among public affairs officers in major corporations in the early seventies that problems could erupt more terribly than before unless all segments of society moved toward some form of integrated social responsibility.

It would not be easy to set policy from the top of major corporations and convince managers down the line that they should embrace social action as an essential part of their job descriptions.

Yet this was done with some effectiveness in many companies, including Borden, where performance goals were agreed upon and achievement was tied to incentives: promotions, bonus payments, and the like.

As the pressure eased, or at least took a more deliberative form, many of the urban-oriented social programs mounted by industry, with government's help, were cut back, however.

Attention once again focused on the marketplace, cash flow, product development, and improving the bottom line. The notion of raising the bottom line to adjust to the new realities had not yet surfaced. Business executives had been trained to maximize profits and to avoid activity that would draw time and attention away from running the company.

Lyndon Johnson had pleaded for social legislation in the heat of the riots, and Congress had responded.

Richard Nixon and his secretary of commerce, Maurice Stans, had formed the Office of Minority Business Enterprise to assist minority-owned firms. Things were under control, or so it seemed. Even Charles King, the effectively audacious race relations confrontationist, was retained by the Army, Navy, and private industry to hold his encounter sessions. Minority leaders appeared on national television, and some of them were invited to serve on the boards of major corporations.

Given the historic mind set of business and the general perception that the problems were "under control," it is remarkable that so much real integration took place in the early seventies among fifteen or twenty big companies: General Electric, International Business Machines, Xerox, Quaker Oats, Standard Oil of Indiana, General Motors, Borden, Cummins Engine, Control Data, Dayton-Hudson, and Bank of America chief among them.

Not all the integration held. Minority affairs committees had a way of disappearing or being "institutionalized." But the election of prominent minorities to seats on the boards of major companies made a permanent difference. In certain cases, the appointments were token gestures, mere responses to change. Once there, however, the minorities and women made a profound difference. The Reverend Leon Sullivan, Patricia Harris, Earl Graves, the late Hobart Taylor, Jr., and Vernon Jordan exercized a powerful influence for business's social involvement.

Still, slippage was apparent. Young business graduates again sought traditional career ladders, dropping the demands for "useful social activity" they had voiced to recruiters in the late sixties and early seventies.

New terminology was adopted to ease the conscience of hard-nosed business executives tired of responding to pleas for more "corporate social responsibility." Now, instead, "corporate strategies" were discussed and "future planning" units were established.

Perhaps some of the best social forecasting takes place today in the planning offices of major corporations: Shell Oil, Atlantic Richfield, Aetna Life & Casualty, to name three.

These new "corporate strategies" and "public issues" units within the corporate structures are not always connected by a solid line to the day-to-day struggles of the enterprise, however.

Involvement of the chief executive officer in highly visible and useful activities — the National Alliance of Business, for example — has not usually been translated into action within that executive's own company.

I recall a brief exchange with a woman in Connecticut about the priorities established by her company's public issues office. Near the top of the list was "reform of the criminal justice system," and I congratulated her on the company's willingness to get out front, given the nation's alarming crime rate and the related judicial logjam.

"That may be the chairman's issue, but we're more concerned about the way he's running the company," she snapped.

That chief executive's vision of raising the bottom line to meet the broader realities of the marketplace had not been conveyed down the line. Vertical and horizontal communication in that company is sorely lacking. The public sees the company's top executives on major public platforms, admires the statements they make, and applauds the social investments the company has authorized. Yet, most of the corporate body, even those people in supervisory positions, view the social activity carried on in the executive suites, and even the work of the "public issues" forecasting unit, as rather remote and certainly not central to the success of the company or the private enterprise system.

The fault lies with top management. They need the help of every employee down the line in raising the bottom line. Unless employees know the new rules and are rewarded for their contributions to raising the bottom line — integrating social and economic goals — the whole process is slowed. A change in top management could abolish a company's overt social involvement. Social involvement has not been institutionalized.

The rising executive in any company must be able to earn his or her "star" by contributing to a broader concept of business success and long-term achievement. "Maximizing profits" and "new corporate strategies" can be fused into one dynamic force within business structures without contrivance. What is at stake is the difference between a free or a restricted marketplace; a private or a public economy.

To bring about the integration of social and economic planning — the integration of "social responsibility" — chief executive officers must come to understand that they cannot isolate themselves from middle-level managers or expect their managers to meet new goals under old operating concepts.

Nor can the executive remain aloof from the workings of government or the realities of the political arena, for the corporation is a social, economic, and political force in America. The executive must understand and be responsive to the needs and aspirations of the communities in which his company operates. And he or she must comprehend the social changes that have taken place, the issues that are now emerging, and the changing moods of the citizenry.

These demands, thrust upon corporate thinking in a span of fifteen years, have brought about fundamental changes in American business — for the good of business and the nation.

Historically, the business executive moved along his own path, toward his (or her) own perceived goals, and reacted to outside pressure only when absolutely necessary. Today, sales are influenced by the company's role as a community citizen, as a provider of consumer information, as a protector of the environment (by cleaning up old facilities and the careful selection of new plant sites), and much more.

MECHANICS OF INTEGRATION

Many efforts to integrate social thinking have failed because companies made the function an appendix to the personnel or public affairs department. Social involvement was not perceived to be *everybody's* responsibility but simply a new duty attached to one of the staff departments.

Most managers down the line viewed the whole idea of 'social' involvement as an exercise in appeasing vocal activist groups and a heavy-handed federal government.

Efforts were vulnerable to year-end budget cutting, especially during brief periods of recession in the seventies. Where minorities had been elected to boards, and committees of the board had been established to monitor social activity, the internal programs tended to be strengthened despite dips in the economy.

Social integration succeeded where top management asked staff and line managers to set social goals, approved them, and advised managers that their performance would be measured.

"Show a manager that social involvement will help him (or her) do the job better, and increase his chances for promotion and financial gain, and he will not only support the concept but will also contribute his ideas and skills," said Marusi.

In his own company — which was founded by Gail Borden in 1857 and in the seventies employed almost 50,000 men and women in 100 locations across the United States and in 30 other countries — Marusi had made social goal setting a collaborative effort. Upper management countersigned the objectives set by lower management for hiring minorities, assuring upward mobility for women, keeping plants safe and pollution-free, purchasing goods and services from minority-owned firms, and selecting new plant sites compatible with community interests.

Marusi knew that he personally had to set the tone and that the effort had to cut across divisional lines. He agreed to the formation of a council made up of top-level line and staff executives, including women and minorities, to inventory company activity, set basic rules for collaborative goal setting, and monitor social involvement.

"Auditing may come later," Marusi said in 1971, "but it is a puzzle to me why so many companies are obsessed with the idea of auditing social involvement, which is just developing, and attempting to justify its costs even before most managers down the line are aware of the issues, much less ready to set realistic goals."

But business types were fascinated with the idea of measuring costs. It was a natural bent. If business was going to engage in any activity, it wanted to know what it would cost and what it would get for the investment.

In July 1972, representatives of some sixty major companies met in Boston, under the auspices of the Public Affairs Council, to discuss the rationales and methodologies for conducting audits of corporate social responsibility efforts.

A distinguished panel of educators and consultants presented their views. But participants could not make connections between the theories offered by the academicians and the real problems confronting them within their companies and plants. The forum was an exercise in frustration. Audits can't be defined, much less conducted, until a body of knowledge, or at least boundaries for action, are defined. And the application of social responsibility varies sharply among companies, and even among different locations of the same company.

The men and women who met at Boston reflected the newness of the challenge that social responsibility presented to their companies. Among the conferees were men about to retire who had been plucked from sales or accounting to "tackle this new and important assignment." Some were new employees, right off the campus. Others were personnel and public affairs executives who were familiar with the problems and were attempting, even them, to fuse social and economic planning in their enterprises, to raise the concept of the bottom line to meet public needs.

The Boston meeting also attracted consultants looking for clients, professors seeking materials for articles and books, and a fair number of skeptics who yawned through the proceedings.

The titles of participants verified the diversity of their functions in different companies: urban affairs, minority affairs, public relations, public affairs, special counsel, management coordinator, assistant to the president.

The vast majority of the attendees did not report directly to the chief executive officer of their enterprise — a fundamental weakness in starting up a new program that had to cut across internal jurisdictions in order to succeed. They could not set policy, control funds, or administer such a program from the middle of the pack. One immediately knew that the chief officers of the companies they represented had not grasped either the significance or the permanency of corporate social involvement: "Sure, Joe, you go along to that meeting in Boston. Let me know what you find out."

It is essential that the officer responsible for integrating social responsibility throughout the company report directly to the chief executive officer [CEO]. He or she must have the visible and serious support of the CEO in implementing program and evaluating performance. Without those basic ground rules, integration is an impossible task.

Even with the CEO's constant endorsement and support, integration cannot be mandated. No manager removed from mahogany row, or even any seasoned executive at headquarters, will long ponder social goals, or comprehend that the integration of social and economic planning is a part of his or her day-to-day responsibilities, merely because a persuasive memo comes down from the CEO.

Until the riots, the only time a manager down the line got a memo or a phone call was when somebody up the ladder was raising hell or asking a favor. When a manager has been acclimated in this manner for five, ten, or twenty years, he tends to put a policy-type memo in the bottom drawer until the boss comes around to talk about it.

If the only visit from the CEO is to inspect the plant, discuss the safety record and ways to increase production; if the only time a CEO talks to a sales manager is to whip him about increasing markets, managers cannot

— will not — take seriously some new, fussy concept to which they cannot relate and to which they believe management reacts simply to ease external pressures.

Social integration requires much more: a sense of involvement must be transmitted down and across the company in a very personal way. The CEO must conduct meetings himself at which no other subject is reviewed.

Many business executives chide government for its two-layered management system: the transient bosses — appointed by the President and approved by the Senate — highly visible at the top, and the troops — the permanent Civil Service Corps (now the Office of Personnel Management) — doing "business as usual" down the line.

Business is guilty of the same dichotomy. The CEO may engage with minority groups, serve on government committees, head community programs, take leadership in trade organizations, make speeches on corporate social responsibility on distinguished platforms, but fail to enlist his own enterprise in the effort.

Integrating corporate social responsibility requires much more than pronouncements from the top, articles in company publications and even written policies or detailed instruction. Managers at every level must be personally convinced that social action helps them to make a profit, that short-term losses for long-term gains are blessed by management and that the boss really means what he says.

At Borden, Marusi chaired regional meetings with small groups of managers, usually over breakfast, lunch or dinner. He spelled out the reasons for social involvement in the managers' self-interest and described the way managers were expected to participate and benefit. He invited suggestions and questions. To add weight to his visits, he also addressed local service clubs and business groups so that his remarks were reported in plant towns. This put Borden on record with all area employees, suppliers, and civic leaders. His public remarks, reported in the news media, reinforced what he had told managers privately. But he always met with his managers first. Then he would speak publicly, and meet with representatives of the news media.

Sometimes Marusi, with his local manager, would call on the mayor or congressional representative to discuss ways in which the company might relate to community programs.

Marusi did these things himself, on the local manager's turf. His policies came alive. His managers knew that Marusi understood the problems they would encounter in implementing the new plans and that he intended to help them.

Marusi also agreed to a series of meetings for senior management, called "Chairman's Forum," at which invited guests talked candidly about changing social conditions and the new role of the corporation. Sen. Robert Taft and Gov. John Gilligan, both of Ohio; the late Berkeley Burrell, head of the National Business League; and Elizabeth Hanford Dole, then a consumer expert and now assistant to President Ronald Reagan, were among the invited guests. Governor Gilligan hosted Borden's management group in the executive mansion in Bexley.

Marusi also approved the total restructuring of the Borden Foundation to make it more efficient and responsive to emerging issues, and he scrutinized memberships paid for by the company to make certain Borden was supporting useful and appropriate programs and getting a return on its investment of time, manpower, and money.

He included a segment on corporate social responsibility in the ongoing sales, as well as production and quality control meetings held on a regular basis throughout the company.

Marusi also took over the chairmanship of the National Minority Supplier Development Council (originally the National Minority Purchasing Council) from Robert Stuart, chairman of National Can Corporation.

He found to his dismay in 1976 that Borden had been purchasing only $3 million annually from minority-owned firms. One year later, Borden spent $10 million, and within twenty-four months, the company was buying more than $23 million worth of goods and services from minority entrepreneurs in all parts of the country. Moreover, the Purchasing Council he chaired promoted action nationwide among all of industry, and reported an increase from only $86 million in 1972 to more than $3.7 billion in 1980.

Within his own enterprise, Marusi backed a minority affairs committee that made recommendations for the hiring and training of minority workers and for supporting a wide range of projects in various plant communities.

Marusi, and men like him in the top ranks of American industry, set the standard for integrating corporate social responsibility by their personal example.

Vernon Jordan, Jr., the outgoing head of the National Urban League (and the victim of a yet unsolved attempt on his life in 1980, in which he was seriously wounded), gives industry credit for maintaining most urban affairs units despite economic stress in the seventies. But he warns that industry should think twice about eliminating minority and urban affairs programs in the eighties in the wake of President Reagan's rollback of government support.

"Some companies have merged urban affairs functions with old-line departments, some have trimmed urban affairs programs to the bone, and others have simply abolished the function," he says. Jordan thinks companies are responding more to what he terms "the national indifference to minority needs and the shift from social involvement to more traditional ways of doing business that are more compatible with middle management and administrative preferences.

"Chipping away at urban affairs and affirmative action offices is self-defeating," Jordan says. "The problems that led to their creation are still there. In some companies, the axing of urban affairs may be the warning signal that corporate ardor for socially responsive policies is cooling. Black people will be watching carefully."

The eighties present the greater opportunity industry has ever known for balancing power with government. Whether industry succeeds or fails will depend on how well it integrates social responsibility into the fabric of the private enterprise system.

Chapter Four

Kreps's Busted Balloon

Juanita Kreps was not prepared for the harsh reaction to the speech she gave at Duke University one pleasant October afternoon in 1977. The secretary of commerce, speaking among friends in her home state, at the university she had served before accepting President Carter's invitation to join his cabinet, sent up a trial balloon called "Social Performance Index." It was quickly deflated.

She believed those corporation executives already engaged in social action would applaud her efforts to enlist all industry. The Department of Commerce, she said, would monitor industry's social performance and publish a scorecard. The soft-spoken cabinet officer was semantically insensitive.

Business is not persuaded to take a voluntary role in societal affairs by the notion of a government "index" or "report card."

Secretary Kreps failed to make industry her partner. The idea she articulated deserved a much more understanding response than it received. What she got was a public kick in the shins. The criticism were exaggerated, unfriendly for the most part, and unworthy of industry. But the secretary was basically at fault for her failure to make a joint statement with industry leaders and to encourage industry to issue its own report card. If industry had failed to act on its own in a reasonable time, the secretary could then have toughened her stance.

In fairness to Kreps, industry would probably have ignored her plea. But the gesture would have been an important strategy.

John H. Filer, chairman of Aetna Life & Casualty, and the late John D. Rockefeller 3rd, who shared the dais with the secretary that day, supported the concept of industry's involvement in social issues but cringed at her phrasing. They knew how business would respond to the notion of a government-monitored index.

The secretary told the chief executive officers of major companies seated in the audience that the Department of Commerce intended to publish a Social Performance Index that would give business a way of appraising the social effects of its operations. She said business could use the index to provide data on environmental controls, affirmative action, minority purchasing, resolution of consumer complaints, and product testing. The Commerce Department would compile the data and publish it in order to make the information widely available to the public and the press.

To the executives present, and the hundreds more who would read about the speech and receive caustic notices about it from their trade associations, the scheme constituted a public scorecard that would put corporations in competition with each other for public favor, with the Commerce Department acting as referee.

"By assisting businesses in evaluating their own performance, we can help to ensure that corporations get credit for the constructive things they are doing," the secretary said. That offended serious-minded business leaders who were concerned with the substantive role business could play in resolving national issues, and not with scoring brownie points. It also irritated those executives who had not yet committed their time or company resources to social activity. They heard the voice of "Big Brother" threatening them with embarrassment if they didn't get moving.

Those who supported the concept that secretary Kreps set forth and wanted very much to support her personally, were deeply concerned that the government would intervene in an area of voluntary effort and attempt to establish mores and standards. Those business executives who were laboring in the social arena knew full well that opportunities to succeed varied sharply among plant locations in their own companies, and even more among different industries with diverse operations. Setting standards, they knew, was a futile exercise, except as an individual company or perhaps a single industry — such as the insurance industry with its $2 billion urban investment effort — might conscientiously set goals and monitor its own performance.

The secretary compounded these general fears when she added, "This index would also allow those companies who are leaders in promoting the public interest to bring about an improvement in the behavior of less progressive firms. For the latter companies not to join the former is, I fear, to continue to invite governmental regulation."

FIGHTING WORDS

Those were fighting words, even though thoughtful business leaders recognized the truth of her statement.

History is replete with case studies of industry's resistance to societal needs later converted into laws. But businessmen resented the perceived threat and the seeming indifference to the strenuous efforts many companies had made, since the riots of the sixties, to do exactly what the secretary was preaching.

She promised that the index would bring credit to those companies that had taken leadership. Business leaders believed that a simple review of their efforts could have accomplished the same purpose.

Milton Moskowitz had published his own kind of "audit" twice monthly for several years, in his newsletter *Business & Society*. The modest, well-written, and carefully researched newsletter was read avidly by concerned business executives across the nation. Some strenuously opposed Moskowitz for suggesting that business had any social obligations. But most readers respected his objectivity, his reasoned arguments, and his candor. His criticism of industry's passivity were sometimes barbed, but never unfair.

Many of the major corporations had already established urban affairs departments and social involvement committees of staff and board long before Kreps spoke. A few companies had published their own "social" reports. Atlantic Richfield went so far as to invite Moskowitz to prepare a critique of its social performance — unedited — and published it as part of its own report.

Evidence of industry's response to social needs was available to the secretary. Industry's overall performance may have been lacking, but no more than government's. It was clear that industry had initiated many useful projects, and had worked in partnership with government to form the National Urban Coalition and the National Alliance of Businessmen, to fight the war on poverty, and even to attempt to reform the nation's welfare system.

Business executives believed, therefore, that Juanita Kreps should have recognized those efforts, urged more voluntary action, and pledged the support of the Commerce Department. She then might have asked industry to assemble its own report to share with the government and the public so as to promote even broader voluntary involvement.

The secretary intended only to encourage and stimulate action; to warn industry that the national mood and the urgency of social needs demanded voluntary action to diminish the growing zeal for regulatory mandates. But her message did not register that way.

Secretary Kreps actually presented a test for private initiative: Was industry willing to work with government on a continuing basis to maintain a proper balance of power between the public and private sectors? That her challenge was poorly presented was unfortunate, but not as unfortunate as industry's harsh response. Industry's collective resentment about the presumed "threat" obscured the need for business executives to respond intelligently to the basic message: business is in trouble; it will be regulated in the social arena if it does not step up its voluntary efforts.

David W. Ewing of the *Harvard Business Review* wrote in *Harper's* magazine in January 1978 that "Safety scares, health hazards, energy worries, inflation, and unemployment are making industry the target of increasing public frustration."

Kreps knew that the public would attack industry through the political process if industry did not make its case in a convincing manner through the mass media, with government as its ally. But that vital point was blurred. And industry's knee-jerk reaction diminished the opportunity for reasonable discussion.

One reason, perhaps, for industry's instant rejection of the proposal was the belief that it had Jimmy Carter's stamp of approval and was not simply a trial balloon floated by the secretary among business acquaintances in North Carolina.

Anne Wexler, the deputy under secretary for regional affairs at the Commerce Department, had distributed the speech one day in advance to corporate affairs officers throughout Washington.

There were exceptions to industry's generally negative response. "Gus" Marusi wrote to the secretary, "The task you have outlined deserves the wholehearted cooperation of business and industry, but the means that are adopted to ascertain performance are absolutely vital in terms of generating cooperation and useful data. Even within an individual company, business executives have learned that opportunities for progress vary plant to plant. Measurement criteria among industries presents an even greater challenge."

Most letters were not so polite.

PUBLIC RIDICULE

The syndicated columnist James J. Kilpatrick devoted a column to the proposal, calling it "Mrs. Kreps' silly do-good plan."

"Why this giddy index?" Kilpatrick asked. "Will the Carter administration never be content to get off the people's backs, and simply to leave the people alone? Mrs. Kreps is a nice person. I do not mean to say an unkind word about her. She means well. But this is an especially fatuous idea; it is a piece of solicitous do-gooding, at once silly and symptomatic, and it is the kind of thing that tends to make big governments bigger."

Kilpatrick was riding the corporate horse, and he knew it. He wrote on, "But Mrs. Kreps is not satisfied with what business is doing on its own. Onward and upward! . . . She will assist business in evaluating their own performance. She will ensure businesses that they get public credit for the good things they do. She will thus use the example of the good children to encourage the bad children and it will all be peachy keen. . . . Madam, one would like to say, go help someone else. For the harassed businessman, this is one more form, one more report, one more drain on executive time, one more needless, unwanted, goody-goody intrusion by government."

It can be assumed the Kilpatrick response was gleefully passed around corporate suites, framed and hung in business offices, and Xeroxed by the thousands for display to head-nodding plant managers, salespersons, and public affairs people.

But what exactly did the good lady say to deserve such ridicule?

She pointed out that no fewer than three government agencies — the Commerce Department, Federal Trade Commission, and Securities and Exchange Commission — were examining the public responsibilities of corporations; that business and professional associations, such as the American Bar Association and the Business Roundtable, were also weighing corporate obligations to society.

She said a socially concerned company takes into account the ways in which its daily activities affect its constituents and attempts to integrate public concerns and company goals.

She acknowledged that a corporation's first obligation is to succeed, to be profitable, but argued that the public assesses corporations on the basis of their social involvement as well as their profits. And she noted that youth, especially, are much more concerned with the uses of profits in terms of the general welfare.

She stated flatly that "business [persons] can address the social consequences of their actions far better on their own than with the help of government," and urged businesses to give evidence to legislators of their willingness to "preclude further oppressive legislation." The plea might have been drafted by Richard Lesher, president of the Chamber of Commerce of the United States.

The secretary also praised the work performed by Control Data, Bank of America, Standard Oil of Indiana, Babcock & Wilcox, Avon Products, Owens-Illinois, Prudential Insurance, Honeywell, Equitable Insurance, and Atlantic Richfield. She cited these companies chiefly for their public accountability as well as their innovative programs. She praised their collective efforts to create jobs in urban centers, integrate socioeconomic concerns, develop minority-owned enterprises, assess their social impact on society, buy goods and services from minority firms, take extraordinary measures to control pollution, and renovate housing in poor neighborhoods.

But the positive examples, she cautioned, did not suggest an industry stampede. She called for a series of regional conferences to begin in 1978 to review industry "models" that incorporated social issues into the mainstream of corporate activity.

Kreps also spoke of liaison with the Urban Economic Policy Committee of the U.S. Conference of Mayors, chaired by Mayor Coleman Young of Detroit and by Coy Eklund, president and chief officer of The Equitable Life Assurance Society. She said a commission would be formed to examine ways of involving business in alleviating the deeply rooted problem of structural unemployment.

None of these suggestions alone would have surprised or troubled most business leaders. But when the secretary added her intended liaison with the Environmental Protection Agency to expand the "ongoing regional seminars on 'Pollution Prevention Days,'" the business leaders rebelled at what they considered to be overkill.

The secretary concluded her now famous "index" speech among the fallen leaves at Durham by promising that Commerce Department initiatives would "be developed jointly with the corporations, particularly with those who are providing leadership in these fields, as well as with consumer representatives, environmental groups, and others."

PUT-DOWN BY THE ROUNDTABLE

But it was too late.

The cruelest blow to the secretary's proposal came from the prestigious Business Roundtable. Kreps had announced in her speech that her office would be working with the roundtable to develop and publish the index. Irving Shapiro of du Pont was its chairman; Reginald Jones of General Electric and Thomas Murphy of General Motors were its cochairmen.

In a letter to Kreps dated December 6, 1977, the roundtable's Washington-based executive director, John Post, wrote, "I want to clear up what may be a misunderstanding. . . . Members of the Business Roundtable are recognized leaders in the field of social performance and share your belief that progress in this area should be encouraged and applauded. Having said that, I must tell you that since the public discussion of a proposed index began in October, we have heard from many Roundtable members and they are all against the "index" concept ["all" was underlined in the letter]. They believe that such a measurement would be impractical, unworkable, and unfair.

"It is suggested that the index be voluntary. The history of voluntary government systems, however, leads business leaders to fear that the ultimate result would be the imposition of even more regulation on a burdensomely regulated business community. Thus, the proposal of an index could result in confrontation now between business and government at a time when cooperation is needed."

The balloon-deflating letter concluded by saying, "While the Business Roundtable has taken no formal position on the index concept, the communications we have had from members clearly establish that they are strongly opposed to it. Therefore, it would be most unfortunate and misleading if anyone were to gain the impression that our members support the index idea."

Homer E. Moyer, Jr., the attorney in charge of the effort at commerce, and his colleagues saw the rug being pulled out from under the program with one swift tug by the powerful business group. Obviously, earlier exchanges between commerce and roundtable personnel had been more cordial and mutually supportive. The secretary would not have suggested in her address that the Commerce Department would fashion the index in cooperation with the roundtable if she had not received such assurances, at least from her own staff.

Although a sense of betrayal permeated the fifth floor of the Commerce Building, staff bravely continued to plan a meeting on December 16, 1977, with business leaders.

But attendees had been thoroughly preconditioned by the roundtable before their arrival.

Social activists, academicians, and association representatives also participated in the meeting. The Consumer Federation of America complained about *not* being invited, giving rise to speculation among business people that any government-run appraisal of industry's social action would surface a carnival of special interests and make impossible any sensible accounting of industry performance.

Moyer repeated throughout the day that because of the "misunderstanding" over the word "index" the subject should now be referred to as "Corporate Social Performance Review."

The meeting foundered uncomfortably on generalities, philosophy, and unsuccessful attempts at defining "corporate responsibility."

The social activists objected to the spending of public monies to develop a monitoring device for corporate performance.

Business people sharply questioned the role of commerce in suggesting the index, or review, as it would now be called, and vigorously objected to more reporting to the government.

Work initiated by the Human Resources Network (HRN) in Philadelphia, a respected research firm hired by the Commerce Department to involve the business community in fashioning a "fair" social performance review model, was quickly aborted. HRN had been told to step up its activity following Kreps' speech at Duke. But the negative response to that speech, compounded by the criticisms dumped on the idea at the meeting of December 16, cooled the project permanently. The HRN was put on hold, serving thereafter only as "advisors" to Moyer and his colleagues.

After the meeting, Stephen Nowlan of HRN wrote to a business associate, "unless the project is reconstituted to restore our original role, we cannot participate."

WHAT WENT WRONG?

Why this bungling? The secretary seemed to have selected the right moment, the right subject, the right audience. But she failed to communicate effectively with industry prior to her speech, a speech that reflected her assumptions rather than commitments for voluntary action by business executives.

She intended, it is clear, to help industry coordinate its activities in the maze of conflicting and overlapping regulatory jurisdictions. But her proposal, with trigger words raising hairs on the back of the necks of corporate executives, was heard as still another layer of snooping, a redundancy that would plague the already harried business executive.

Kreps's balloon was busted by poor communication and insensitive strategy. The encouragement of a voluntary program, planned by the heads of the Business Roundtable, the Conference Board, the Chamber of Commerce of the United States, the National Association of Manufacturers, the Public Affairs Council, and others, might have succeeded. If the secretary of commerce, in the company of the President and industry leaders, had announced the program, it might have set the stage for a massive voluntary effort in the private sector.

If such a public-private effort failed to rally convincing voluntary action; if it failed to integrate social and economic planning in most corporations; and if industry, after such a grand send-off, failed to account to the people and the government for its performance on a voluntary basis, it should then suffer regulation in silence.

But Secretary Kreps did not set such a stage. Her position was sound: she urged business to expand its voluntary efforts. But business should have been asked to speak for itself.

She failed not because her proposal lacked merit, but simply because she did not persuade business people to accept the idea as their own, with the government as an ally and supporter.

One can encourage voluntarism. One can inspire voluntary action. One cannot mandate it.

Chapter Five

Measuring Social Progress

Almost from the start, in the period following the riots, cost-oriented business executives were sometimes more obsessed with analyzing the cost of social involvement than the costs of noninvolvement. It was a habit, a mind set hard to throw off.

The cities had been set afire. Government was rushing through regulations that would restrict business freedoms. Social activists were placing new demands on industry. And in many instances, industry was being presented as the villain in a traumatic domestic drama.

Yet, industry, for the most part, reacted in typical fashion, choosing to deal with the "passing" crisis, doing what it could on a stopgap basis to train and employ minorities, offering rebuttal and defending against attacks by environmental and consumer groups, and watching the costs.

I called on one company chairman in New Jersey in 1968 to ask his support for the recently formed National Urban Coalition in Washington. He was an open, caring individual. I had known him for several years, and he had regularly attended the series of dinner meetings I had arranged in Washington with Dan H. Fenn, Jr.

He was sensitive to the problems that beset the nation and anxious to help. But he claimed not to know how. He said he needed more time "to sort things out" and pointed to a stack of mail on the corner of his desk. "Those are requests for money from more than twenty groups who say they can help solve the urban crisis," he gestured. "Most of them have the word urban in their titles. One of those letters is from your organization. Let me think about it."

When I reported my friend's reaction to John W. Gardner, the coalition's chairman and a former secretary of Health, Education, and Welfare, he was visibly irritated. "The nation is in crisis and he is sorting mail," Gardner snorted. "We need commitment and involvement as well as money. I'm disappointed."

I heard a lot of silly talk from intelligent men and women in 1968 about "maintaining a low profile until this thing blows over," and I witnessed a discouraging amount of foot-dragging in industry's response to social pressures.

Government regulation rushed in where private initiatives were wanting.

A dozen of the big companies were way out front, training minorities for jobs, "adopting" urban schools, setting up minority distributorships, depositing money in minority banks, establishing minority businesses, and increasing purchases fivefold from minority companies. They loaned executives to the government and community organizations. They revised their contributions programs to include social change groups critical of business.

"Gus" Marusi at Borden would agree to a program in which his line and staff managers set goals for social performance on which they were measured. Failure to perform could cost an errant manager a promotion or a healthy percentage of his or her annual bonus. Western Electric and Standard Oil of Indiana in Chicago would spearhead the minority purchasing concept (long before the riots) and give access to minority entrepreneurs previously cut off from the mainstream of commerce and industry.

But the majority of American companies could not comprehend that they were not simply caught up in a passing crisis, but rather a basic revolutionary change in socioeconomic thinking.

Bill Norris of Control Data in Minneapolis saw opportunity in the change. So did Kenneth Dayton of Dayton Hudson. Most of their peers saw only government intervention and the loss of public esteem.

"Gus" Marusi recognized the need for leadership, and headed the National Association of Manufacturers' [NAM] Urban Affairs Committee and chaired a Business-Industry Council in support of the White House Conference on Children and Youth. Most executives preferred to play a more passive role.

Milton Moskowitz and other social writers served to remind industry leaders of their new role in a changing society. Press attention to business's public accountability spread from the business pages to the front pages, and eventually to food sections, consumer columns, and occasionally, to the editorial pages.

By the end of the sixties, business was sitting up straight and taking notice. By the early seventies, the big-name companies had appointed directors of urban affairs, vice presidents for public affairs, and even vice presidents of corporate social responsibility. E. B. "Burt" Knauft at Aetna and Phillip T. Drotning at Standard Oil of Indiana (SOI) were among the first to be so titled. They have not been empty titles at Aetna and SOI: Aetna has established an extraordinary record of pragmatic social involvement, including enormous financial investments in urban centers, and aggressive efforts to curb "redlining" practices, in which residents and business owners in poor neighborhoods find it difficult to obtain either mortgages or insurance coverage. Aetna has also shown uncommon leadership in relating philanthropy to emerging needs.

SOI and Western Electric pioneered the minority purchasing plan, enlisted other companies, and set the pace. Long before most companies had begun to organize minority purchasing goals, SOI and Western Electric were each spending $60 million a year with minority-owned companies. (Eight years later, only General Motors had topped $200 million a year with minority suppliers. Ford exceeded $100 million. SOI had reached $75 million, and Western Electric continued to purchase in excess of $60 million, year after year.

Bank of America and Atlantic Richfield were publishing social reports on a voluntary basis, and were soon followed by Aetna Life & Casualty, Standard Oil of Indiana, and other large companies. Still, in most companies, the "social" effort was separate from day-to-day activity. Integration would come slowly, moved forward by the internal persistence of public affairs executives.

Step by step, social planning was fused with marketing, personnel administration, plant closings, site selection for new installations, purchasing practices, legal debates on product safety and consumer interests, and finally, long-range planning.

New structures were set up within the corporate organizations to deal with regulatory requirements: packaging and labeling, environmental safeguards, worker health and safety, and much more.

The means of compliance necessarily differed from company to company and from plant to plant within the same companies. No clear definition had or could be drawn to explain "corporate social responsibility." Still, there persisted among academicians and management consultants, and among business executives with a bent toward engineering and accounting, a desire to quantify and qualify the new function.

The late Prof. Raymond A. Bauer, and Dan H. Fenn, Jr., had become deeply interested in the notion of a social audit. They collaborated in holding seminars, drawing up theoretical models and writing articles.

Bauer was professor of business administration at the Harvard

Business School (HBS); Fenn, in addition to his duties as director of the John F. Kennedy Library, was a lecturer at the HBS.

Bauer and Fenn saw that a fair number of the large — and even medium-sized — socially oriented companies had put together programs of one sort or another, and that many executives were attracted to the idea of finding measurement tools to assure themselves and the public that they were responding to social pressures in useful ways.

However, corporate social efforts in the immediate post riot years were little known and not universally adopted.

BIG INFLUENCE

No entity in American society has more social influence than the biggest private employer, taxpayer, borrower, and spender — the corporation. The fortunes of business and society are totally enmeshed.

But this fact was not generally perceived until the riots of the sixties.

Until then, the government was little more responsive than business to the simmering racial crisis. When the inevitable eruption came, business and government, for a precarious moment, became two victims looking for a villain. They struck out at each other. But the severity of the problems cooled animosities and brought business and government together, almost as if the country had come under attack from some outside force, rather than from within.

Not in a hundred years had the nation suffered such internal splintering and trauma. Youth could not accept the world according to Lyndon Johnson and a jingoistic Congress. Blacks, Hispanics, American Indians, and other minorities could no longer tolerate the back of the bus, the end of the employment line, the dregs of housing in seething urban centers.

But even if companies were willing to act, how could the tasks be accomplished? Where would the money and manpower come from?

Logically, they would come from a partnership with government, for neither business nor government could do the job alone. The problems must be shared, most observers agreed. It was more comfortable after the riots to say that all Americans were the victims and none of them the villains. It was reassuring that no single element of society could be made totally accountable, that this national trauma had simply fermented and erupted.

DIFFERENT MIND SET

The eighties have indeed started as the sixties ended. But we are not at all the same people we were then. We have been conditioned. Our mind set is different.

Business-government arrangements to accomplish social objectives are more commonplace: to meet the challenges of environmental health and safety, assure employment, and even the survival — or at least the extended life — of basic industries.

The corporation as a social entity is better understood and accepted; its integrated role in society is undeniable and important.

Have some companies backed off from their social role? Are some companies less dedicated to social issues, more concerned with short-term, bottom-line pressures now that the economy is on a decline, a conservative administration is in power, and foreign competition is on the rise?

There has been a certain amount of regression. But America's second civil war, fought on the city streets a little more than a dozen years ago, is not forgotten. Industry has always had the choice of taking initiatives in the public arena or waiting for government to set the rules. It has rarely opted for the former, and has suffered historically for the latter. That business is overregulated is apparent; that business often has invited regulation by its inaction is equally apparent.

In the eighties, business has the opportunity to balance power between the public and private sectors by facing the consequences of the information it has, and acting on the predictive data it regularly collects from futurists and social research firms.

Industry has the knowledge and the power to lead. It is industry, as William Gorham, longtime head of the Urban Institute, points out, "that decides where plants will be built, what will be produced, how much will be produced and how many people will be employed."

Gorham and other knowledgeable observers of change in American society applaud recent efforts by industry to coordinate their urban investments with federal expenditures; to encourage community revitalization through new, privately funded programs such as the Local Initiatives Support Corporation, which is financed by the Ford Foundation and six major corporations.

More and more, industry is not only meeting government halfway but also initiating action, building models, and demonstrating how business and government can and must relate their goals and actions in order to anticipate and solve socioeconomic problems. To maintain a healthy balance of power requires uncommon cooperation between agencies of government and private organizations. Our elected officials and our business executives must understand their public and social obligations and replace their traditional adversarial posturing with continuous two-way communication and mutual planning.

The splintering of America by special interest groups in recent years has also fragmented the Congress, scattered leadership among self-interest crusades and causes, and blurred national goals. The splintering has rendered the nation vulnerable to attack from both within and without.

By taking pragmatic initiatives and being publicly accountable for its performance, industry can assure a balance of power with government and help to bring the nation together. Its leadership would not only assure the survival of the private enterprise system in America, but of America itself.

No nation can endure divisions and subdivisions and multidivisions and remain whole. The pluralism we have cherished in America keeps us free and independent; it sets us apart as a people. But it is our recognized national goals that keeps us together as a people.

In the eighties, the development of a business-government alliance is essential. Public-private planning and coordinated action can mobilize diverse interests in support of national goals.

Every organization needs to define the larger purposes within which its legitimate self-interests can be achieved. This does not mean that the distinction between business and government should be blurred, but only that socioeconomic planning must be shared.

PART TWO

Adversarial Mania

Chapter Six

The Rise and Fall of Government Regulation

Someone once said — probably a businessman — that a government regulation is a compassionate impulse converted into an economic monstrosity.

Surely the railroad barons felt that way when in 1890 the Interstate Commerce Commission decided to oversee their operations to protect the public from monopolistic practices.

Once started, government regulations multiplied like rabbits, and the bureaucratic agencies created to administer them became entrenched.

Regulatory excesses hit their peak in the troubled sixties when activists for special interest groups — minorities, consumer advocates, and environmental protectionists — put enormous pressure on the Congress.

Overregulation and its transfer costs to consumers became a critical political issue. Ronald Reagan campaigned strongly for dismantling the expensive regulatory machinery and "getting big government off the backs of the people."

It was a popular appeal. Computers had already invaded the personal privacy of many citizens. Voters were increasingly wary of more government intrusion in their lives.

Voters also saw that the nation's automobile industry was going downhill as more efficient, lower-priced imports flooded the market. Jobs were being lost in Detroit and in other cities dependent on a strong domestic automotive industry.

The voters tended to side with automakers, who complained bitterly to the Carter administration that safety and environmental regulations were pricing U.S. cars out of the market.

Skeptics argued that the regulations governing mileage, emissions, and safety had already proved their value and had in fact made the U.S. auto industry more competitive with foreign manufacturers. They pointed out that for many years America's automakers had ignored the need to produce more efficient cars, and that it was their own lack of planning, not government regulations, that had caused the alarming dip in domestic auto sales.

But the regulatory issue was more political than intellectual, and, as columnist James J. Kilpatrick wrote after Reagan's impressive victory, "The President scarcely had taken off his top hat on Inauguration Day" before he named Vice President George Bush head of a Task Force on Regulatory Relief. While applauding the President's action, Kilpatrick warned that the new administration might find that the rule-making disease "can only be temporarily slowed."

The focus was clearly on the dismantlers, however, and business executives across the nation began to slap each other on the back and pour money into massive campaigns mounted by the Chamber of Commerce of the United States and the National Association of Manufacturers to get public support for the President's new budget (for reducing social expenditures and unwanted regulation while increasing military expenditures).

Not all thinking executives were so quick to rejoice. A. W. "Tom" Clausen, outgoing president of the Bank of America (and the new president of the World Bank), and Andrew C. Sigler, chairman of Champion International, convened a meeting in New York City of several chief officers of major corporations to discuss the new burdens that would be imposed on business by the rollback of federal funds and the relaxation of government regulations. Clausen and Sigler, who both played key roles in the Business Roundtable, argued that the social and health problems of the nation would be exacerbated and that industry would have to develop its own voluntary programs.

The rapid dismantling of regulations and government-sponsored social programs would require, they said, a redefinition of industry's role in society.

The general euphoria among business celebrants would not be diminished, however, and a quick telephone survey I conducted of a half-dozen corporate contributions managers in May 1981 confirmed that most companies — including those represented at the Clausen-Sigler meeting — were restricting rather than expanding their giving programs.

The rise of government regulations had given business a headache. The fall of regulations might give business gas pains as well.

The swing of the pendulum was predictable. Regulations had gone too far, had become too costly, and industry was determined to go on a removal binge, with the support of the new administration in Washington, and toss out all that unwanted machinery. Industry would get back to a free market system and then, most thought, everything would be just fine. Except, of course, for those industries that needed and wanted regulation.

The general conclusion was that Reagan's men would relieve industry of economic constraints but keep a watchful eye on regulations that protect worker safety and public health. But there was an eagerness to get on with as much dismantling as possible as quickly as possible.

Arthur Andersen & Company had conducted a study of regulatory impact (commissioned by the Business Roundtable) in which it noted that the Lord's Prayer contains 56 words, Lincoln's Gettysburg Address 268, and the Declaration of Independence 1,322, but a government regulation on the sale of cabbage ran 26,911 words!

Examining the impact of only six federal agencies on forty-eight roundtable companies, the Andersen study found that regulatory compliance had cost a total of $2.6 billion in 1977 — 43 percent of what the same forty-eight companies spent on research and development that year, and 16 percent of their combined net income.

Murray Weidenbaum, before he was appointed chairman of the Council of Economic Advisers in the Reagan administration, had called for a careful balancing of bona fide considerations — clean air and lower unemployment, safer products and less inflation, healthier working conditions and rising productivity. He recommended phasing out economic controls that interfere with marketplace competition, and mandating cost-benefit analysis and cost-effectiveness studies prior to issuance of new regulations. Even the regulators could agree with Weidenbaum's sensible approach.

Other voices raised within the new administration were more rash and controversial. Office of Management and Budget (OMB) chief David Stockman claimed that if the beleaguered Federal Trade Commission (FTC) were eliminated, the world would never know the difference. "The more money they have," he said, "the more regulations and interference they're going to generate."

Stockman had equally harsh things to say about activist groups. "They've created this whole facade of consumer protection in order to seize power in our society. I think part of the mission of this administration is to unmask and discredit that false ideology."

There were those who strongly opposed Stockman's ideology and brashness. And the battle lines were drawn.

The Carter administration had sensed the growing political importance of the regulatory debate during the 1980 campaign. In May of that year, President Carter grudgingly signed the Federal Trade Commission Improvements Act, saving the FTC from extinction but requiring its staff to conduct "sound economic analysis" and "find the least burdensome way of achieving its goals."

Leveling his ire at industry, President Carter said, "If powerful interests can turn to the political arena as an alternative to the legal process, our system of justice will not function in a fair and orderly fashion."

Business had, in fact, been operating in the political arena for several generations.

By the fall of 1980, Carter was talking about "stripping away needless and costly regulation in favor of marketplace forces wherever possible."

When, on October 14, he signed the Staggers Rail Act that provided incentives for railroads to improve equipment and attract shippers, Carter sounded more like Reagan than Reagan: "This Act is the capstone of my efforts over the past four years to get the Federal Government off the backs of private industry by removing needless, burdensome regulation which benefits no one and harms us all."

Carter noted that his administration had deregulated the airlines, freed the trucking industry from "archaic and inflationary regulations," and deregulated financial institutions to eliminate many restrictions on loans and improve services to small savers.

"Where regulations cannot be eliminated, we have established a program to reform the way they are produced and reviewed. . . . We have established a sunset review program for major new regulations, and cut federal paperwork by 15 percent. . . . I am hopeful for Congressional action on my broad regulatory reform proposal," Carter recited. But it was too late.

Public officials argued for some regulations — and against others. Many business executives seemed ambivalent. One could not blame the public for being confused about who was for and against regulation.

Donald MacNaughton pointed out in 1976 the confusion generated "when the businessman who normally advocates minimal interference by government, reverses himself and seeks government help when his own company is in trouble. If we truly believe in the [market] system and want to convince others of its value, we must act consistently."

MacNaughton might have been forecasting the Chrysler dilemma to come, and the general demise of the automobile industry, which for years had fought all forms of government intrusion, then begged the government to slap import quotas on Japanese cars to protect its home market and even accepted outright financial subsidy.

BUSINESS AND POLITICS

Laws governing business's conduct changed little in the first hundred years of the Republic. Few constraints were placed on business as an institution in society. In fact, politics were strongly influenced by business, and industries, such as railroads and shipping, received substantial government subsidy.

Important changes occurred between 1895 and Franklin D. Roosevelt's New Deal, cooling the business-government love affair. The labor movement strengthened and challenged the monopoly of business interests in the political arena. The subsequent institutionalization of the Civil Service System and the reform of the electoral and legislative processes also weakened the business power-brokers. Further, the growth of powerful newspaper chains and an increasingly literate public created a new and more open political climate. Business became a player rather than the dealer.

Perhaps the most radical change in the American political process took place between the New Deal and Lyndon Johnson's Great Society. The federal government was transformed from passive overseer to the granter of benefits — benefits never before considered the responsibility of the national government. The role of granter also made government the rule-maker. It began to publish guidelines and instructions, and the library of regulatory jargon was founded.

In the beginning, little of the progovernment thrust was antibusiness. Actually, business was very much a partner in the political process chiefly because of its generous financial support of its favorite candidates and incumbents, thus building powerful friends in Washington. Business also often developed close — sometimes uncomfortably close — relationships with the agencies that regulated its practices.

Still, the public had faith in business and usually perceived that business interests and the national interest, if not always in harmony, were really not incompatible.

The riots of the sixties, the divisive Vietnam war, and the Nixon capers of the seventies eroded public trust in business and all large institutions. With activist groups on the attack, and a Congress eager to respond and calm the nation, business found itself increasingly regulated. Demands for safer products, cleaner air and water, and jobs for minorities pushed business away from traditional bottom-line considerations. Success was no longer confined to making and selling products, or providing services. Business was forced to address the social needs of the nation. Regulations told them how.

In the past, the typical business attitude toward social legislation was to ignore it as long as possible. When business could no longer ignore it, it opposed it. Business had been opposing social legislation that the majority of citizens supported since the turn of the century. Now social legislation was pouring through the Congress, almost all of it impacting on business. Not only was business involved, but it was losing power, and losing face. Business got no credit for abiding by laws it had so fiercely fought. The public mood, as Daniel Yankelovich would record in the early seventies, changed from "I demand" to "I am entitled."

Gradually, and reluctantly, business assumed a role in societal affairs and came to demonstrate its concern for the national welfare. But it continued to lose power and prestige — and to suffer overregulation.

Aetna Life & Casualty's chairman, John H. Filer, chided business and industry for their failure to take modest initiatives that might have minimized government mandates: "We failed to take reasonable action on our own, so now we must abide with unreasonable restraints."

Most business executives agreed with Filer's observation. It was not that business people could not see the scenario unfolding; it was simply that the situation was beyond their traditional experience. They were not prepared. They responded too slowly.

Business executives believed the attacks were unfair and unwarranted; new regulations were unnecessary and burdensome. They resented the public's displeasure with business, considered it disloyal, and were more angry than responsive. Most business leaders were not ready to face reality.

A paper sent to participants in a colloquium on corporate priorities in 1975 pointed out that data compiled by Yankelovich, Skelly & White reflected a widespread sense that business's influence on government worked against the public interest and therefore must be curbed.

The colloquium was held immediately following the Watergate affair and President Nixon's forced departure from the White House. At that critical moment in American history, close cooperation between business and government was needed to harmonize efforts among units in the public and private sectors. But the public was suspicious of relations between business and government and, in fact, wanted business's freedoms contained.

Because of blatant chicanery among business organizations in the funneling of political contributions in the Nixon years, campaign-spending laws were tightened. Lobbying laws, virtually unchanged since 1946, came under scrutiny. The appeal for reform was basically for more openness and less hidden influence and not against lobbying itself. People simply wanted to get everything out in the open.

The zeal for regulatory constraint of business in the seventies stemmed not only from business's past isolation from societal needs but also from its alleged manipulation of government in its own self-interest and — it was commonly believed — against the best interest of society.

In 1976, S. John Byington, chairman of the often unpopular Consumer Products Safety Commission, chided industry for its failure to provide data to the government when regulations were drafted. "Regulation in a data vacuum will result in bad regulation," he told a business audience in Chicago.

But business did not trust government. It held fiercely to its proprietary information and was conditioned to resist any request for data, any suggested intrusion into its affairs. Many business executives still believed in their minds and hearts that "things would get back to normal."

Because of business's basic distrust of government and its suspicion — sometimes with justification — that any information it provided would not be safeguarded, business was to foreclose many opportunities to help shape and mold regulation.

Industry might have addressed societal needs on a voluntary basis and avoided overregulation. With certain splendid exceptions, it did not opt to do so. A ponderous federal government, itself under attack, was thus able to shift the focus to industry.

The excellent work of the National Urban Coalition and the National Alliance of Businessmen, and business's support of the Urban League, the NAACP, and the National Business League were genuine and constructive. The heading had begun. But it would take much more to offset the negative perception of business. Business would become the victim of overregulation. It was not immediately understood that society would also become the victim.

"Any time the pendulum swings too far in one direction, we get in trouble," said Augustine R. Marusi. "The benefits of regulation to end pollution, promote worker safety, secure pension rights, and equal opportunity seemed to outweigh by far any possible costs from more government intervention in public life back in the sixties. Indeed, as I recall, scholars, journalists, and the public tended to dismiss any business objection to more regulation as self-serving; an attempt to preserve private business convenience at the cost of the public welfare. It even seemed that way to many business executives of conscience.

"But things have gone too far. The evidence is all round us. Not just the impact on business, but the change in all of society. The government rulebook is not only telling industries how to control pollution and the like, but also instructing universities and hospitals and social welfare agencies and foundations how to conduct their affairs. Even the individual citizen is told how he or she should behave."

The federal government gives back to the municipalities the tax monies it has collected from them. But with the allocation of funds goes an increasingly complicated, comprehensive set of rules and regulations.

According to Marusi, "The federal government has no business telling any local school board, local library board, or local health agency what is important and not important in their home town."

Indeed, when business executives talk about overregulation, they are speaking about a shared experience, whether the listener is an academic, a member of a profession, a journalist, or even a government official.

Marusi and many other executives complain that business must employ staff that has no direct connection with the production or marketing of its products in order to comply with government regulations: additional lawyers, accountants, engineers, personnel specialists, hygienists, and so on. They do not believe citizens are conscious of the costs they share for the new bureaucracies set up within industry to keep pace with the regulatory bureaucracy of government.

Business, like the universities and social agencies, suffers from having federal officials substitute their judgment for that of the men and women on the scene.

"I recall a dispute we had in a processing facility where the regulatory agency insisted we install a quarter of a million dollar treatment plant at the end of the process to clean up what was coming out. Our engineers found a better way to do the job by changing the process itself and recycling the effluent. The agency would not accept our alternative even though it produced more clean-up at less cost," Marusi said, shaking his head. "There was no room in their regulations for a different, innovative approach."

The imposition of decision-making authority from top to bottom is perhaps the chief reason for universal discord in the implementation of government regulations.

The nation would be in deep trouble if the innovative spirit should be diminished in the private sector.

John W. Gardner, an extraordinary man of new beginnings (Carnegie Corporation, secretary of Health, Education, and Welfare, chairman of the National Urban Coalition, founder of Common Cause, leader of the Independent Sector) and one of America's great thinkers and writers, talked often about the loss of independence that accompanies government regulation.

"One thinks of the agencies supported by the United Way as private agencies, yet the federal money going to those agencies averages 25 percent of their budgets. And with federal money comes the federal rulebook. Never before have private sector agencies been more plagued by governmental regulations," Gardner said.

"This poses the familiar conflict between the government's requirement of accountability and the private institution's requirement of independence. As long as private institutions have multiple sources of support and the federal money is only one among several sources, independence is a possibility. But even with modest federal funding, we're going to have to work toward arrangements that reconcile independence and accountability. Otherwise, private sector institutions will all eventually become arms of the federal government."

Regulation not only restricts the action of private institutions and increases the costs of their administration to comply with regulations but also transfers decision-making authorities and discourages innovation.

Business and industry might have taken initiatives in the fifties and sixties that would have greatly diminished government intervention. The mind set of the average business executive toward social involvement worked against that possibility. But business faced no barrier other than its own traditional way of viewing the bottom line.

I do not suggest that business could or should do the job of government. That is not its role.

I am suggesting that industry can fully engage in social and economic planning where it has heavy investments in plant facilities; where it is a significant employer and taxpayer. Total involvement means much more than giving generously to the United Way or supporting levies when money runs low for social programs. It requires the planned involvement in education, transportation, social services, pollution control — and philanthropy.

Business has a choice: become fully involved in the life of the nation through plant-town leadership or continue to suffer the restrictions of federal regulation and rule making.

REFORM, NOT ABOLITION

It is a good bet that even Theodore Roosevelt, the great trustbuster and early regulator of industry, would be appalled at the mass of federal limits imposed on American commerce today. The goal of the twenty-sixth President's vigorous moves toward control was to protect "the little man," never to destroy individual or corporate initiative and achievement.

Theodore Roosevelt could no doubt join in leading today's movement to give individuals greater freedom and get the government "out of their hair." The demand for less government interference in the details of individual lives and the conduct of commerce and industry draws almost total agreement to the proposition, "Cut down on government regulation."

Leaders of business call for freedom from costly compliance at a time when industry and the economy need revitalization, not restraint. They are joined in the eighties by a broad range of lawmakers, professionals, educators, and thousands of single-interest constituencies, and a good share of the public.

The majority demand is for reasonable regulation at reasonable cost; reform, not abolition.

The pendulum swing toward reform reflects deep-felt concerns for satisfying the high cost of regulations; the seeming foolishness of some; the overzealousness of regulators and those who write the rules; plain proliferation of regulatory agencies and regulations; the regulatory rein on innovation and development; and, finally, the question of whether, and how well, many regulations actually serve the public good in the end.

In 1980, Sen. Charles Percy of Illinois asked, "Who will regulate the regulators?" He said the high rate of inflation was coincident with the rising cost of regulatory activity. He noted that the Federal Register, the daily index of government regulations, churned out some 20,000 pages of government directives in 1970 and that by 1977, such directives required 60,000 pages. During the same seven-year period, Percy said, the expenditures of federal regulatory agencies had increased over 400 per cent and that their employees had tripled.

While emphasizing that great benefits flow from regulation, the senator cautioned that "none of us will win when regulation becomes counter-productive." He called for reform and accountability to the public. He urged a "cost-conscious" attitude toward regulation and "sunset provisions" that would retire those regulations that proved ineffective or simply not worth the cost of their implementation.

Reformers immediately ran into serious problems, however, because regulations designed to protect the public well-being were supported by strong constituencies. Reform government regulations, they agreed, but not *my* regulation.

There was really no organized conspiracy of regulators who sought to enlarge their empires, as weary business executives sometimes imagined. The lawmakers were simply responding to the voice of the people, expressed through special interest groups and the news media, for the preservation of perceived rights and protection from hazards.

Because laws are incomplete, achieving the intent of laws is made the responsibility of regulatory agencies and various departments of government. Congress exercises a certain amount of "oversight" and sometimes reconsiders laws, but the process is inadequate. Once on the books, a law or regulation is extremely difficult to modify, much less erase. The supporters of a given regulation, having worked hard to see their objectives realized through congressional action, are not easily persuaded to remove the regulation from the books.

COMPLICATING FACTORS

In an age of growing complexity and rapidly changing technology, the rules of the game change quickly. Problems unheard of in the recent past must be faced now. Today's scientific breakthrough must be weighed for its problem potential at the same time it is hailed as an achievement. Old laws to cover old problems remain on the books to clutter and conflict with new statutes and their regulations. One attempt to solve a problem may duplicate or contradict another solution when the problem is viewed from a different angle.

Almost no one questions that a certain amount of regulation is absolutely necessary to protect mankind and the Earth itself. But how much is too much?

Perhaps we should put the issue in perspective; if we could sign an agreement to ban weapons in space, we might begin the process of banning weapons on Earth. That single compact would do more for the protection of mankind than a million lesser regulations.

But the talk of killer satellites in space goes on, and surface regulations increase from Maine to California, most of them originating in Washington. The unanswered questions are: How much regulation is needed, and at what cost? The pendulum is swinging hard toward deregulation, but it cannot be allowed to swing too far for fear of failure to protect society against the hazards, known and unknown, that exist.

A DIFFERENT IDEA

Gus Marusi has proposed that some measure of control over proliferation and regulatory redundance might be achieved in the eighties by a public-private advisory review board. "Most problems don't stop at a state border or an international boundary line; we need to work with our friends in Mexico, Canada, and all over the world to address our common problems and agree on sensible, cost-effective regulations."

The independent panel Marusi envisions would be made up of scientists, government officials, industry representatives, academicians, and consumers. It would screen, evaluate, and monitor existing and proposed regulations and maintain liaison with similar groups in other countries.

Initially, Marusi believes, the board could review the most clogged areas of federal regulation and make recommendations to the government, industry, and the public. This purely advisory body would consider specific "hard" cases over which there is seemingly insoluble controversy. "I know how much can be accomplished through dialogue from my participation in the informal dinner discussions in Washington for seven years. I know the review board I recommend would save money by helping to eliminate unnecessary regulation and would more fairly represent the coalition view."

The concept is not new with Marusi. As the former U.S. chairman of the U.S.-Canadian Committee of the National Planning Association, he presented a paper to an international conference on the environment in Vienna in which he said, "Business and government can and should work openly for effective national and international standards on measures that are incontestably in the public interest. There is no other rational approach and no other pattern that provides the order required for sensible planning and investment."

Through the International Chamber of Commerce and the British-North American Committee, a plan such as the one Marusi advocates could be carried out. It would appear to respond to current needs, the philosophy of the Reagan administration, and the mood of the people.

PERSPECTIVES ON THE PROBLEMS

John Filer puts the burden for reform on the back of the business community: "Business resisted reasonable environmental control efforts, so now we can't avoid unreasonable ones. We resisted work safety improvements and have to deal with regulatory excesses. We discriminated against minorities and women and now have impossible government requirements. . . . we lost public confidence not only by domestic and foreign bribery and political contributions, but also by an incredible insensitivity to changing public expectations."

The dangers of federal overregulation were foreseen long ago and, in considering today's quandary, perspective might be gained by noting two views separated by nearly 150 years.

In 1835, Alexis de Tocqueville saw a "centralized government" in America, not a "centralized administration," and said: "If the directing power of the American communities had both these instruments of government at its disposal and united the habit of executing its commands to the right of commanding; if, after having established the general principles of government, it descended to the details of their application; and if, having regulated the great interests of the country, it could descend to the circle of individual interests, freedom would soon be banished from the new world. . . .

"The secondary affairs of society have never been regulated by its authority; and nothing has hitherto betrayed its desire of even interfering in them. . . . When the central government which represents the majority has issued a decree, it must entrust the execution of its will to agents over whom it frequently has no control and whom it cannot perpetually direct."

Speaking to the Kennedy School of Government at Harvard in June 1980, David Rockefeller noted that President Franklin Delano Roosevelt had issued "a portentous warning" on government regulation in January 1936. Rockfeller quoted FDR as saying: "In 34 months, we built up new instruments of public power in the hands of the people's government. . . . [but] in the hands of political puppets of an economic autocracy such power would provide the shackles for the liberties of our people."

"It is now 45 years since President Roosevelt issued his warning," Rockefeller said. "During those years, the mass of regulatory powers has mounted steadily. Yet, I believe that during the last 34 months or so — the last three years of the seventies — the U.S. government has launched a body of new regulatory measures even more portentous than those of the thirties. Despite all talk of deregulation; between 1976 and 1979, the number of new rules in the National Register rose by more than 50 percent.

"The shackles of the seventies, like the shackles of the thirties, were created with the best of intentions, and have achieved some good results. But. . . . it is hard sometimes to tell the solutions from the shackles, the problems from the programs."

The Interstate Commerce Commission dates back to 1887. In 1906, the Food and Drug Act produced a regulatory agency to protect public health. During the Depression years, there were established the Civil Aeronautics Board, Federal Communications Commission, Federal Maritime Commission, Federal Power Commission, Securities Exchange Commission, and other agencies.

In the mid-sixties and early seventies, traditional federal regulatory objectives were broadened, with new goals to encourage cleaner air, safer and healthier working conditions, and equal employment opportunities for all. To achieve these goals, new regulatory agencies were formed whose impact went beyond historic boundaries.

By 1977, some eighty-five federal agencies were involved in regulating one or more areas of American economic or social life, and more than one-fourth were created between 1969 and 1975, according to an American Bar Association study. As the agencies became more numerous, their budgets grew larger and, with increased power and the funds to use it, the agencies issued increasing numbers of regulations.

THE COST OF REGULATION

Just how much does governmental regulation cost Americans annually? It is estimated at between $50 billion and $150 billion — figures comparable to industry's outlay for new plants and equipment.

Murry Weidenbaum estimated that the cost of a new automobile in

1978 was increased by about $666 due to federal government-mandated safety and environmental equipment, amounting to about $6.7 billion in the total bill passed on to automobile buyers.

The Council of Environmental Quality estimated the costs of federal and state-local environmental controls for private industry (excluding emissions from consumer-owned vehicles and municipal expenditures for water and solid-waste facilities) at $24.4 billion in 1977. Other estimates place the cost at more than $25 billion, with a projected rise to $44.7 billion by the mid-eighties.

The Business Roundtable acknowledged that "most government regulation originated from genuine concern for achievement of desirable economic and social goals," but contended that "some regulations have resulted in the imposition of large cost burdens on the private sector and ultimately on the U.S. economy."

They have also generated confusion and put small companies in jeopardy, for they can not easily bear the costs of compliance.

BENEFITS OF REGULATION

Former Environmental Protection Agency administrator Douglas Costle believes that if it were not for environmental rules, the nation could face a $10 billion annual bill in health damages. He told the Consumer Federation of America in 1979 that "no matter how much progress we make. . . . the fact remains that in a society as intertwined as ours, characterized by a technology as complex and massive as ours, a substantial amount of regulation is necessary. We have to protect health, safety, and environmental integrity in situations where such protection exceeds the jurisdiction or self-interest of any corporation."

Why should only the government be expected to regard protection of the public welfare as its responsibility? Why should industry exclude the public interest from its daily deliberations? How can business succeed if society falters?

Companies are social institutions, with a clear responsibility to the people of the nation, as well as to their shareowners and employees. By raising the bottom line to accommodate societal concerns, business could engage in socioeconomic planning at the national and community levels, and erase unwanted regulatory constraints by its own leadership and voluntary action.

Costle admitted that many regulations were outdated in the seventies and that some should never have been written: "We are trying to get both types off the books, but what we don't need is a regulatory witchhunt, for in the interest of reducing costs today, we may create nightmares for ourselves tomorrow."

A Senate report said flatly that "substantial benefits have been realized from federal environmental, health, and safety regulations. . . . direct economic gains, improvements in public health and in the standard of living, and enhanced environmental quality." The study was conducted for the Senate Committee on Governmental Affairs by the Center for Policy Alternatives of the Massachusetts Institute of Technology.

It raised the question of placing a monetary value on human life and suffering. "A strict cost-benefit approach in federal regulation does not appear advisable," the report said. "The philosophical and ethical issues raised by placing economic values on such intangibles as human life, chronic disease, injury, and pain and suffering will continue to limit the ability of analysts to perform benefit studies without unavoidably making value judgments that are more properly performed by publicly accountable decision makers or by society at large."

ATTITUDES TOWARD RISK TAKING

Elizabeth M. Whelan, reseach associate at the Harvard School of Public Health, believes that most Americans have a very poor concept of the nature of the risks regarding environmental cancer. "A real risk is something you can identify and quantitate, then either accept or reject: driving a car, flying in an airplane, smoking cigarettes. We know the risks. Americans appear to have little trouble accepting these real risks," she observed. But, she added, Americans are not so willing to accept hypothetical risks, such as the use of food additives, pesticides, and low-level exposure to occupational chemicals.

"As a society we seem to be drifting toward a policy which tolerates known, major risks that are chosen by the individual — and rejects hypothetical risks that might be assumed by industry and society as a whole. This was clear in the fall of 1979," Whelan said, "when nearly a quarter million individuals gathered in New York to protest nuclear power. The newsclippings I saw revealed that a significant number of them were smoking cigarettes."

Citizens may choose to act foolishly or recklessly, but they demand information on which they can make a judgment. The question is one of informed free choice: personal liberty. The unknown risk — the pesticide or chemical in the environment, is not an option of the individual. Until scientific evidence is available, citizens will continue to protest and challenge the use of unknown or questionable substances over which they can exercise no personal choice.

OTHER CONCERNS OF INDUSTRY

Business leadership acknowledges that real benefits have accrued from regulation but contends that the sheer volume and detail of compliance presents an unreasonable burden. Many business leaders regret the lack of private initiatives in the fifties and early sixties that might have given industry more control of its own affairs in the seventies and eighties. They take a more enlightened view of the bottom line and are determined to reduce regulation and assume greater public accountability on a voluntary basis.

But they share the concern that as regulations proliferate the chances rise continually that business will be in violation of something, sometime, somewhere. And they object to the great discretion of regulators over what to move on, whom to charge, and when.

"When little is left to the judgment and discretion of the business executive, plant manager, or anyone on the scene, we have cause for concern," says Marusi.

One notorious example is the Occupational Safety and Health Administration's [OSHA] regulation on workplace safety that dictates such things as the size of toilet seats and the permissible number of knotholes in a stepladder.

Thus, the concern of business over the thickening web of federal regulation goes beyond the matter of costs, needless red tape, or even the growth of government power. The fear is that the complexity, the manner of federal regulation, are stifling the economy and business incentives when the opposite is desperately needed. It appears to business that rather than working closely with industry, regulators are seeking to bureaucratize the entire economy, and government itself is seen as a major anticompetitive force.

No one intended these negative results when regulation boomed during the past twenty years. Legislators and officials meant to address only such purposes as job safety, pollution control, fair employment, and protection of pension rights. Few foresaw the cumulative effect of myriad laws and regulations.

REFORM: THE REAL GOAL

As the Business Roundtable pointed out in its study, some government intervention is needed to achieve the social goals most Americans support, and it conceded that in many instances, specific regulations are well-conceived and carried out.

On Capitol Hill, regulatory reform is a popular issue. Lawmakers seek to require economic impact analyses of new rules, to allow Congress to veto regulations that overstep congressional intent and to put entire agencies out of business.

Reflecting Marusi's proposal, one congressional measure would make it easier for companies and private citizens to challenge federal regulations in court. Currently, a company or individual that wants to challenge a regulation must prove the government unit acted arbitrarily or capriciously in issuing the regulation. Under Senator Dale Bumpers' proposal, the *agency* would have to prove to the court that the rule is fair.

The American Bar Association has suggested several regulatory reforms and noted that "the mechanisms surrounding much government intervention have become so unwieldy and slow that private citizens, even when organized into groups, and small business often cannot afford the huge cost of effective participation in the regulatory process."

Various economists have suggested that a regulatory agency's budget be cut when its activities generate more costs than benefits.

CONCLUSION

At least two messages come through clearly in considering the matter of protection of public well-being through law and regulation: rules and regulations are essential and, given the decentralization and complexity of modern society, will remain in force and perhaps even increase in number; and all parties involved, in the public and private sectors, are agreed that the tipping point has been reached in the massive buildup of regulations, that something must be done to bring order and control to the situation.

Neither a continuation of piecemeal repair and reform, nor more Topsy-like growth of regulation, will serve. The regulatory maze that exists has prompted a hardened adversarial relationship at a time when business and government should come together in partnership to meet socioeconomic challenges.

In the eighties, public opinion and the mood of government and industry are moving toward a greater degree of free choice and local and individual options. No reasonable businessperson would welcome a reaction that would destroy the positive legislative initiatives of recent years.

But this may happen if middle ground is not identified soon for joint review of regulation by business, consumers, and government. Creativity, imagination, and cooperation are needed. Reason and joint effort are necessary to halt — at precisely the right level — the continued descent of the central government into what de Tocqueville called "the circle of individual interests" and to avert the threat to freedom that he foresaw as a consequence.

Business can raise the bottom line if it joins with the federal government in setting goals, and is itself set free to find the best ways of achieving those goals across the nation. To earn such freedom, business must redefine its role in society, set standards of performance for managers in merging social and economic interests, and establish incentives for performance and penalties for failure, just as it does for every other phase of the manager's responsibility.

Business's relationship with national issues and community objectives must be seen as an integral part of the manager's job. That is the best way for business to design a new relationship with the government that will prevent government from dictating all the rules.

No one I know suggests the lifting of prohibitions against imminent health hazards, or fraud — but the regulatory maze we have erected goes far beyond such clear and present threats to the public welfare. There are many areas where the creativity and imagination unleashed by an incentive approach within the private sector, and especially within the business community, would produce far more real progress toward the nation's social and economic goals than the present bureaucratic system ever will.

Chapter Seven

Lobbying, Ethics, and Common Sense

For thirty years business executives have been making the same basic mistake in Washington: telling the Congress and the Executive Departments what they do not like rather than what they support in the national interest — interests that also encompass their own legitimate goals.

Charles Wilson of General Motors (GM) once said that what is good for GM is good for the nation. Some claim he said it the other way around. But the first version stuck.

President Calvin Coolidge once said that the business of America is business, and that wisdom was pretty much accepted until the sixties and seventies when people began to ask hard questions about business's lobbying practices, ethical standards, and plain common sense.

People didn't necessarily have to go to Washington to ask these questions. They found plenty to criticize where they lived: streams and rivers polluted and no longer suitable for swimming or fishing, waste dumps allegedly causing illnesses and surely causing fear and disharmony. They saw business leaders playing key roles in almost every community organization, running the town, some said. And mostly, people didn't like the secretiveness when something went wrong at the local plant.

The brass always seemed anxious to get front page when they sponsored the summer band concerts and raised money to build a new wing on the hospital. By George, they deserved front page too. No one was complaining. But the brass wasn't always available to explain an explosion in the plant, or the effects of a new chemical said to injure workers, or to report pollution of water and air.

People didn't like that much. And this influenced the way they felt about the company as well as its managers and its products.

In Washington, veteran members of Congress nodded politely when business leaders came to testify. They could recite the "house of cards" testimony by heart; they had been hearing it for thirty years.

Don't pass the law, the theory went, because it will reduce the profit on my widget, and the widget is a part of the retogismo; you can see that, can't you? Well, sir, the whole damn thing will come tumbling down around that widget. So don't ask me to clean up the plant, or compete with that French product. After all, I am providing jobs, sir, and the folk have to learn to put up with a little dirt. And you can surely raise the trade barriers a mite to keep that foreign product off the shelf right here in the good old U.S. of A.

During the thirty years of hearing such testimony, the Congressmen had watched the marvelous growth of American industry and technology. They were impressed by what they saw, not by what they heard.

The change in industry's approach began during arguments for and against the Kennedy Trade Expansion Act of 1962 — the most important piece of legislation the young President would see enacted before his tragic assassination.

The House Ways and Means Committee and the Senate Finance Committee listened attentively to those who offered a balanced view, who gave constructive suggestions for working with the European Common Market and strengthening America's competitive capacity, without hiding behind unreasonable trade barriers. The legislation was debated in an era of growing international trade and international investment. The multi-national corporation had been born and was growing up to be a big, strong boy.

In the late fifties, an old friend in Utica, New York, had said of the Eisenhower administration, "Americans are expecting less and less of government and industry and getting it."

In the sixties, Americans began to look for leadership from their government, and statesmanship as well as success from their business leaders.

The domestic riots and the Vietnam war forced business to deal with myriad problems it had previously been able to avoid.

In the seventies, business fashioned a new attitude toward government. The National Association of Manufacturers shocked the business world, for example, by testifying in support of Richard Nixon's welfare reform measures.

The Conference Board, always out front, emphasized public affairs and social responsibility.

The Public Affairs Council convened international seminars to discuss trade, foreign investments, and the conduct of U.S. industries abroad.

Perhaps the most significant change in business circles was the determination to have a constructive voice in Washington. Not simply in the legal debates, but in the actual process of forming laws and regulations and policies.

Special interest groups had sprung up representing every conceivable interest. And in the late seventies, political action committees commanded attention because they helped to elect and defeat candidates for public office. The voice of business continued to grow stronger in Washington and in state capitals.

At times, the voice was as crass and self-serving as it had been at any time in history. In other instances, the voice was refreshingly statesmanlike, moderate, and oriented to the public interest. The latter voice reflected, as Irving Shapiro of Du Pont said, an awareness that business executives have "got to meet the needs of society or they are not going to be successful."

The life insurance industry's Committee on Social Responsibility, directed by Stanley Karson, promoted social investments in urban neighborhoods and elimination of "redlining" practices.

But most efforts were even more pragmatic and conservative. The Chamber of Commerce of the United States intensified its legislative support of traditional business objectives on Capitol Hill and formed an affiliate called "Citizen's Choice" to lobby against government regulation and high taxes. The Chamber also launched a new Office of Corporate Relations to increase the involvement of corporate leaders in the activities of the Chamber.

The Chamber pushed liaison with nonbusiness voluntary organizations in order to broaden its constituency, and it formed special task forces to monitor the actions of individual government agencies.

The Chamber also claimed to promote long-range planning — but on the basis of its own objectives. The Chamber continued to score legislative "victories" in terms of its own goals. Head man Richard Lesher would contend, of course, that the Chamber's objectives were consonant with the national welfare.

Some of the Chamber's victories on Capitol Hill came about through genuine support for the Chamber's objectives and the defeat of so-called antibusiness proposals. Other help came directly from the White House, especially when Gerald Ford sat in the Oval Office.

The Chamber advocated tax incentives to encourage investment, permanent tax cuts, the abolition of any form of wage-price controls, zero-based budgeting for federal programs (which might have been advocated for some business programs as well), reform of the Social Security system to limit benefits, and reform of public pension plans to bring them in line with private pension plans.

In addition, the Chamber promoted the deregulation of natural gas to encourage exploration. It stressed the need to amend the Clean Air Act to balance economic growth and environmental protection, and asked for a special minimum wage for unskilled youths so they might be employed, at least during the critical summer months.

The Chamber's board approved the building of an extensive, multimillion-dollar communications complex in the atrium of the Chamber's historic building on Lafayette Square across from the White House, and embarked on an aggressive public relations effort, including a professionally produced public service television series, "It's Your Business."

Lesher appears in every segment with three different guests and a moderator for discussion of issues impacting on business. The program appears on commercial and public stations, usually on Sunday, and increasingly in prime time.

The U.S. Chamber was formed in 1912, a dozen years after Booker T. Washington had formed the National Business League [NBL], the black chamber of commerce in America. The NBL has depended, in recent years, on government contracts to carry out its programs. The Chamber avoids government involvement other than meetings and conferences with government officials. In the Reagan era, as in the Ford era, Lesher will walk across Lafayette Square more frequently for meetings and social events.

Under Lesher's direction, the Chamber has addressed critical social issues: health care, consumer redress, and greater reliance on initiatives in the private sector.

The Chamber failed in its efforts to merge with the National Association of Manufacturers (NAM) in the seventies, not so much because the philosophies of the two Washington-based organizations were in conflict, but rather because of a surprising breakdown in communications.

The clear objective had been to fuse the resources of the two organizations so that business might speak with one powerful voice in the nation's capital. The merger did not jell, although most observers believe the two groups will eventually come together.

The merger would not even have been considered in the early seventies when the NAM sported an active urban affairs comittee and endorsed a guaranteed floor for welfare recipients. NAM was headquartered at 277 Park Avenue in New York at that time and was busy putting out publications urging business to engage in the revitalization of American cities.

That changed when the NAM moved its headquarters to 1776 F Street, a short walk from the old Executive Office Building next to the White House. The NAM came to Washington with its sleeves rolled up to engage in political warfare. Its urban affairs committee was quietly "absorbed" within staff functions. Studies for involving business in urban redevelopment were put on the back shelf. Concern for "social" issues faded. The hardliners took over. And the NAM became more and more like the Chamber, and thus more attractive to the Chamber's management.

Not only was industry critic Ralph Nader unacceptable to the new NAM management but even an esteemed Republican liberal, like John W. Gardner, was seen as a threat to the accomplishment of business's goals.

Real liberals thought Gardner wanted "nice people in station wagons to make the hard decisions for the citizenry," while real conservatives considered Gardner's Urban Coalition and Common Cause as antibusiness organizations.

NAM's new posture was to defend and attack. It did not seek to bring groups together in any pattern of common interest. Its own conservative political positions polarized.

Most observers saw little philosophical difference between the Chamber and the NAM. If anything, the Chamber was, at that time, becoming more statesmanlike in its approaches, if not always in its objectives. A merger seemed desirable. But tactical failure, not philosophy, kept them apart.

The Chamber was insistent on limiting the size of the new board — to reduce it to the size of the Chamber's own board as soon as possible. The action would have eliminated two-thirds of the NAM's board members almost overnight.

Still, a public announcement was issued saying that the merger was imminent. But the infighting went on, fed by the alleged insensitivity of the planners in failing to accommodate the egos of NAM board members. It was a stunning public defeat for the two groups who prided themselves on their smooth handling of issues on Capitol Hill.

"The idea got off the track as soon as it was announced," said a former NAM official, now a tax expert in Washington. "First, the memberships didn't like the secrecy. The idea was discussed at high level, agreed on, and then sprung on the national members across the country. They didn't appreciate the strategy. The NAM boys naturally resisted being thrown out and losing face. And there were a few honest philosophical differences here and there. But Lesher could have brought everybody around if the communications and human relations had been handled differently. Staff people at the NAM were concerned about having a job. It was a stressful time. And communication was lacking."

The tax official says he won a $10 bet with a colleague that the merger would not take place. "We all heard about it [the merger] for the first time at one of our regular Monday morning staff meetings. The press release announcing the intended merger was already in the mail. That was in the spring of 1976. By fall it was a washout. The principals loved each other in September as they had in May, but their respective boards wouldn't let them marry."

Today, working relationships between Alexander "Sandy" Trowbridge at the NAM and Dick Lesher at the Chamber are excellent. The organizations share common goals and interests. Lesher was clearly disappointed by the failure to consummate the marriage, however; he would have been the top man.

In the wake of the failed merger, the distinguished Business Round-table assumed even greater prominence in Washington and throughout the business community.

The roundtable is an organization of some 200 big companies who are represented by their chief executive officers. Exxon, Ford, General Motors, General Electric, Du Pont, IBM, U.S. Steel, Bank of America (and other large financial institutions), Merrill Lynch, some of the big utilities, and Metropolitan Life are among its members. It is perceived as the most formidable, educated voice of business, and therefore is sometimes resented by — and even in conflict with — the Chamber and the NAM.

At the start, the roundtable floated lofty phrases about developing more sophisticated and cordial relationships with government in the interests of healing and strengthening society. As time moved on, the roundtable's real purpose seemed to be that of forming a lobbying umbrella over lesser business groups; defining positions on issues important to big business; and lobbying for those positions with the help of chief executive officers. That was the critical difference between the roundtable and other business groups: the use of CEOs as lobbyists.

Persuasive, informed men — like Irving Shapiro, Reginald Jones, Clifton Garvin, and Thomas Murphy — learned how to take Capitol Hill in stride. Doors opened wide for these famous men of industry. They had access.

The roundtable was criticized by those who believed that the CEO should not engage in such activity, that his presence undercut the work of other business associations, and even other executives in his own organization. Moreover, the argument went, if the CEO got turned down on an issue that hadn't been fully explored by executives down the line, there was no fallback position.

Roundtable supporters brushed aside such criticisms as sour grapes. They stressed the role of the roundtable as a kind of think tank to redefine the role of business in a changing society and to assist the Chamber, the NAM, and other business groups to do their jobs better.

Where parochial interests have conflicted, however, the roundtable has not always served as the arbitrator. It has at times remained silent; at other times, it has joined with the Chamber and NAM in fighting battles, such as the defeat of a proposed consumer protection agency and labor's efforts to assume more power. Pretty traditional stuff.

Later, the roundtable began to discuss such issues as central planning for the nation's economy, and its leaders were called into the Oval Office for conferences. Shapiro advocated compromise, arguing with his colleagues that industry can't always say, "It's this or nothing."

Shapiro's successors have taken his advice to heart, praising as well as criticizing government programs and striking bargains rather than demanding total support for business plans.

The thinkers in the sometimes rarified air of roundtable discussions agree that business must take positions on welfare and education and health care because business is inescapably caught up in the implementation of social programs, locally and nationally.

The hardliners in the roundtable scoff at business-government interchange and stress single-minded efforts to achieve "bottom-line" objectives. Not all members of the roundtable have discovered that it is necessary to raise the bottom line in order to protect business from the heavy boots of its critics. The roundtable's long-standing task force on welfare reform, for example, has never reported out.

At the start, the roundtable distinguished itself from other Washington trade associations and lifted its sights above even the broad objectives set by the Chamber and NAM. Many observers were dismayed, therefore, that it did not leave most of the lobbying activity to the NAM and the Chamber. "Clout diminishes when it is overused," commented one business executive based in Washington. "The White House doesn't trot the President up to Capitol Hill to push every issue. Industry also should use its power in a more selective way. CEOs can be overexposed."

Prof. Kim McQuaid, a professor at Lake Erie College in Ohio, who has written some of the most insightful analyses of the roundtable's activities, sees the organization as a "sort of super holding company for big business political influence." He points out, however, that the roundtable was originally a loose alliance of groups interested in lessening organized labor's powers — particularly in the construction industry. It evolved from the old Business Council, which was formed in 1933 to provide a confidential forum for chief executive officers during Franklin Roosevelt's New Deal.

After Watergate, McQuaid notes, the federal bureaucracy fragmented into many agencies, and special interest groups proliferated in the private sector. Business executives found it increasingly difficult to know where or how or when to speak out. The roundtable provided the answer.

The roundtable's leaders were wise enough to see that the nation had entered an era of big government; that big business had to work together. By proposing realistic ideas and moving out front of developing issues, the roundtable tried to fashion a new and more constructive relationship between business and government. It usually succeeded when it addressed broad national issues. It sometimes failed to fulfill its stated purpose when it joined with the lobbyists in fighting for relatively narrow legislation. Men like Shapiro privately expressed unhappiness that the roundtable had become what McQuaid calls a "super lobby" and less of a long-term policy forum.

By any measure, the Business Roundtable is a powerful instrument. It is not always used for noble purposes; it is run by imperfect human beings who do not always agree on objectives or strategy. But given time and astute leadership, the roundtable may be the best hope for raising the bottom line, conducting socioeconomic planning, and breaking down unnecessary adversarial proceedings between business and government.

The roundtable, the Chamber, and the NAM must understand the extent to which the public marketplace has changed in order to form strategies that will succeed in the eighties. As Donald H. Haider of Northwestern University observes: "The current public mood does not suggest a growing love affair with the corporate world but rather that business is the temporary beneficiary of a rather pervasive anti-government feeling. Corporations survived the seventies, bruised and tarnished, but remarkably well adapted to changing circumstances. They learned the political process and how to win legislative confrontations. . . . however, the armament employed in the previous decade may not be appropriate or adaptable to what lies ahead."

Most business executives, tempered by the events of the sixties and seventies, take a broad view of industry's role in society. Lloyd B. Dennis, senior vice president of the United California Bank, presented this point of view: "I believe that the most influential segment of the business community has accepted the notion that business should — nay, must — be socially responsible. That is certainly true of a large and growing number of the Fortune 500 companies, the multinational companies and many large national and regional firms. They are now recognizing that it is important to combine maximizing profits with upgrading the quality of life. A key reason: Many corporate heads are finding that their peers who are attempting to solve profit-threatening problems are further ahead —

not only in profit, but in many other ways — than if those problems are ignored."

It is a matter of lobbying with common sense and ethics. A business can't succeed in a vacuum. Profits can't be maximized in a declining market. A business cannot find strength by exploiting the weakness of those it intends to serve. If business wants to sell, it must protect its markets.

The paradox is that government, under President Reagan, is moving back from social problems. Every type of community and national organization is now turning to business for financial and technical help. Business must protect its workers, save the environment, rebuild the inner cities, and support social and cultural organizations with its contributions.

The probability is that many national and community programs will go out of existence. Other programs will be consolidated. The challenge for business is to respond but avoid unreasonable public expectation for its performance. It must communicate effectively.

Business wanted government "off of its back." It got its wish. Now the burdens fall largely on business to respond to the needs of society. Business can't have it both ways. The problems of society are real and pressing. The rollback of federal funds has not erased the problems, but rather exacerbated them.

Business can't run society alone. Nor should it try. Nor do people want business to assume that role. But business can redefine its role in order to work cooperatively with city hall, the state mansion, the White House, and Capitol Hill. It can, as Dennis says, combine the pursuit of profits and the quality of life.

Pulpit talk, critics say.

The Reverend Verne Henderson might agree, but without disparagement. Henderson works "both sides of the street" as a United Church of Christ minister with a degree in management from the Massachusetts Institute of Technology's Sloan School. He has spent much of his life analyzing the church and business.

In recent years, Reverend Henderson has conducted leadership seminars for the clergy and served concurrently as a consultant to business. "Generally," says the cleric, "I've found the church to be as uninterested in leadership as business is in ethics." Henderson says he has made a career of finding out why people do what they do.

To be effective among business executives, he says, the ethicist has to do a better job of speaking the language of industry. When Henderson called on industry to see what companies might offer a minister with a sheepskin in business, he told Susan Trausch of the *Boston Globe*, "No one was interested in me in any way, shape, or form. In fact, some were hostile."

Henderson teaches a course, "The Ethical Side of Business," at the Arthur D. Little Management Education Institute. Students have told him they'd be fired for bringing up issues in the workplace that they had discussed in his course. His students are mostly middle managers from foreign countries.

Former commerce secretary Philip M. Klutznick, upon receiving the Business Statesman of the Year Award in April 1980 from the Harvard Business School Club of Chicago, warned, "Without leadership from business committed to a public spirited pursuit of its goals, the society will increasingly look to the political process to develop solutions to the nation's economic problems."

Klutznick spoke of a mutual accountability by business and government to the American people that should override short-term expedient behavior and unethical conduct.

But industry cannot easily erase the record of the seventies in which disclosures of illegal campaign contributions by a few business organizations cast a cloud on the character and credibility of the entire business community.

Shapiro at Du Pont responded in 1975 by announcing a policy of publicly disclosing all political contributions by Du Pont's top executives to U.S. candidates and incumbents. In addition, Du Pont made public all political solicitations for more than $1000 and responses to those requests.

Archie Carroll of the University of Georgia said almost 60 percent of respondents to a survey he conducted after Watergate agreed that young managers in business would have done just what the junior members of Nixon's reelection committee had done, however. Carroll believes that managers are under strong pressure to succeed, to conform to what they perceive to be their superiors' expectations of them, even though it may require the managers to compromise their personal values and standards.

The answer lies in the ethical conduct and standards and examples established by top management, and its stated expectation of employee behavior. A company that condones unethical behavior, much less encourages it, is not going to worry much about polluting the environment or marketing shoddy products, but only about getting caught.

In today's open society, they will fortunately, probably get caught sooner rather than later. Business, the members of its boards and management teams, and those who invest in American businesses share the responsibility for the character of lobbying practices and the degree of ethical behavior and common sense applied day in and day out in their enterprises.

Chapter Eight

The New Competitors

The notion that American industry has fallen behind and lost its competitive edge is an overstated proposition, according to Irving S. Shapiro, former chairman of E.I. du Pont de Nemours & Company and the Business Roundtable. "One can make the case that not enough capital is being generated to permit the kind of investment that we need to stay healthy," he told an interviewer upon his retirement from Du Pont in February 1981. "But that doesn't say that we're running behind the pack as a nation. It does say that we've got pockets in our industry where that's happening. Steel is obviously one. Short term, the automobile industry is another like that. But you have to take it in terms of specific industries and what's happening in those industries."

Shapiro essentially blamed the citizenry for not accepting the reality of an energy crisis, rather than poor planning by the automobile industry, for the influx of foreign made small cars. "The industry couldn't produce that many small cars in a hurry," Shapiro explained, "and so there was an obvious market opening for Japanese and Germans and others. The Japanese had been making small cars for a long time because Japan always knew it had an energy problem."

Shapiro also blamed government regulations for hobbling American industry in the face of foreign competition. "There are fields in which regulation is a necessity, and only government can do it. On the other hand, government has no self-restraint. Once it has power, it tends to exercise maximum power without reservation. That's the heart of the problem."

The lawyer-business executive said he believed that "most businessmen are sensible and rational people. They recognize that they've got to meet the needs of our society or they're not going to be successful."

Shapiro agreed, however, that business executives are "pushed by quarterly financial reports into judgments that measure you on today's results rather than building for the future."

George Allen, president of Fawcett Publications, a unit of CBS, believes that the emphasis on short-term profits at the expense of long-term planning is at the heart of the business decline in America.

"We don't produce services and products anymore," Allen laments, "we make money. There is no corporate loyalty or consistency. Traditional products are sacrificed. Top brass divests and it acquires. They don't want grief from board members or shareowners. Businesses make dollars. They're banks; they've lost their original character."

The veteran publisher compares many business executives to politicians on the move. "The mayor spends himself into popularity and tries for country executive. He makes his mark there and quickly shoots for the governor's chair. That is a hot seat, and so he campaigns for the Senate. Those who follow the politician on the move usually pick up a lot of broken glass and unsolved problems. In business, the successors to the fast-climbers inherit a lot of grief, too. We ought to be asking: Who is building for the future?"

General Electric's former chairman Reginald Jones, who, like Shapiro, was a power in the Business Roundtable and a counselor to presidents, also retired in 1981 with these words of caution: "What we have today is a bunch of money managers who are under tremendous pressure from Wall Street to have every quarter a little bit better than the last, and I'm sure it's not realistic." He asserted that profits may occasionally slip if a company is going to make long-term improvements.

Jones complained that the quest for profits at any price has brought a spate of illnesses to American business — a decline in quality, a fall-off in productivity, a slump in corporate investment, and a lag in research and development. He places the blame on the board of directors, who, he contends, must encourage management to make investments that will enhance longer-range opportunities, even if they mean some diminution of profitability in the short run.

In the early part of the century, family-owned businesses were criticized for their paternalistic and sometimes arrogant behavior. But the executives of that era took the long view, envisioning the day when junior or grandson Willie would run the enterprise. Family owners not only provided jobs and security for the entire community, but also built hospitals, parks, marinas, and playing fields. They created their own class distinctions and problems to be sure. But not often could they be accused of expedient action at the sacrifice of long-term planning.

Today, those family-owned businesses have become public institutions. Shareowners want a return on their investment. The pressure is on for immediate profits, as Jones, Shapiro, and Allen point out. Old-line products are dumped when their profits decline. Old plants are closed. Old-time employees are fired. New companies are acquired because they have a good earnings record and not necessarily because they produce a compatible product line.

Critics of American industry often refer to the high productivity achieved in Japan and in Japanese-run plants in the United States. They ask why management skills taught in American universities and practiced in American industry do not seem to work as well.

"The Japanese are very good at managing workers," said Shapiro. "They've transferred that talent to the United States, and they're very successful. They have built a close relationship between workers and management. It's been a lifetime relationship. There is a national ethic that says that work is important. It contributes to the nation. When you go into a Japanese hotel, even the chamber maid works at her job as though her life depended on it. And Japanese managers have been able to transfer that attitude and teach it to American workers."

Shapiro also pointed to the close relationship between government and business in Japan that enables heavy public-private investments to be made in certain industries: "For example, the Japanese decided they would take on IBM in the computer industry around the world. They've poured resources into the area, and they're doing a good job."

Japan may be the new competitor of American industry, but many U.S. communities are courting Japanese investments nonetheless and the jobs those investments bring.

Labor unions do not always court the Japanese so enthusiastically. In Smyrna, Tennessee, for example, labor unions disrupted a groundbreaking ceremony for a $300 million Nissan Motor Company assembly plant in February 1981, protesting the selection of an open-shop construction firm to build the facility. Fear of labor problems has discouraged many Japanese manufacturers from locating plants in the United States. Still, Japan remains the number-one competitor of the United States at home and abroad.

Another form of competition relates to alleged government rewards for inefficiency. Supposedly, the free market system provides strong incentives for corporations to increase their efficiency. Supposedly, profit and the fear of failure inspire managers to produce quality products with a minimum of wasted motion and wasted materials. Efficiency is rewarded. Inefficiency causes companies to fail. That's the free market system.

Not necessarily.

The multibillion-dollar loan guarantees by the federal government to Lockheed and Chrysler to keep those companies going under adverse conditions suggest that Japan is not the only nation to build alliances between its businesses and its government.

The American manager's aversion to government intrusion in the marketplace is selective. When things are going well, he wants to be left alone. When foreign competition and internal inefficiencies tumble his fortunes, he wants Uncle Sam to bail him out.

In July 1971, former senator James Buckley said, "If the inefficient or mismanaged firm is insulated from the free-market pressures that other business firms must face, the result will be that scarce economic and human resources will be squandered on enterprises whose activities do not meet the standards imposed by the marketplace — standards which have assured us of the efficiency on which our industrial supremacy had been built."

In the seventies, the new Japanese owners of a United States producer of television sets sent its technicians to look over the U.S. plant. They were especially interested in the daily reject rate for sets that came off the assembly line but didn't perform well at quality-test levels.

The Japanese were told that the reject rate sometimes was above 100 percent — meaning that on some occasions, some sets had to be gone over not once but twice before getting an okay for shipment. The Japanese were horrified; a reject rate in their plants in Japan of 2 percent is considered unacceptably high.

A major reason the Japanese put so much emphasis on quality is that their products are shipped all over the world, often to places where service and repair facilities are skimpy or nonexistent. Thus a product has to be capable of giving long service without failures. By contrast, a U.S. manufacturer with service facilities countrywide may not be so concerned if every TV set doesn't measure up; a local serviceman can patch it.

At that same plant taken over by Japanese owners, it was found that employees were able to buy at a discount radio and TV sets that came off the assembly line with scratches or dents. Again, the Japanese were shocked. They asked why there should ever be a set that was marked, scratched, or dented. The new managers beefed up quality control and abolished the employee discount.

These examples are only illustrative, but they indicate that competitive forces are often self-created and controllable.

Technology has also played an important role in competition. Japan leads the world in the use of robots, for example. The United States is second; West Germany, third. Robots often mean fewer jobs for humans, but organized labor until now has not offered much criticism.

Sophisticated computers also monitor the flow of materials, conserve expensive energy consumption, and help to control pollution.

Robots and computers not only make the workplace more efficient but also relieve humans of tedious, boring, high-turnover jobs. Robots also save money, once their initial cost is recovered. In February 1981, for example, the automobile industry claimed that robots could weld and spray paint at a cost of $5.50 per hour as compared with a human pay scale of $18.10 per hour. Robots, said the automakers, helped to keep the U.S. carmakers competitive.

Technologists nonetheless criticized American industry for being too late with too little, claiming that the Japanese had many more robots of greater sophistication. James S. Albus, head of the National Bureau of Standards' robotics-research laboratory, opined, "The manufacturing process in the U.S. is probably about where it was 10 years after the invention of the steam engine."

President-elect Ronald Reagan made the automakers feel better about themselves, however, in a campaign speech to the Detroit Economic Club in May 1980. He said that the domestic automobile industry was being wrecked by government because it had been forced to build cars "that meet the needs of politicians rather than consumers." He claimed that "Washington" was hostile to the industry and was "regulating it to death."

Reagan's cry ignored the public demand for safe and pollution-free cars that had prompted the regulations in the first place. He also ignored the obligation of the giant industry to plan ahead, to anticipate changes in the market, and to stay competitive with foreign automakers. Even Thomas A. Murphy, chairman of General Motors Corporation until November of 1980, said, "We should be devoting our energies to making American business generally more competitive with foreign merchandise."

Perhaps federal financing of troubled business shouldn't be all that surprising. After all, government has entered into just about every other phase of business's operations — areas in which business did not take the initiative: pollution controls and safety regulations, for example. Industry is regulated because it did not act voluntarily in response to public demands and expectations. Those demands and expectations represented changes in the marketplace. And monitoring the marketplace is what industry is expected to do under the free enterprise system.

In 1979, Elsa A. Porter, then an assistant secretary in the Department of Commerce, held long discussions with top-level executives of eleven major companies about improving efficiency and economic return on investment. Her questions also centered on worker satisfaction — indeed, their enjoyment of working life — as a critical factor in raising productivity. Porter prepared a statement of philosophy after completing her discussions, and sent it to business leaders who would participate in a two-day seminar near Washington in February 1980, under the auspices of the Conference Board.

Porter and Michael Maccoby, director of the Harvard program on technology, public policy, and human development, served as discussion leaders at the seminar.

The executives who participated exchanged experiences about programs they had initiated to protect the security of workers who make suggestions for increases in productivity that may reduce jobs. They also reviewed programs of profit-sharing; autonomous, or self-directed work teams, not unlike models in Japan; elimination of needless distinctions between workers at different hierarchical levels; and many other innovations that both reflect and strengthen management's respect for the capabilities of employees at all levels.

Believing in the capabilities of their employees, the management people in these companies also believe that they can profit by using the ideas as well as the skills of the entire employee group.

The view of the bottom line in these companies becomes one of encouraging employees to contribute to the improvement of the total enterprise. In addition to productivity increases, quality improvements, and cost savings reported by the companies participating in the seminar, they emphasized even more the "improved spirit" of their workplaces and the "improved quality of life" experienced by their employees, because they are able "to use themselves more fully in their work, and have more opportunities for receiving awards from their work than just their paychecks."

Implementing modern managerial methods in American industry is not an easy task. Traditional roles of the manager and the managed are deeply ingrained. "It has taken us two years to convince people that we are not trying to manipulate them," one executive told Porter during her preseminar discussions.

Much more time is required for communication and coordination to keep things moving when following the new management procedures; less time is required for managing subordinates and making decisions for them. The difference is crucial.

The effort should begin in colleges and universities, not on the plant floor. But there is no choice at the present time. Educational curriculum changes slower than the assembly line or office procedures. Top management must act now, in their own enterprises, to change working conditions in order to improve employee attitudes and productivity, and thus meet their new competitors head-on.

Business leaders must also begin to build new coalitions among national institutions and organizations to meet competition. For example, Jones and Shapiro led the effort to revive a top-level business-labor advisory committee to seek solutions to the nation's economic and energy problems, and thereby contribute to America's competitiveness in world markets. The committee was disbanded in mid-1978 after existing in various forms since the sixties. Labor members were unhappy that some of the business members had helped to defeat changes in federal labor law sought by the unions.

Labor leaders, led by AFL-CIO president Lane Kirkland, agreed to reestablish the committee after a formal charter was drafted recognizing the legitimacy of a "free labor movement and a free-enterprise economy" in the "process of free collective bargaining."

In reviving the committee, Jones, Shapiro, and Clifton Garvin, head of Exxon, strengthened business-labor relations at a time when congressional conservatives were attacking both large corporations and large union organization. While agreement on President Reagan's social budget cutting surely could not be reached through any business-labor alliance, the committee did verify that business and labor could stand together on broad issues in which they and the nation shared an abiding concern.

It is not long ago that most business executives would shut off all government contact if they were caught up in a single difficult issue in Washington. The same was true of their relationships with labor: one issue could stop all communications. During the sixties and seventies, business executives learned to agree on issues where they could, to fight issues only when they must, and to keep channels of communications and decision-making options open as long as possible. That is why Jones and Shapiro struggled to revive the broad-based business-labor committee to consider the economic and energy problems of the nation.

The old bottom-line mentality would have prohibited collective reasoning. The new bottom line demands it.

Chapter Nine

Changing the Mind Set

Good deeds *can* be prescribed. A manager will follow instruction when his job or next promotion are at stake, when his bonus payment might be cut if he fails to perform. If the boss says, "Jack, hire more minorities, recruit disabled persons, promote a woman to manager, support anti-drug abuse programs in Jonesville," Jack does it, or looks for another job. Jack may even learn to like the new activities and become personally involved through his implementation of company instruction.

But prescriptions do not change the basic mind set of managers down the line.

When social involvement depends on prescriptions and the personal conviction of the chief officer, it is vulnerable to budget cuts at every turn and is not likely to become part of operating policy.

Awareness must be fostered among all employees, up, down, and across the enterprise, that their ideas, as well as their compliance, are needed to improve a deteriorating social and physical environment. Management must also continuously emphasize that the company's success depends directly on public acceptance of its products and services and a generally healthy society.

If business persists in pushing economic education programs, those programs ought to focus on the interdependence of all units in society and the critical need for business and government to work together.

"Each of us must convince the other of our sincerity and willingness to cooperate," says John Filer. "Only then will we be able to bring the full power of our society to bear on social problems." Filer believes business and government are the two keys in the struggle to address social issues in America.

"We are likely to see more and more cooperation between government and business in finding solutions to our social problems because neither one can do the job alone. It is imperative that each acquires a better understanding of the other's function." He notes that business and government have worked together well in meeting external challenges, "but have yet to learn how to do so in the face of challenges that arise from within. I think we will."

Mind set, according to Filer, is changed by considering the effect on society of business's day-to-day activities, especially its investments. "We have a responsibility to place our investments where they will inure to society's benefit. This is not inconsistent with [the objective of] maximum yield because in determining yield we must take into consideration the effect of our investments on society as a whole, over the long haul."

Mind set, says James Langton, is changed by remembering that the dinosaur did not survive because it was unable to adapt to changing conditions. "An analogy between the plight of the ancient monster and the contemporary large organization may strike some as whimsical," smiles Langton, "yet the corporation is in a similar predicament. The dinosaur was dependent on its natural habitat, the corporation is dependent upon its social milieu."

Langton believes that many executives still perceive the social environment as hostile or threatening to corporate survival.

"Social forces have a drive of their own and therefore it is more constructive to view the social environment as an existential fact and deal with it accordingly. Like the environmental changes that finally did in the old dinosaur, these social forces eventually will sweep away the nonadaptive. It is a matter of perspective. A question of mind set."

Langton is convinced that corporations can raise the concept of the bottom line and assure industry's survival by integrating social and economic goals.

In the sixties, busines relied on familiar avenues to tell the public about its efforts to meet social needs: films and brochures, advertisements and news releases.

It would take time for most companies to upgrade their public affairs operations so that they could monitor corporate developments having some impact on the social and political environment, and communicate those developments to the news media, government agencies, and private institutions.

The change of mind set demanded uncharacteristic behavior: corporations were asked to reach out to consumers, counsel with employees, inform stockholders, and meet with public interest groups, legislators, regulators, and the news media. After all, voluntary disclosure had been an "unnatural act" in the executive breeding grounds.

Changing the mind set of American business is an arduous process. Progress is uneven among corporations, but can be accelerated overall by adaptive chief officers who see the advantages of getting out front of changing public expectations.

Procedures for institutionalizing the adaptive process — changing the mind set — are varied and imaginative. Most companies involved in the adaptive process provide some kind of mechanism for board overview and share responsibility among top executives for integrating social responsibility.

Board involvement tells both external constituents and employees that the company is serious about relating its own goals to the larger goals of society.

Making sure that social involvement develops across the board, rather than being confined to a single office, such as public affairs, helps to share the responsibility for success and assures implementation throughout the corporate body.

Still, someone has to be in charge, to lead and monitor the overall process, to summarize progress, and report to the top officers and board.

The man or woman in charge — a public affairs vice president, perhaps — must report directly to the chief executive officer and chair the management committee responsible for across-the-board implementation of social responsibility programs.

Over the years, many of these positions and committees have evolved into future planning and public issues operations. Where such effort is continually linked to day-to-day operations, the company's government relations and marketing strategies have usually improved. Social planners are able to relate economic plans to social realities and public expectations. They can function in a similar way with research and development experts who guide the company in adapting its products and processes to the changing technological environment.

The business response to domestic strife developed in three stages: the cautious experimentation in job training and increased financial support for minority institutions in the sixties; the adaptive process in the seventies, in which management set up structures to cope with external changes and made internal adjustments; and, by the end of the decade, the emergence of corporate futurists and public issues experts to help chart plans. The use of pollsters and social research firms in this process was important.

One of the most dramatic stories to emerge from business's response to the riots took place in California. In January 1964, an ominous footnote appeared at the end of a story in one of San Francisco's daily newspapers: "Civil rights leaders have hinted that Bank of America is the next scheduled target for fair employment demonstrations and picketing." The Ad Hoc Committee to End Discrimination and the Congress of Racial Equality [CORE] were active in San Francisco at that time.

Through demonstrations, the groups had secured agreements from automobile dealerships, a prominent hotel, a supermarket chain, and other businesses for hiring quotas and the right to supervise the process.

Bank of America denied any allegation that it had discriminated. At the time, the bank employed a large number of minorities, including 600 blacks, some of whom occupied supervisory positions. Over 12 percent of the bank's total workforce were minority citizens: blacks, Orientals, and Hispanics.

"Obviously, the bank's minority hiring efforts could and should have been improved," reflects Langton, "but our performance was more than defensible. We were picked out because we were big, not because we were bad."

Management agreed that the bank should take its appeal to the public. They knew the bank would have to address the urgent problems of the minority community in California, candidly and with a resolve to work with other organizations.

The traditional mind set about confidentiality had to be changed. Full public disclosure would be essential in gaining a fair hearing in the news media to earn public support. The bank would have to publicly pledge to accelerate its minority recruiting. Management approved.

The bank agreed to sit down with any minority groups to hear their views, with the understanding that the bank would proceed voluntarily but would not sign any agreements.

To authenticate its record, the bank asked the California Fair Employment Practice Commission (FEPC) to serve as a validating agent.

The bank appealed to the FEPC in an open letter and called a news conference for all Bay Area news media, including minority and campus media, to state its position.

CORE officials responded by saying they did not intend to demonstrate against Bank of America and asked to meet with the bank's management. But relations deteriorated during a series of meetings over the next four months. CORE wanted to set quotas and see confidential files. The bank refused. CORE complained through the news media, broke off discussions, and started picketing. The bank sent detailed materials to editorial writers and stated its position in full-page newspaper advertisements throughout California.

Langton provided the bank's 850 branch managers with speeches and statements to help them during the period of picketing. Finally, the bank and the FEPC held a joint news conference announcing an understanding regarding the timing and content of information that the bank would provide to the FEPC, and the use of the information by the agency.

CORE continued to picket but sought additional meetings with management. Management agreed to meet if the picketing would stop. Picketing continued, and no further meetings were held.

By summer's end, CORE pulled its pickets off the line.

"The paradox of the controversy was that CORE's dispute with the Bank of America really had nothing to do with the bank's position as an equal opportunity employer. It was not even related to the bank's willingness, even eagerness to hire qualified black applicants," said Langton.

The principle upheld, said Langton, was that no business organization should award "police powers" to any pressure group under any circumstances. "We agreed with CORE on objectives; yet we could not convince their leaders that progress could be improved without confrontation. But then we met in an era of confrontation.

"Our job was to change the traditional mind set within the bank about the institution's public accountability. We couldn't refuse to deal with CORE on its terms if we did not establish terms of our own that the public would respect. Third-party validation was important through the FEPC."

Langton points out that the bank was the only picketed corporation in California at that time where ministers, and prominent civil rights leaders were conspicuously absent from picket lines. Moreover, by appearing on campuses and communicating directly with campus editors, the bank avoided large-scale student demonstrations.

"If there was a single factor that contributed most to our earning public support, it was our willingness to make public disclosure of detailed statistical data on a regular basis to the FEPC. We had two issues: one to maintain the nondisclosure policy with private groups, which would have violated every principle of banking; and also to maintain public confidence and respect by proving we were acting properly and responsibly and sensitively.

"Obviously, any company which consciously or unconsciously, overtly or subtly followed a discriminatory hiring practice could not have acted as we did. No rhetoric, or advertisement, or public relations program, or pious platitude can conceal a racist policy. Full disclosure does more to change public attitudes about the company and more to change the mind set of management within the company than any other single factor."

Walter Barlow recalls a different kind of trauma on college campuses in the sixties. Barlow heads Research Strategies Corporation in New York, an attitude and opinion research consulting organization. In the sixties, he was president of Opinion Research Corporation at Princeton, New Jersey, working daily with the heads of large corporations. He was also a trustee of Cornell University when the student riots erupted high above Cayuga's waters.

James Perkins was president of Cornell. When rebellion came, the Board of Trustees established a campus commission of seven trustees. Barlow was the only one of the seven with a research and communications background.

"We were no better prepared for violence on campus than corporations were in their board rooms," Barlow confesses. "We worried our way through the situation for many months. The student were against the war, against business, against Perkins and against the trustees. It wasn't that we hadn't been alerted. We had been talking about and reading about the powder keg of discontent in our nation, but I think most of us related it exclusively to the long-standing racial problems that were finally being addressed to some degree. We really didn't comprehend that a whole generation of youth saw a world they didn't want to live in. Kids also discovered they had visible, effective levers to pull on campus to get public attention for their views. And they pulled them."

Barlow shakes his head in remembrance: "The universities thought the corporations were the bad guys, too. In that regard, they sometimes sided with the kids. As our band of seven saw the depth of alienation among the young activists at Cornell and the degree of collusion among some young faculty members and demonstrators — actually seeing faculty members aid and abet student capers and feed the fires of their resentment against the business world — we were deeply troubled and convinced that changes had to be made."

Jim Perkins was sympathetic to the problems, Barlow recalls, but stunned by the demonstrations. Similar problems were hitting campuses all over the nation, of course. "We talked with our friends at Columbia University to compare strategies. No one had certain answers. The people at the top of university life were taking the heat and sometimes were forced to take a walk. That's what always happens when the heat is on. It isn't always justified or fair, but it happens. Universities just didn't have any mechanisms for handling social complaints. Lord, universities were still in the Dark Ages in the way they handled their own administrative affairs, much less student protests against a divisive war, the production of chemicals used in war, and racial riots on the streets of our cities.

"At Cornell, the administration simply had lost touch. Out of that realization our commission developed a new communications program. It wasn't enough to get people to act, but we began to pull people together, establish dialogue, identify practical things we could do to relieve tensions, and the like. Very fundamental. But desperately needed. The mind set of the administration changed within a few months. This could not have happened without the impetus of traumatic outside forces. But that was true of all of society. We were sitting on information. We didn't act until we had to."

Barlow said he learned many basic lessons along with his friends in corporate life: neither universities nor companies can live as if they are isolated slices of society rather than integrated entities affecting each other and society at large. "That seems terribly fundamental now, saying it, but it was an honest discovery in the sixties," said Barlow. "No corporation of any consequence today believes it is possible to conduct business in a narrow sphere. If it tries, government soon steps in with laws and regulations and rule books."

All of us were caught in the sixties, says Barlow. "We didn't comprehend what was happening or what would happen. We were not accustomed to measuring social impact. We thought in terms of market share and sales. Hell, if we couldn't put it in a package and place it on the store shelf, it wasn't worth talking about. If we couldn't identify it by sticking a pin in a map, it wasn't there."

Through that trauma, Barlow believes the nation learned that "We *are* our brothers' keepers," not only in a personal sense, but also in an institutional sense; that business and government began to understand that they had to invest in people and societal aspirations.

The methods of involvement within corporations were varied, imperfect, inconstant. But the notion of corporate social responsibility was established. The mind set began to change.

Barlow believes space flight helped people appreciate how much they needed each other. "When we saw 'Spaceship Earth' in photographs taken by our astronauts, I think it changed forever the way we could think about protecting the environment and each other."

Most elected officials and community leaders would agree, however, that evidence of man's unity is sorely lacking in the eighties. Military armament, hostilities among nations, cruelties beyond description levied by power-mad dictators, and rising violent behavior in so-called free and civilized societies depress the spirit. Still, the photographs from space are relatively new, the problems of mankind relatively old. Given time, Barlow may be right.

Chapter Ten

Business Responds

"Running a company isn't worth a damn unless it contributes to the nation, unless it provides jobs," Irving Shapiro said on retiring in 1981 from the Du Pont Company where he had served as chairman and chief executive officer since 1974. During most of the seventies, the former government antitrust lawyer had not only directed the fortunes of one of the world's largest and most diversified corporations but also chaired the Business Roundtable.

Shapiro was President Carter's first choice for secretary of the treasury, but he turned it down to continue his leadership at Du Pont.

"Most businessmen are sensible and rational people. They recognize that they've got to meet the needs of our society or they're not going to be successful. I don't know anybody that believes you ought not to have safety in your plants — that you ought to be indifferent to accidents. So I would make the case that you get rid of the adversary approach [with government] and simply say we have common objectives — one as the representative of the private sector, the other as a representative of the public sector."

The regulatory machinery is too cluttered and packed with rules, says Shapiro. It has too many barriers to communication and people tied up in knots. "There is so much that can be done by industry, on its own, without government prodding," Shapiro believes.

When he was challenged about industry's ambivalence in accepting government support, Shapiro answered candidly, "Businessmen are just like everybody else: they sometimes talk out of both sides of their mouths, depending on their self-interest. They sometimes use slogans to mask their real thinking. And 'free enterprise' is that kind of thing. It's a slogan. It means different things to different people. You pour your own meaning into it."

Shapiro said the Business Roundtable adopted a resolution opposing the bailout of Chrysler, although individual members held different views.

"I think that industry has come to have a new perception of its role in our society and of its role opposite government. The chief officers have come to be a lot more sophisticated about what government really has to do to function, what it takes to make policy decisions, how business ought to participate in those decisions in terms of producing facts and alternatives — as distinguished from an earlier period in which business viewed government as a place where you exercised political muscle. It was a period in which you opposed fresh ideas without offering alternatives of your own. . . . Now I think we've reached a point in history in which people will be supportive of business if business levels with the citizenry."

Shapiro is critical of the Carter administration for worsening the economy. He claims that counselors to Carter, like himself, did not influence the administration until it was too late; that the damage had been done by staff who were "just not knowledgeable enough about the economy to call the shots right. They needed help. And they weren't listening to the people who were the experts. They approached everything on a political basis ... the three martini lunch [Carter had criticized] was political garbage. It had nothing to do with solving the problems of the economy."

To get the economy moving, Shapiro would "turn people loose to experiment and devise their own ways." He is confident that the market system would find innovative solutions faster than government.

"Our belief at Du Pont has always been that you can't conduct a business in isolation. You're a part of the community in which you function. And you'd better be sure that you're helping to make the community a good community. . . . I don't see the dichotomy. I don't see how anybody can run a business and justify dumping waste on the side of the road or shipping a product that is obviously inappropriate. If you think about it carefully, business is a means to an end, it isn't an end in itself."

The fact that the Department of Commerce would need to form an Office of Business Liaison says a great deal about the previous mind set of Commerce Department bureaucrats in working with their principal constituent. Isabelle Hyde was put in charge. She had served on the Carter transition team when the Georgian entered the White House, and then was assigned to Secretaries Kreps and Klutznick.

"It's difficult to get industry's reaction to a developing issue," she said, "because each company has its own objectives which may not mesh with the next company's objectives." Hyde recognizes that public affairs has increasingly come to mean not merely a response to change within corporations, but a positive role in the management of change itself — in the shaping of public policies and programs and in the development of corporate activities to implement change constructively.

She believes, however, that the integration of social responsibility is still dependent on the motivation of the company's chief executive: "The subject requires his continuing active involvement and organized efforts to forestall emerging problems."

James Joseph, one of the highest-ranking black officials in the Carter administration, served as under secretary of the interior for four years. He came from Cummins Engine Company in Indiana where he had earned a national reputation as an astute fighter and eloquent spokesman for equal opportunity.

Joseph found his four years in government "wonderfully educating," but sees a troubled world outside Interior's door: "The surfacing of the Ku Klux Klan and sentiment that is clearly anti-black and anti-women is deeply discouraging. Industry should join with government at every level in speaking out against blatant racism. Racism is still the root of our problems. Sure, it goes underground for a spell, but rises quickly in times of economic stress or on any suggestion from Capitol Hill that help for minority and disadvantaged citizens may be relaxed."

Joseph is also concerned about the apparent lack of leaders in America: "We tried to hold some seminars at Interior to bring consumer groups and industry representatives together to talk things through. They screamed at each other. And the industry types thought they were selling out if they simply met with their adversary. Perhaps we should have given the project more time and patience. But frankly, I had hoped industry had matured in the seventies. I didn't see much sign of it.

"The industry leaders who felt the heat of the sixties are mostly gone. The present crop of managers is less concerned, less pressured. The idea of corporate social responsibility has not been institutionalized. So where do we look for our leaders?"

Joseph smiles. "A whole generation of bright young people went outside the system, outside institutional America in the sixties. Many of them have since come back into the system. There are many good innovators and thinkers among them. Maybe we have to be more imaginative about searching for our leaders. We're not likely to find them in traditional places. It worries me that both industry and government may not be wise enough and relaxed enough to identify and welcome leaders who have earned their stars in unconventional ways."

The government-industry executive says flatly that public policy must be based on the public interest: "If a policy maker can't identify public interest he or she ought to challenge their own project. In industry, companies should refrain from advancing programs unless they can clearly identify with the public interest. A company must be able to meet its own goals, but those goals must also relate to the public interest."

During his four years in the executive suite at the Interior Department, Joseph said he was delighted to give time and attention "to those rare industry executives" who had done their homework and sketched their proposals in terms of the public good: "The vast majority came in there squawking about their self-interest and pressuring me to support their point of view. It surprised and disappointed me that a CEO of a major company would come in there and try to strong-arm. It was offensive and disturbing.

"When a class person came in, sensitive to the issues, knowledgeable about political realities, with something useful to say, he or she had our undivided attention. Unfortunately, that may have happened twice in four years."

Joseph thinks lobbying practices are basically unchanged: "Everybody is still hammering away for personal advantage. I don't think business learned much in fifteen years. The concept of social responsibility was not in evidence. Top executives did not train their successors vis-à-vis social responsibility. The oil companies may appear differently on television, in advertisements, and the like, preaching in ads and sponsoring good programs on public television; but in there, around a conference table, they looked and sounded alike. Social concerns have not been integrated with the day-to-day gut concerns of the marketplace. I told a dozen friends in industry they should align their company interests with the public interest. I told them I'd help any guy who came in there with a thoughtful, broad-based approach. And they still didn't do it."

Joseph was associated with a "caring, open, sophisticated group of managers" at Cummins before accepting the government appointment: "I was surprised and disappointed to find that the majority of business people walking in there [to Interior] didn't measure up to the people I knew at Cummins. They were narrow of mind, to put it kindly. They had no sense of national destiny or mutual purpose."

Jim Joseph is happy to have had his experience in government. He believes it will help him in his new duties for Cummins Engine in Washington.

"I know how the system works in both the public and private sectors.

Unfortunately, I don't think most people in either sector are trying to make the system work better."

Isabelle Hyde and Anne Howard, a niece of the late Hubert Humphrey, who worked in the Commerce Department in the Carter administration, are less critical of business practices at Commerce and more critical of perceived departmental shortcomings.

"Commerce serves business. Yet, we didn't have a single coordinating unit to help steer business executives through the maze. So we created one to help business people put information together among the agencies of the department. We wanted to form a partnership of sorts with business. The adversary relationship will persist, and it should. But we should be friendly adversaries most of the time. The liaison office should help to keep things friendly."

Hyde and Howard think the Chamber of Commerce of the United States looks upon the Department of Commerce as a weak sister. They were determined to change that perception: "We formed the business liaison office and began to call on companies to discuss ways in which the Commerce Department could help them. Quite frankly, we think the Commerce Department should enjoy the same relationship with business that the Labor Department enjoys with organized unions."

The Business Roundtable is "astute" and "more conciliatory" than the Chamber, and the NAM is "quite agreeable," says Hyde. The biggest skeptics, she alleges, are the Washington representatives of corporate offices: "They're not used to working with Commerce."

The relationships among Commerce, the big associations, and Washington reps of big corporations should improve in the probusiness Reagan administration.

Union Carbide responded to government with a full-page advertisement in the *Wall Street Journal* (and other publications) in November 1980, entitled "Adversaries — Or Allies? How Best Can Business and Government Stimulate Economic Growth in the 1980s?" The ad ticked off the danger signals: loss of share of world markets, reduction in economic growth, negative impact of foreign competition, and said citizens were expecting business and government to "provide workable and practical solutions." Carbide called for removing regulations, of course, and advocated tax cuts. More important, it called for a kind of Neutral Zone for mutual planning and cooperative action in the public interest by having business and government work together.

Quaker Oats had made substantial deposits in minority banks after the riots, and soon stepped up its training programs for minorities, opened up its purchasing department to minority entrepreneurs, depicted minorities in its print and broadcast advertisements, and set up a whole new range of policies to deal with rapid social change. It worked with minority insurance companies and demand grants to TV's "Sesame Street" in the program's formative years. Quaker also prepared a black history quiz for commercial television featuring inner-city high school teams.

Quaker executive Thomas Roeser took a leave of absence to organize the Office of Minority Business Enterprise in the Department of Commerce.

Internally, Quaker established a plant reporting system to help its managers respond to government mandates and activists' attacks.

Quaker also got into tenant housing, developing coalitions of business and government resources to work with community leaders. Joining with other Chicago companies, Quaker also tutored inner-city youth for many years.

Equitable Life Assurance Society pushed the hiring of school dropouts.

Bell Telephone of Pennsylvania worked with black clergy to ease community tensions. In Buffalo, Bell people carried employment applications to the homes of black applicants who were reluctant to visit personnel offices.

The Interracial Council for Business Opportunity, working with IBM, Pepsico, and other companies, provided counseling for minority entrepreneurs.

Work Opportunities, Inc., in St. Louis, trained and employed 900 undereducated, previously unemployable persons.

Smith, Kline & French Laboratories set up an information center to tell area residents in Philadelphia where they could get food, clothing, housing, jobs, and training.

Major corporations also managed Job Corps camps: Westinghouse, Xerox, Litton Industries, Burroughs, General Electric, RCA, and IBM among them.

George Champion, then chairman of Chase Manhattan Bank, put the whole matter in perspective when he said, "I can think of nothing that would put the brakes on big government faster than for business to identify critical problems and take the initiative in dealing with them before Washington felt the need to act."

In Watts and Tampa, after the riots, job training programs were established. Business-sponsored self-help housing projects, employment referral services, and employment clinics sprang up in burned-out riot corridors of major cities.

Government and business worked together through the new Economic Opportunity Corporation sparked by former senator Jacob Javits.

Senator Robert Kennedy, a year before his murder, mobilized the resources of private business to improve the Bedford-Stuyvesant area of New York.

Eugene M. Zuckert, former secretary of the Air Force and a Washington attorney, urged business to help shape the social and political climate by taking the initiative.

Businessmen began to react like businessmen, even in the middle of chaos. Said James Cook, president of Illinois Bell: "To state it quite flatly, when we help in the improvement of a community, we enhance the chance for business success there."

These first tentative ventures into the inner city represented a radical departure from traditional business practice — and the beginning of a new era. While many of these tentative programs vanished, either because they were poorly conceived or management did not sustain the effort, a start had been made. As the years passed, business's social programs became more sophisticated.

Chapter Eleven

Philanthropy and Social Investments

In giving from their hearts, it seems Americans think first of their souls. Organized religions in the United States receive almost half of all voluntary contributions, followed by educational and health organizations.

Corporate philanthropy, which now surpasses the amounts given by private foundations, focuses chiefly on education, community-based social agencies, the arts, and minority organizations.

But inflation is reducing the value of philanthropy at a time when government funding of social programs is also being diminished.

The rate of all charitable giving has gone down steadily for more than a decade. In that period, government funding of social agencies actually equalled private gifts, a fact that many people believe has changed the very character of our society.

The Commission on Private Philanthropy and Public Needs, chaired by John H. Filer, chairman of Aetna Life & Casualty, established that half the $80 billion contributed annually in the United States comes from individuals in households with incomes under $20,000, and millions of hours of volunteer time devoted to charitable institutions are not even counted.

The Commission was formed at the initiative of the late John D. Rockefeller 3d, with the strong support of the then chairman of the House Ways and Means Committee, Wilbur D. Mills; Secretary of the Treasury George P. Schultz; and Under Secretary William E. Simon, who subsequently succeeded Schultz before the Commission's work was completed in December 1975.

Privately convened and privately funded, the Commission set out to make recommendations to the voluntary [or "third sector"] of American society, to the Congress, and to the public about ways in which voluntary institutions and private givers might strengthen their relationship.

Terming corporate giving "a relatively new element in American philanthropy," the Commission observed that the corporate charitable contribution provision had been in effect since 1936, but that there were those who still questioned whether corporations should be involved in philanthropy at all.

The Commission concluded that while charitable giving "can only be a minor element in the corporations's role in society," only 20 percent of corporate taxpayers in 1970 had reported any charitable contributions and only 6 percent made contributions of over $500. The record of corporate giving, the Commission said in its report "Giving in America," is "unimpressive and inadequate."

The Commission recommended that corporations set as a minimum goal — to be reached no later than 1980 — the giving to charitable purposes of 2 percent of pretax net income, and that means of stimulating corporate giving be pursued.

Part of the Commission's latter expectation came true: by 1980 corporations were contributing more than $2.3 billion annually to causes and institutions of all kinds, surpassing the amounts given by private foundations and bequests.

In 1970, private foundations had given twice as much as industry.

The $2.3 billion represented corporate gifts that were labeled as contributions. When added to the value of gifts of property and equipment or contributions made through advertising and marketing budgets, plus the value of time contributed by corporate personnel, the figure tripled. But financial contributions in 1980 still amounted to less than 1 percent of pretax profits for those companies that gave, and three-quarters of the nation's 1.5 million corporations reported no cash contributions.

The $2.3 billion gave industry many opportunities to increase its influence in the third sector, however. It also turned the public spotlight on industry as a social and philanthropic leader, as well as a provider of jobs and economic security.

And it presented industry with some brand new problems, especially after Ronald Reagan's rollback of federal funds for social programs.

A fierce scramble for corporate funds among recipient groups has raised three fundamental concerns: industry's financial ability to respond, industry's new role in society, and its possible influence over the institutions that benefit from its contributions.

Some corporate executives view philanthropy as a way to help the company while helping others. Corporate contributions to the arts have increased most dramatically, up more than 5 percent during the seventies, and now represent 10 percent of total business donations.

"It isn't charity at all. The basic reason is to make ourselves known," said Gordon Bowman, who supervises grants for the arts at United Technologies Corporation. "We decided to make art the way of building our reputation. We could have done outboard motor races or tennis matches, but we chose art.

Others take a quite different view.

A. W. "Tom" Clausen, president of the World Bank and former president of Bank of America, thinks business "should pick up some of the slack" in correcting social ills with its philanthropic dollars and involvement in public issues.

Critics of corporate giving claim that company gifts go consistently to the same "safe" traditional establishment causes year after year — the United Way, local hospitals, the Boy Scouts, the Red Cross, the local symphony orchestra, and museums.

There are many exceptions.

Cummins Engine Company in Indiana has made contributions to groups promoting equal opportunity.

Reliable Life Insurance Company of Missouri matches employee gifts to any bona fide recipient group.

Metropolitan Life in New York supports medical research.

Seagram's and Sons, the Canadian distillery, gave $5.8 million to Harvard for research in alcoholism.

Oil giants Exxon, Mobile, and Atlantic Richfield are key supporters of public broadcasting.

But Brian O' Connell, president of the Independent Sector, an organization representing a broad range of private agencies, is fearful that the Reagan administration may give the impression that voluntary organizations and private industry can subsititue for government in providing a vast array of services — such as enforcement of civil rights laws and public welfare.

Leaders of charitable organizations actually believe that cuts in federal spending for social programs will put some private agencies out of business.

John W. Gardner, the chief organizer of Independent Sector, recommends that taxpayers be allowed to write off all charitable deductions. He said studies show that while the Treasury would "lose" $3.7 billion in revenues, private donations would jump $4.2 billion a year.

Andrew Heiskell, former chairman of Time, Inc., said the formation of the Independent Sector was needed because the private sector is seriously threatened by relative declines in personal, corporate, and foundation gifts.

There is much at stake.

Six million voluntary organizations dot the United States; 1 out of 10 service workers and 1 out of every 6 professional workers are employed by a nonprofit organization. The third sector is an $80 billion enterprise. About $25 billion comes from private philanthropic sources, including corporations. Another $23 billion in government dollars — now being substantially reduced — flows through private organizations from grant-making bodies. In 1981, the Council on Philanthropy said real dollar giving had increased to $47 billion.

Some $32 billion is received from service charges, tuition income, endowment income, payments to private hospitals, and other direct payment for services. Not counted, but vital to the success of the third sector, is another estimated $26 billion in volunteer time devoted to philanthropic causes by citizens in every walk of life.

Tight dollars and new demands for performance are changing the style and substance of many volunteer groups. The third sector shares with business and government the pressure of coping with emerging public needs and expectations. "Business as usual" is not acceptable in either the public or private sector — or the third sector.

Money giving dropped from 1.98 percent of gross national product in 1969 to 1.8 percent in 1974, setting a disturbing downward trend that has not abated. Action to stimulate private and corporate giving is needed, even though the scope of philanthropy in America is still unmatched any where in the world.

Taken as one element of corporate social responsibility — and given the fact that some executives exploit their contributions for public relations and marketing purposes — philanthropy alone is viewed with suspicion by some of business's critics.

"To zero in on philanthropy and neglect the basic operations of companies is to beg the question of corporate social responsibility," wrote Milton Moskowitz in a paper he prepared for the Commission on Private Philanthropy and Public Needs. "Alms giving is not what corporate social responsibility is about."

Phillip T. Drotning, who manages corporate social responsibility programs at Standard Oil of Indiana, wrote in *Business and Society:* "At the outset, most companies developed social programs, largely in the urban-racial area, as an extension of traditional support for charitable endeavors. As a consequence, social expenditures were largely applied to the symptoms of public problems, but had little impact on causes. They represented minimal actual involvement of the corporate organization in social problem-solving. As the appalling ineffectiveness of most of this effort became clear, recognition developed that if corporations were to develop significant programs in social areas, they must be integrated into normal business operations, not treated as a separate and often ephemeral responsibility."

Moskowitz continues to criticize corporate giving to select organizations "by consensus" resulting from the regular exchange of information among corporate officers responsible for making contributions.

In a nation where fewer than 1 percent of companies control almost 90 percent of the total industrial assets and receive over 90 percent of the net profits of all industrial activity, it is not surprising that perhaps only 6800 companies accounted for all corporate giving in 1970 and that only 850 corporations accounted for half of all corporate contributions in 1977.

E. B. "Burt" Knauft, Aetna's vice president for corporate social responsibility and manager of its foundation, served as John Filer's chief lieutenant during the work of the Commission on Private Philanthropy and Public Needs. It was Knauft, with Commission director Leonard Silverstein (a prominent Washington tax attorney) and Gabriel Rudney (who served as research director for the Commission while on leave from his post as assistant director of the Office of Tax Analysis, Department of the Treasury) who argued for protraction of the Commission's work to consider more fully the complaints of emerging social action groups.

Knauft analyzed corporate giving in the seventies and discovered that its growth rate of 12.4 percent was higher than that for all giving, but that the effect of inflation had reduced the value of corporate giving to $1.26 billion, or a real growth rate of only 5.2 percent.

Corporate giving as a percent of GNP did follow an upward trend through the seventies — from 0.081 percent in 1970 to 0.097 percent in 1979.

Corporations gave to a broad range of recipient groups in the seventies, but many executives also began to see what Bill Norris of Control Data had urged them to consider immediately following the riots of the sixties: "Make business opportunities out of social problems!"

Control Data gives away as little money as possible. When it is approached for a contribution, management sends a staff member out to see what the problem is — and how the company might make money by devising a solution. Norris says Control Data makes cash gifts only "where there is no other option." Control Data's philosophy is straightforward: if business doesn't engage in social problems on its own, it will pay much more later on (to the government) and have no control of either the expenditures or methods used.

In spring 1981, Kenneth Dayton, of the Dayton-Hudson Corporation in Minnesota, urged his colleagues to step up their corporate contributions to the full 5 percent of pretax profits allowed by the IRS. Some forty companies of all sizes had banded together in the Minneapolis — St. Paul area, he reported, and agreed to give at the 5 percent level. What could be done in Minnesota could certainly be done elsewhere.

As a matter of scale, the general adoption of Dayton's recommendation would make a tremendous impact. The Atlantic Richfield Foundation, for example, under the astute baton of Walter D. Eichner, gives $17 million each year to a variety of national and local organizations. The $17 million represents less than 1 percent of ARCO's pretax profits.

The full 5 percent would make more than $80 million available to Eichner. "The board would never hear of it," Eichner said without hesitation when I asked him about the prospects for ARCO's upping its giving to the 5 percent level.

"But it's a question of scale, not principle," I persisted.

"No," he smiled, "it's a matter of very real dollars."

Millionaire New York attorney-realtor-entrepreneur Lawrence A. Wien thinks it's a question of principle and scale. And he's busy encouraging his business associates to increase their philanthropic giving. Unlike the Commission on Private Philanthropy and Public Needs, Wien is not relying on persuasion alone. He is showing up at the annual board meetings of major corporations (nearly 60 by the summer of 1981) and presenting proxy proposals requesting that the companies increase their contributions to the full 5 percent of pretax profits allowable under the rules of the Internal Revenue Service. Wien's committee includes such business dignitaries as C. Douglas Dillon, John T. Connor, Charles F. Luce and William S. Renchard.

By August 1981, Wien had issued and distributed seven reports commenting on the philanthropic habits and promises of more than fifty corporations. Wien's forthright and often unpopular approach seems to be generating results. He claims he will push proxy fights all the way if that is necessary to get a company to increase its philanthropic giving. But he much prefers to see the company make a public commitment on its own. When a company acts voluntarily to increase its dollar giving, Wien withdraws the proxy proposal.

Reporting on American Telephone and Telegraph, Wien wrote: "With its associated Bell companies, AT&T made charitable contributions of $28,100,000 in 1978. One percent of their earnings before taxes in that year would have totaled in excess of $110,000,000. A proxy proposal was filed recommending an increase to 1 percent. The company has agreed that it and its associated Bell companies will establish a budget target of 1 percent of pretax income which they expect will be achieved by 1981 or perhaps 1982. In the meantime, there will be a steady increase in philanthropic giving. The 1979 earnings exceed the 1978 earnings, so that 1 percent will exceed $110,000,000. The total increase within two years should be at least $85,000,000. The proxy proposal has been withdrawn."

Reporting on Amerada Hess, Wien wrote: "Amerada Hess Corporation has indicated that it would move to distributions of approximately 5 percent of earnings before income taxes, which plateau they expect to achieve within three to five years. The proxy proposal has been withheld."

Wien may not know it, but he is of the Lyndon Baines Johnson school of corporate giving. The former President would chide friends in industry from time to time about their reluctance to give up to the allowable 5 percent when they complained about the wisdom of federal spending for social programs. The President delighted in saying that business leaders could assume social leadership and show the government how to spend funds more wisely anytime they wished.

The Reagan administration is looking to the private sector to fill the gap left by the cutback in federal spending for social programs, and Wien is pushing industry toward a position of leadership in social affairs by presenting his case in the form of proxy proposals. He has assembled a powerful group of business supporters and they are convincing an increasing number of shareowners that industry ought to raise its philanthropic giving not only because community agencies urgently need help, but because private industry can respond much better and faster to social needs than the federal government.

Still, corporations seem more inclined to use their resources to invest in community rejuvenation and job formation than to increase charitable contributions alone.

The investments may be high risk and provide a slower and lower return when they succeed, but they can be managed as part of the normal business of the company, in communities where the company already invests in plant and equipment and employs a substantial number of workers. It is not charity; it is business. And it gives the company a full stake in the outcome of the ventures. Such investments involve company personnel across the board: planners, technicians, accountants, attorneys, not just the public affairs and contributions people.

Contributions may become a part of the "package" of services a company brings to bear to solve a given problem. But the investment factor minimizes the possibility that Moskowitz and Drotning warned about years ago, that a company might tend to write a check and never look out the window to understand the problem.

As business responds to social pressures in the eighties, it is much more likely to follow the example of Bill Norris at Control Data.

Honeywell, for example, bought homes in its headquarters neighborhood and paid its employees to rehabilitate them. Northwestern National, one of the largest banks in Minneapolis, now places nearly half its conventional home mortgages inside the city limits, as opposed to about 12 percent in 1976.

General Mills pushed the formation of the Greater Minneapolis Housing Corporation; chief executives of area companies make up the board of directors. Each corporate member adopted a different neighborhood, making multimillion-dollar investments to improve the quality of living and the economic base.

Control Data established a day-care center in cooperation with the government, provided legal help for its own employees during business hours, and set up financial counseling services for employees on matters ranging from how to get loans and mortgages to obtaining scholarships for their kids.

Control Data also set up a program to help ex-offenders find jobs, and to train recovered drug-addicts, the disabled, and the unskilled to qualify for jobs.

Robert A. Beck, chairman of the Prudential Insurance Company of America, pinpointed the shift from contributions to investments — and true social involvement — in a speech at Duke University in 1977: "We [business] are powerful socioeconomic institutions and we must recognize the responsibility of our power and the need to provide leadership in anticipating and resolving society's problems. . . . The scope and range of the problems of today's society exceed the capacity of our government to deal alone with them — the sixties were proof enough of that. . . . I believe that a sound program of social responsibility is the ultimate in enlightened self-interest and totally consistent with the long-range goals of all enterprises that expect to remain viable and productive organizations into the eighties and beyond. In fact, there is no other alternative."

Franklin A. Thomas, president of the Ford Foundation, believes the expanded corporate role in society is likely to take the form of "social" loans and investments parallel with philanthropic gifts, stimulated less by appeals to conscience than to pragmatic instincts. Thomas contends that business executives are more likely to stake money that may come back than simply to make gifts. He believes that "balance-sheet philanthropy" has a potential for aiding in the redress of social problems that is at least as great as that of traditional philanthropy. Thomas believes that professionally staffed foundations are uniquely qualified to facilitate balance-sheet philanthropy in the eighties.

Thomas had been president of the Bedford-Stuyvesant Restoration Corporation for ten years before becoming head of the Ford Foundation. He recalls that corporate gifts came into Bedford-Stuyvesant at an average rate of about $500,000 per year. Corporate investments over the same period included $24 million in mortgage loans for the purchase and renovation of one- to four-family homes in the area; $29 million in mortgage loans for the construction and renovation of multifamily housing; a $13 million manufacturing plant, producing needed jobs; a $6.5 million private shopping center, bringing jobs and decent food and merchandise at fair prices; and several million dollars in loans to locally owned businesses. The ratio of corporate investments to corporate gifts was in excess of 15 to 1!

Businesses are serving society through an entrepreneurial mode in many parts of the nation.

The Connecticut Housing Investment Fund was made possible by loans totalling $10 million from several insurance companies, at concessional rates. The Fund opens housing opportunities for minority families by helping them meet down-payment requirements.

Between 1967 and 1972, the insurance industry provided $2 billion in urban investments, mostly in the form of mortgage loans for residential, industrial, and commercial buildings in older neighborhoods.

Master urban planners and investors, such as Felix Rohatyn, think it will take much more than social investments and balance-sheet philanthropy to revitalize our cities. Rohatyn is head of the Municipal Assistance Corporation in New York, but is also taking his old-line investment firm of Lazard Freres & Company to the most depressed neighborhoods in Cleveland, Detroit, Chicago, and Washington. He believes that nothing short of a second industrial revolution will set American cities right. He wants the federal government to give more business to firms in "older America" and launch a coal-based energy program that would develop production, transport, and harbor facilities in the East. He thinks the tax base of cities should be expanded to include the suburbs.

Rohatyn is listened to, but Congress is not likely to enact his urban support programs during the Reagan administration. He envisions a vast public-private partnership that would not only create jobs and improve neighborhoods but actually reestablish fading industries. And big spending is not the current mode.

But most industries may be backing off from social concerns in the private sector, just as government is backing off in the public sector. If this is true, and evidence supports the premise, then the gap between social expectations and social fulfillment in the eighties is sure to widen and social problems worsen. But there is hope.

Although the massive investments by the insurance industry in the late sixties and early seventies have faded, individual insurance companies continue to organize their own social investment and contributions efforts.

"Loans under the massive industry-wide program proved to be about ten times as likely to be delinquent as conventional investments," recalls James S. Dailey, an Aetna vice president and mastermind of that carrier's social investment program. "We continue to be sensitive to the fact that our investment decisions — how we invest approximately $20 billion in bonds, stocks, and real estate — have an impact on society that imposes responsibilities we cannot shun. In some measure our concern could be called self-serving, for when there are rents in the social fabric that are not mended — when a significant segment of the population is denied the promise of a matured economy — the system itself is threatened."

Dailey and his colleagues agree that cash grants are preferable to the pretense of investment. But they are convinced that successful investments with positive social consequences can be developed if the investor is committed enough to expand the effort to uncover them, evaluate them, carefully structure them, and work with the borrower as long as that may be necessary. Aetna's goal has been to achieve a few well-developed projects in a few fields rather than engage in many small efforts.

"Probably our major impact thus far has been in urban areas," Dailey said. "Reclamation of the decaying core of so many of our major cities is of vital importance in restoring confidence in what is, after all, an urban society. And yet lenders have been wary of rehabilitation commitments; it is much easier to invest in a new suburban shopping center. We have proven that we can identify attractive investment opportunities in the very worst neighborhoods — opportunities that we once would have walked away from."

Aetna has set up subsidiary companies to handle certain social projects; poured money into developing minority-owned businesses and broadcasting facilities; established revolving funds for the acquisition of residential properties; and backed the Local Initiatives Support Corporation [LISC] with $1 million in cash. LISC is sponsored by the Ford Foundation and a half-dozen corporations. Its purpose is to identify and activate local projects that will employ people in efforts to improve their neighborhoods and economic stability.

Aetna also entered into an agreement with the leadership of the National People's Action to erase real and alleged redlining barriers — areas of cities "lined off" and excluded from investments and insurance coverage.

Aetna is not alone. New York Life's diversified investments have aided big business and small, including the construction of the first industrial building in ill-fated Soul City, North Carolina — a dream city invented by Floyd McKissick and funded by the Department of Housing and Urban Development, but which never received the kind of private sector involvement required to make it grow.

New York Life also supported the efforts of a group of black physicians and dentists in Houston with a $1.2 million loan to construct a medical complex. Similar financing made possible the black-owned

Garwyn Medical Building in Baltimore; the Matthew Walker Neighborhood Health Center in Nashville; and medical facilities in seven other cities. Hospitals and moderate-income housing programs also have benefited through New York Life's aggressive social action program. Alan E. Pinado coordinates the company's urban investment program which includes minority business development, housing, and job-creating activities.

Pinado believes that the problems of the sixties have already returned to plague America in the eighties: high crime and unemployment rates — which go together — and antisocial behavior of all kinds: "The educational system is a mess. It's really discouraging. Many companies have to provide entry level literacy training for kids who have a high school diploma."

As a result of the general social environment Pinado describes, most managements are getting more nervous about making out-and-out social investments. It's a harder sell inside. The overt pressure is off of industry. Ronald Reagan is in the White House. The economists are pushing the old bottom line, not the new bottom line. They're not thinking about social responsibility, but strictly return on investment. Who wants to take a high risk when there are a dozen safe investments begging for attention? In the seventies business was willing to go the extra mile. The support for corporate social programs has cooled, and government's ardor is cooling too. But industry leaders are aware of the need to raise the bottom line in order to avoid recycling the problems of the sixties.

James Langton, senior vice president of Bank of America in San Francisco, acknowledges that California banks have very large real estate portfolios: "In the seventies, the Bank of America was the second largest real estate holder in the world. We know the mortgage business, and we've seen the problems brought on by FHA 'redlining' practices. Yes, government started the practice of redlining. And, yes, there has been de facto redlining in the private sector. It is a continuing problem that requires constant attention."

Corporate social responsibility and corporate giving have been pretty much institutionalized at Bank of America. Committees of the board and staff have functioned for a decade. Board member Andrew Brimmer, the famed economist and former member of the Federal Reserve Board, serves on the Public Policy Committee, monitors social programs, and makes recommendations to top management.

"We apply the same disciplines in carrying out our corporate social responsibility program as we do in every other department throughout the enterprise," Langton said. "I'll be the first to say the rules may not work out as neatly or the results manifest themselves as clearly as in other more precise areas of banking activity. There are many ambiguities in the social arena. But my point is that the function is a part of the bank's normal operations. The function is truly integrated."

Langton views government encroachment in the private sector as the most dramatic change of the seventies: "The laws have obscured issues and made simple statements almost impossible. Compliance with regulation is costly. The well-intentioned 'truth in lending' provisions are so tied up in legalities that the customer is poorly served.

"We're investors. Bad loans are poor investments. We're careful. That's our business, to be careful. But we do make high-risk, low-return loans for social projects we've analyzed and want to support. We think that's good business too."

The new openness among corporations in reporting their contributions — some even publishing special annual reports — and their willingness to meet with emerging groups and be fully accountable for their social actions attests to the new norms in corporate life.

PART THREE

Business Power/
Media Power

Chapter Twelve

On Wearing Black Hats

Businessmen and businesswomen suffer many fears: the fear of failure, the fear of competition, the fear of labor unrest, the fear of government regulation, and the fear of high blood pressure, heart attack, and ulcers.

But most of all, they fear the news media.

The fear is neither reasonable nor intelligent, but it is terribly real.

High-level executives, who coolly manage the affairs of multimillion-dollar international corporations, crumble at the sight of an unfavorable story in a newspaper and reach instant boiling point when confronted by a misleading headline.

The feeling toward the news media is so negative that many executives would actually welcome restraints on the news media, even as they cry for relief from government regulations in their own industries.

As Herbert Schmertz, the aggressive spokesman for Mobil Oil, has pointed out, until recently business executives have been poorly prepared for their role as public spokespersons.

Fortunately, business and the media are striving for mutual understanding in all fifty states. But harmonious relationships may never be achieved, and perhaps should not be set as a goal.

More than one hundred years ago, Alexis de Tocqueville wrote in *Democracy in America* that to enjoy the inestimable blessing of a free press, it is necessary to endure and tolerate the evils that a free press will engender. To believe that one can enjoy the first without suffering the second is to indulge in illusion.

In the eighties, business executives and media executives seem to agree on at least two major points: the media must perform more responsibly; business must be more open and accessible.

The media have come under increasing attack for their alleged lack of responsibility: contrived news stories, payments to criminals for story material, docu-dramas, and news-entertainment shows that, critics claim, confuse the viewing audience.

On the other hand, John Leonard reminded the business community in 1977 that its leaders had never been considered the men in white hats by the news and entertainment media. Writing in *Forbes,* the brilliant *New York Times* reporter said business executives are subject to inept reporting on the news pages, are maligned in the theater and media entertainment shows, and portrayed in novels as being oppressive and corrupt.

Money, it seems, is a metaphor for evil.

"Has a businessman ever been portrayed as decent, much less heroic, in an American western? When was the last time you saw a happy businessman, except in commercials for airlines, rental cars, and motel franchises, and not counting Colonel Sanders?" he wrote.

According to Bob Dylan, the businessman is one of the masters of war. And Tennessee Ernie Ford complains in song of owing his soul to the company store.

In the theater, Willie Loman's employer was ungrateful and uncaring.

"In high culture and in low, judging by our novels, plays, movies, TV programs, magazines, comic books, and pop music, except for Ayn Rand and Little Orphan Annie, Americans don't like businessmen," Leonard wrote.

"Oh, the highbrows tolerate businessmen in and around the various palaces of culture, and on the boards of museums and symphony orchestras, in the columbaria of the great foundations, philanthropizing . . . . But when the chlorophyll people from Sirius the Dog Star arrive to sift our volcanic ash, to crack open our tiny time capsules, to muck around among our artifacts in search of a clue to our values, they aren't going to find any coins stamped with the heads of businessmen. On the whole, the Mafia gets a better press."

Businessmen agree. In 1981, a television show titled "The Gangster Chronicles" appeared on prime time and quickly attracted a large audience. In docu-drama form — with liberties taken to invent characters, alter situations, and glorify the bums who hustled booze, broads, and violence in the thirties — the series glamorized punks. The producers claimed to be showing a piece of American history, and viewer response, they said, proved that millions of citizens were enthralled.

Perhaps so. But out on the real streets of America, crime rates are soaring. Sixty million citizens carry or keep handguns in their homes and cars. Twenty thousand real men, women, and children are killed by those handguns every year; eleven thousand of them murdered. Arson, theft, and child abuse are rampant. Old people and children are held captive by fear in their own homes.

Business is affected. Who wants to saunter through a shopping mall at night or risk a hassle in the parking lot?

Why glorify violence on TV when the nation is trying to get it under control on the street where people bleed real blood?

"Hell, man, we've got corporations buying time on our show. Who's mad?" the producers ask.

No thinking person argues the right of the producers to air the show, of sponsors to support it, of people to watch it. But thinking people question the judgment, sensitivity, and responsibility of the entertainment media for glorifying the scum of society while ignoring the efforts of other citizens to make our nation strong and safe and to improve the quality of life for us all.

The challenge is to make good news *news*. The battles and triumphs of people who build a better society are certainly equal to chronicles of people who would destroy society. The good guys won this debate: "Gangster Chronicles" was cancelled.

John Leonard does not believe the poor image of American businessmen can be blamed solely on the peculiarities of the recent past, the laundering of campaign contributions, the buying of foreign governments, the bribing of congressmen, the fixing of prices, the energy crisis, and the polluting of the environment. It goes back further and down deeper, Leonard says, almost to a mythic level.

Leonard's sardonic appraisal of the role of business in society is reflected in Michael Harrington's view that businessmen and the economists who advise them (*Twilight of Capitalism*) are themselves the greatest threat to free enterprise.

Veteran economist Robert L. Heibroner, in his book *Business Civilization in Decline*, opines that capitalism will probably disappear within a century. He sees a vast increase in national economic planning in which the corporation's role will grow continually smaller, that of government correspondingly larger.

The Reagan administration rejects Heibroner's prognosis out of hand.

But the future may more closely resemble Heibroner's vision than Reagan's if industry fails to take its case to the public and work effectively with the news media.

Business leaders have been notoriously unsuccessful in taking their case to the public. Pervasive myths about the business system and the use of profits persist. Business must improve its communications with the media, the government, and the citizenry to establish beyond a doubt the vital efforts it is making to help solve the problems of society.

Business has already paid a painful price for its indifference. And at times, its arrogance.

In the seventies, the Chamber of Commerce of the United States said that business confronted the most antibusiness Congress since the New Deal, even with Republican Richard Nixon in the White House. But Congress was listening more attentively to a man named Ralph Nader whom General Motors had made into a hero by snooping into his personal life when he challenged the safety of one of its cars.

Proposals to federalize large corporations were entertained with some seriousness at that time. Perhaps if corporations had been more accessible and less heavy handed, they would not have made such inviting targets for attack in the seventies by social reformers, conservationists, and consumerists.

Under all the rhetoric, these groups articulated one basic goal: give us a piece of the action! Let us participate in making decisions that affect us. Business's critics were not so much trying to change the private enterprise system, as seeking to be a part of it, to benefit from it.

Industry could not at that time understand the need to embrace many different points of view under the banner of private enterprise — to stop fighting fellow citizens who held different views about profits and their uses.

Industry began to hire urban affairs experts, former government officials, and former media representatives to "deal with the new — and hopefully passing — crisis." In the sixties and early seventies, industry had not accepted the idea that both publicly and privately held companies had to redefine their roles and restructure their operations on a permanent basis to cope with the dramatic changes in society.

The media began to report more fully on the day-to-day efforts of companies.

Many newspapers assigned writers to the business beat on an exclusive basis. Political cartoonists raised their pens to characterize life in the corporate boardroom.

Businessmen and businesswomen were not usually pleased by their offerings.

A comic strip about a cold and surly chief executive began to appear in major newspapers in the eighties. Called "Graves, Inc." the strip had a cutting edge and made some executives so uncomfortable that they aimed angry attacks at its creator, Chicagoan Pat Brady.

In one segment, Winston Graves, the insensitive, unsmiling chief executive of Graves, Inc., puts his arm around Bill Balding, his sickly vice president, and urges him to take a week off. "Get some rest, see your doctor," Graves urges, as Balding grabs his stomach. "I want those ulcers cleaned up by the fifteenth, understand?" Graves looks at his watch and turns away.

Chapter Thirteen

Farewell "Low Profile"

A whole new industry has sprung up across the nation to help business executives cope with editors, reporters, and electronic journalists. Simulated television interviews are held daily in company-owned studios that rival the facilities of local stations.

The process, commonly called "adversarial training," speaks volumes about the mind set of management in dealing with a free press.

Gone are the days when a busy executive could tell his speech writer, "I'm too rushed to see you today; I'll read the speech on the plane." Today's executive is coached on style, manner, dress, and delivery.

Speeches are rehearsed in front of a video camera. Media interviews are preceded by simulated interview with staff.

Historically, business executives have preferred a "low profile," believing that company actions were not the concern of the press or public. They shunned opportunities to be interviewed by reporters, unless, of course, they sought attention for a good earnings statement.

Attitudes toward the press changed sharply after the domestic riots, not because management's basic mind set had been modified but because social pressure required that the executive respond in a public way to new demands upon the corporation.

The Freedom of Information Act also altered management's attitudes toward the media because it opened government files to the information they contained on American industry.

Executives began to understand what most of their public relations people had been telling them all along: the press wants direct access to the principals of the company, not secondhand statements. It was at that point, in the late sixties, that public relations entered the boardroom and the top circle of management in many corporations. Public relations people prepared top executives for their new public roles. They counseled on the social and political implications of business actions and statements.

Not all executives were ready and willing to wear blue shirts, powder their noses and bald spots, and go before the cameras, however. Even today some executives seek coaching in the art of obfuscation, although it is a futile and unworthy exercise.

The upheaval in society since 1965 has opened communication and placed uncommon demands on all institutions for public accountability. These demands have forced business to deal more forthrightly with the news media in good times and bad. Business firms are now recognized as social institutions. They must act accordingly or face the consequences: loss of public confidence and increasing government intrusion.

But old habits die slowly. Executives did not immediately embrace their new role in society. It would all go away, many thought, and things would somehow return to "normal". Businessmen reacted to a perceived crisis, not to the fundamental change in society that was taking place.

It took a decade to instill the idea that private institutions are accountable to society, that they must communicate with the public. It will take another decade or more to institutionalize that concept.

It is not difficult to understand why time and patience are required to modify the practices of large organizations. Bureaucratic structures in both the public and private sectors are like fortresses, teeming with internal jealousies and burdened with procedural waste but resolute in their determination that no outside force shall intrude on their misery.

The news media is the most powerful outside force in the life of a business executive. He can't control it, manage it, package it, or put it on a shelf. It has a power of its own, and it is turning its attention on him, the businessman, the big taxpayer, the provider of jobs and bonuses and summer picnics and Christmas parties, the supporter of the United Way and a hundred community causes. The media, says the typical executive, does not appreciate business. It is out to get business. And, by George, business is going to prepare itself for the fray.

It was raw fear and resentment that prompted businessmen to listen in the sixties. Fear of more domestic violence. Fear of government mandates. Fear of a press they considered to be hostile and ill-informed. Resentment of a public turned sour on business.

Not to a man, of course. William Norris of Control Data and Donald MacNaughton (then chairman of Prudential) saw opportunity in the turmoil, and said so. But most business executives were inclined to build defenses, even as they engaged in the work of the National Urban Coalition and the National Alliance of Businessmen, as it was then called, and met with community leaders where they lived and worked.

Businesspeople played constructive roles in bringing the nation out of its crisis. Some played starring roles. But their basic mind set about the role of business in society, and especially their ingrained fear of the news media, could not change overnight.

An invitation to be interviewed by Mike Wallace on "60 Minutes" — the popular CBS Sunday evening news magazine — put fear and trembling into the bone of any chief executive officer. He or she was convinced that Mike would be "out to get them," to embarass them, or to expose some real or alleged wrongdoing. The name of Mike Wallace is synonymous with expose. He is, by his own standard and in the opinion of most of his peers, a top-flight investigative journalist. But in the eyes of fearful business (and government) officials, he is a hatchet man.

It is the exceptional business leader who views the media as strong allies, which indeed they can be. It is the rare executive who enjoys dealing with the media.

Out in Hawaii, on the state's number-one television station, CBS affiliate KGMB-TV, "Hotline to Business" is aired twice a year to dispel the common belief that business executives are stuffy, indifferent to societal ills, and unwilling to hear public complaints.

Five corporate executives answer telephoned questions for ninety minutes. The questions reflect little reverence for business, in keeping with the name of the program. Executives who agree to appear are severely challenged: "How many women managers do you have in your company? Why are you paid so much?"

The program was created by the local Business Communication Council in the mid-seventies and competes successfully with prime-time shows, attracting at least 10 percent of the viewing audience. Said one corporate member of the council, "People are seeing business executives as humans, and, therefore, believable."

Old habits die hard, however. When C. Dudley Pratt, Jr., executive vice president of Hawaiian Electric Company, came prepared for critical questions about a 40 percent rate increase, no caller asked him about it. Rather than taking the opportunity to praise the consumers for their understanding and cooperation, and explaining the rising costs for providing service, Pratt remained silent. "I would have welcomed the chance to explain the situation," he said. "That was a big reason I went on the show. But since nobody asked, I certainly wasn't going to bring the subject up."

MacNaughton thinks business executives should work hard at improving their performance in working with the media. While deploring the inaccuracies he finds in the media, MacNaughton believes it is the responsibility of business to learn to deal with the news media and to live with some of their deficiencies. He also believes it is the basic obligation of a free press to exercise prudence, to police its unprofessional members, and to challenge the questionable practices of some publishers and broadcasters.

MacNaughton thinks business and the media should concentrate on cleaning up their own houses and developing a more productive and mutually respectful relationship.

The stresses and strains are not all on the side of business. In February 1981, the tough-talking Mike Wallace and his "60 Minutes" colleague Morley Safer were themselves the center of a news item for allegedly scrapping a critical film segment on Haiti because of the concern Wallace's wife felt for a cousin living on that Caribbean island.

Wallace denied the charge but admitted that his wife was distraught after he had broadcast a "very straightforward and very tough piece on Haiti in 1972, the year after young Duvalier came into power." Wallace also acknowledged telling Safer how he and his wife felt about it. The 1981 version did not air. And critics were quick to accuse Wallace and his colleagues of applying a double standard: one for themselves; a tougher, less sensitive one for those involved in the stories they chose to report.

In 1975, MacNaughton told a conference of the Institute of Life Insurance in Chicago, "Sixty seconds on the evening news tonight is all that is required to ruin a reputation, turn a politician out of office, or impair a company's profitability. The power of the press with today's methods of mass communication has become, in short, the power to destroy."

MacNaughton did not confine his remarks to the power of the press. He urged business to become more open in its affairs — more free with information, more candid about its plans and problems, much readier than it has ever been to respond to questions and criticisms. He also urged his fellow executives to understand the nature of their relationship with the press.

"Investigative reporting and an adversary press have taken on new dimensions since Vietnam and Watergate," he said, "and this new vigor on the part of the press is now being employed in its dealings with institutions other than government, including business, and we in business must face up to it."

Other businessmen have expressed fear about the "pack" mentality of the press. "When one bird gets a sniff of something, the whole flock comes in," one of my business associates complained in 1972. "Just look at the covers of *Newsweek* and *Time.* They rarely differ week to week. Even the style is similar. The sameness of reporting of government actions and

White House statements suggests that these guys are all reading from the same script."

Is the observation accurate? To some degree, yes. But reporters will say they follow the news; they don't make it. And all good general news publications are going to have approximately the same priorities on any given day.

A good cover, publishers say, can increase sales well above the normal 4.2 million copies per week sold by *Time* and the 2.9 million copies sold by *Newsweek*. No one wants to play follow the leader, they claim.

By Tuesday of each week, editors from both weeklies have decided what they will use on the cover. By Friday, at the latest, each editor will know the intentions of the other, if not by direct information from within the other organization, then easily from people interviewed for stories and gossip among writers and researchers about the articles being developed.

Occasionally, covers will differ sharply, but their usual similarity reflects concurrence among experienced editors on the items that are top-of-the-news in any given week.

Still, it is not difficult to understand why business executives hold on to the pack theory.

When President Jimmy Carter said the holding hostage in Iran of fifty-three United States citizens was his biggest concern, Iranians took him at his word and staged daily demonstrations which were covered by the media of the world. The hostage story was page one day after day after day.

Then, following a devastating failure to rescue the hostages, which cost eight young American lives, the President proclaimed the issue "manageable" and said he would commence a belated political campaign for a second term in the White House. The vast majority of editors accommodatingly put the hostage story in the middle of their papers. Only when one ill hostage was released did stories again appear on the front pages of most newspapers — and again, later, when the hostages received a joyful and emotional welcome home by their fellow citizens.

Columnists Jack W. Germond and Jules Witcover wrote in June 1980: "That the hostages are no longer Topic A with Jimmy Carter or the campaign is not all the responsibility of the President. Both the voters and the news media, it seems, have an attention span roughly equivalent to a 4-year-old boy's."

In the first weeks of the hostage crisis, ABC's Ted Koppel did such a fine job of covering the event night after night, following the eleven o' clock news, that his management decided he should continue to report on just about everything following the news. A new television star and a new program were born.

The State Department's Hodding Carter III, a respected journalist in his own right and the son of a famed crusading Mississippi newspaper publisher, found himself before the cameras every day, telling what little was known and could be said about the fate of the hostages. As newscasters counted off 100, 200, then 300 and more days of captivity for the human pawns in the international power play, Hodding Carter by day and Ted Koppel by night became part of the drama. Their skills and manner, and sometimes their humor, were somehow comforting to the nation.

LOOKING BACK

The United States has enjoyed the fruits of the free market system and a free press for more than two centuries. Yet, business leaders and editors have looked at society in quite different ways.

The business entrepreneur sought to build and create, to fight for advantage and power, to own and to control. His ingenuity and fierce determination helped mold a nation — an imperfect nation, as the free press in America would often point out.

Those who create want their successes reported, not their shortcomings or alleged improprieties. That was true at the beginning of the Republic, and it is true now.

The adversarial relationship between business and the press, as between business and the government, was as inevitable as it was helpful. The power of a free press, with its own imperfections, also helped to build a nation far different and better and stronger than any other on earth.

Powerful newspaper chains were developed between 1895 and the New Deal, feeding the interests and curiosities of an increasingly literate population. In doing so, newspapers became a critical force in the political and social affairs of the country.

Later, when radio and then television became major avenues for mass communication, politicians, and then business leaders, became more conscious of reflecting, or seeming to reflect, the public interest.

Social researchers surfaced after the war, matured in the fifties, and multiplied in the sixties. Everybody suddenly, or so it seemed, wanted to compare and evaluate political candidates, study social causes and the emerging public issues pursued by vocal and persistent activist groups.

Activists seemed to be self-taught in capturing media attention through bold statements, harsh accusations, and public demonstrations. Civil rights spokesmen, environmentalists, and consumer advocates commanded space on front pages and business pages, in food section, and in medical columns. Their leaders were featured on the six and eleven o'clock news, talk shows, and television interviews.

Business tended to respond slowly to activists' attacks, even as the public formed negative opinions of business based on unanswered accusations. The polls verified that public regard for business had dropped drastically.

Business was playing "catch up" ball and not doing very well. It had missed the opportunity to get out front by forming its own strategies for social engagement and preparing sensible statements to defuse attack.

The activists were on the move, and business and government were the defenders but reacted separately, rather than as friends under common attack. Of the two, government responded more quickly and surely.

Business was in trouble, and it would take more than the *Wall Street Journal*, the predictable defender of industry practices, and the *Journal of Commerce*, the sympathetic friend of industry, to counter the stings of the likes of the *Wahington Post*, the inquiries of skeptical columnists, and the probes of special interest newsletters. Still, the events moved business and government toward middle ground.

"In a real sense," says Arthur White, vice chairman of Yankelovich, Skelly & White, the international social research and marketing firm, "the development of the news media, particularly the electronic media, and its use by leaders in business and government, helped to make our whole system more democratic and open in terms of knowing the public mood and responding to it."

Studies by Yankelovich, Skelly & White; Harris; Roper; Opinion Research; Gallup; Research Strategies, and other well-known firms helped business, government, trade associations, and the news media to understand public opinion and expectations and chart societal trends.

In the short term, business was able to fashion statements and policies that the public would find acceptable and that would help to defuse the ardor of activist attacks.

New information, and the demands of "cutting edge" groups that sought changes in society, also sparked the formation of unlikely alliances. In the environmental arena, for example, the demands for clean air and water, leveled at both business and government, pulled the old adversaries together in an odd way.

Industry, which had fought so hard to be independent of government, now said it needed government guidelines.

Government became the master planner and enforcer of myriad regulations.

Business became the unwilling implementor of new laws, and the public whipping boy.

In developing their response to public demands, business people found that phrases and images often became more important than the actual balancing of interests, the negotiating of reasonable compromises, and getting down to the hard work of solving social and economic problems. Answers were difficult to find. Tempers were short. Meetings with activists were testy, noisy, and often crude. It was more comfortable to deal in phrases and visions of what might be — if people would only stop shouting.

But the new dialogue, the new openness, increased the pressure on industry to communicate persuasively, to train its leaders to be better public performers, in a constructive sense, and to devote the resources of business and commerce to rebuilding a sound, healthy, more tranquil society.

Perceptions varied, of course, as to what should be done or could be done. To the visionaries in business, men like Dan Yankelovich were providing the data on which the nation might advance toward its major goals. To the pragmatists in business who imagined that the nation was passing through a temporary crisis, Yankelovich and his peers simply were providing a surer means for calculating one's own narrow course through a sea of screaming activists.

The citizenry withheld its trust in the late sixties and early seventies because the government disseminated misinformation during the war in Vietnam and the Watergate scandal, and industry made questionable payments to foreign governments — revealed after the fact. There was a general feeling among the citizenry that big government and big business had taken over the affairs of the nation and rendered the individual powerless.

The new openness and candor, amplified by the mass media, can do much to restore public trust in all institutions, public and private. Without public trust, the nation's problems will intensify and tranquility will become even more elusive.

Chapter Fourteen

Facing the Red Light at Taues

The associate producer, a beautiful Japanese-American woman named Jur-l Hall, smiles warmly and produces a cup of coffee for the nervous guest before escorting him to the studio.

Student crews are setting up lights, adjusting microphones, and moving chairs. The interviewers, Peter Gamble and Glen Ford, are engrossed in conversation. They greet him perfunctorily and return to their discussion.

The guest says the television studio is a bit chilly. No one responds. He is seated between Ford and Gamble on a swivel chair. The unfamiliar lights bother him.

Jur-l Hall fastens his mike. He has to unbutton his vest to hide the cord, then quickly button it up again as the director barks, "One minute."

Now Jur-l looks at him reprovingly. "Thirty seconds," shouts the director, a short, bearded student at the University of Maryland.

Jur-l leans forward, frowning, staring at his nose, "Geez, why don't you cut that ugly black hair out of your nostril?" she hisses, shaking her head in disgust. He reaches for his nose. "Get your hand out of your face," Gamble says coldly, fixing the guest with an icy stare.

The director kicks over a metal chair on the cement floor. The guest jumps. "Cameras," barks the director. A camerawoman moves in for a close-up. The music comes up, and Gamble, smiling, looks at the red light and opens the simulated television program.

"Good morning, welcome to 'College Park Comments,' a public service program devoted to the exposition of issues of importance to all citizens. I am Peter Gamble. My colleague is Glen Ford, and our guest today is an alleged scientist from the Edison Electric Institute who is going to tell us how acid rain pumped up in the air by power plants in midwestern states is killing fish in Canada and causing an international crisis. Viewers, this is Dr. Jack Taylor, one of the utility industry's defenders. Dr. Taylor, don't the private utilities have any conscience about the damage caused by acid rain? Aren't you, a research person, just a little sheepish coming on this program to defend the industry's atrocious indifference?"

The director holds up a cue card telling Taylor to take off his watch. He does, hesitating in his response to Gamble. Ford breaks in, "I'd be speechless, too, if my industry was responsible for putting resort owners out of business, killing fish, and probably endangering human life."

Taylor turns in his chair toward Ford. "I repeat," Gamble says stridently, "how can you defend such behavior?"

Taylor laughs nervously, tugs at his tie, and begins, "Mr. Gamble, you must understand that acid rain is caused by many conditions. For example . . ." Ford cuts him off, "Are you trying to tell us that the industry is blameless?" Taylor tries again, "Not at all, Mr. Ford. What I am saying is that acid is in the environment. It has always been present in rain."

Gamble, a large, imposing man, sneers, his voice dripping with sarcasm. He leans toward Taylor, "I suppose it's in the trees. President Reagan said pollution comes from the trees. You are some kind of a comedian, Dr. Taylor. Is that why your industry puts you on these programs, to tell jokes and fool the people? The trees! Good Lord, I imagine you suffer from hay fever. The pollen gets to you. Does the pollen cause acid rain, Dr. Taylor?"

Another nervous laugh. Taylor, young, handsome, turns toward Gamble. Ford asks softly, "Now how in the world, Dr. Taylor, did you get off on pollen and pollution from trees? I thought you were here to talk about acid rain and how the private power utilities are killing fish. Can't you tell us anything about the Canadian claims against you and your associates?"

The director holds up a cue card telling Taylor to cross his legs. He does. "I really don't understand your reluctance to talk about acid rain, Dr. Taylor," chides Gamble. Taylor, now a bit flushed, but still smiling, slouches in his chair. One of three cameramen moves in for another closeup shot. Two minutes have elapsed. Taylor has eight minutes to go — an eternity.

The audacious behavior of the interviewers is rehearsed. Jack Taylor is one of five executives and research experts going through "adversarial" training in the Taues Arts Center on the University of Maryland campus at College Park on this cold day in January 1981. It is a learning experience for the students as well as Taylor. Authentic studio conditions are created down to the last detail. But in this studio, the interviewers and crew are testing the poise and knowledge of the guest.

Later in the morning, the five participants in the training session are asked to rate their own performance.

The critique team arrives later. They have watched the five performances on the monitor in the control room.

Prof. Ray Hiebert gives an overview of broadcasting, pointing out that television is a business that sells advertising. Interview shows must be exciting and provocative, he says, and the interviewers are chiefly entertainers. The interviewees, he points out, become part of the entertainment package.

He cautions the trainees that style is often more important than content; any sign of nervousness or anger is magnified.

The participants discuss their performances among themselves. Now Hiebert turns on the monitor in the classroom. He and other members of the critique team study the ten-minute interviews with the participants. They stop the monitor to make key observations.

"What was Gamble trying to do there?" Hiebert asks.

"Confuse me," Taylor laughs.

"Why did you take off your watch?"

"Because the guy held up a card saying I should."

"And what was he trying to do?"

"Divert my attention?"

"Right."

The objective is achieved: the participants see themselves as others see them on the television screen. They are helped in critiquing their own performances. Some remain slightly angry. But most are good-natured and understanding and anxious to have a second chance.

The group takes lunch together in the faculty club. They continue to discuss the morning's events. Those who have done well are praised. Those who did poorly are encouraged. On the walk back to Taues Center, there is kidding back and forth, and expressions of confidence in "putting those guys" (the interviewers) in their places.

Gamble and Ford make an excellent team; Gamble is brash, uninhibited, forceful. He stands 6 feet 3 inches, with a shock of curly brown hair. He is smart, irreverent, does his homework on the subject to be discussed and the people to be interviewed. Before starting the Public

Interest News Center in Philadelphia, he had worked for public broadcasting and Mutual News, conducting daily interviews.

Ford is small, intense, with a Fu Man Chu mustache and a clipped, precise manner of speaking. He smiles engagingly, but sparingly. In the mid-seventies he originated and moderated a syndicated television interview show, "America's Black Forum," which attracted such guests as the Reverend Jesse Jackson, Vernon Jordan, Andrew Young, James Farmer, Carl Holman, industrialist Thomas Murphy of General Motors, and Borden's Augustine R. Marusi.

Every week for several years, Ford greeted a new guest and a new subject — from racial prejudice to redlining practices, from minority business development to crime in the street. Ford absorbs the detail of complicated subjects with remarkable ease, and can be relentless in his questioning when a guest falters or tries to be evasive.

Jur-l Hall was born and raised in Japan. She disarms interviewees with her gracious manner and flashing smile. By the time the guest reaches the studio, Jur-l is his (or her) friend and ally.

Her sudden rude manner and snide comments just before show time are designed to startle and upset the guest.

The director's clumsiness in knocking over a chair and his silliness in holding up cue card instructions are part of the test: Will the interviewee ignore such instruction? Probably not, since he or she is in a strange environment.

When Gamble and Ford throw their verbal punches, will the interviewee know when to laugh, argue, interrupt, and maintain control? Perhaps not, at least the first time around. But almost certainly after lunch.

On this bitterly cold January morning, Jack Taylor, immaculate in his dark suit and blue shirt, does not have an ugly hair growing out of his nose. His watch is not throwing off a glare, but when he crosses his legs on cue, he does reveal skin between sock and pants cuff, a television "no-no." The ploys are all part of the Gamble-Ford treatment.

The second interview of the day is superior to the first. The learning curve is apparent.

Taylor is more confident during his second try. He insists on answering the questions to his own satisfaction. Gamble and Ford ease up just slightly, creating a more realistic interview environment. But they keep the pressure on.

The second interview runs seven minutes. And the same critique process follows. Participants measure their own progress. Hiebert hands out a sheet listing five major guidelines and twelve do's and don'ts.

Gamble joins the group at the very end of the day, relaxed and friendly. He offers his comments and observations as they view the monitor together.

"Look, Al, you were gripping the chair as if you were afraid you would fly away," he tells Al Courtney of Commonwealth Edison, who has flown in from Chicago to participate. "You hesitated too long and allowed us to pose a second question before you responded to the first. You appeared to be unsure of yourself." Al Courtney agrees.

Gamble turns to Dr. Harold Hughes of Potsdam, New York, an inventor and retired professor who will moderate a public forum on acid rain the following week in the Adirondack Mountains.

"You are so forthright and calm I don't think anyone could rattle you," Gamble says admiringly. "But you ought to correct me quickly when I state erroneous information. You have as many rights under the lights as the interviewer. For example, you have the right to finish your answer. You have the right to correct misinformation."

Richard Swantek, a community relations executive with Niagara Mohawk Power Company at Albany, New York, had performed well. In his initial interview, he smilingly held up his hand to ward off a question Ford attempted to interject as he was responding to a previous question from Gamble, even turning his back on Ford until he had fully responded. Gamble recognized Swantek's poise and played the video again for the benefit of the group.

"The interviewees should walk out of here more confident of their ability to go head to head with the media on difficult subjects. If we accomplish that in one day, we've accomplished quite a lot," Gamble says.

Many media training courses are available, dating back to the original curriculum put together by the J. Walter Thompson Company. Almost all the training is useful. Some programs are brilliantly conceived. Not all of them deal with the substance as well as the style of performance, as is emphasized by Gamble and Ford at the University of Maryland. The university also provides a natural learning atmosphere, and the simulated interviews benefit students and faculty, as well as the participants.

Real success will be recorded when the simulated interviews are part of the manager's basic training and not crash courses in defending business against attack.

The idea is to prevent attack, resolve issues, and improve understanding.

Chapter Fifteen

Working on the Firing Line

Industry is not only hiring former broadcasting personalities to train management but is also bringing media experts on staff.

At the Atlantic Richfield Company in Los Angeles, a former CBS reporter, Anthony Hatch, serves as manager of corporate media relations. He joined ARCO in 1977 after twenty-three years in journalism, sixteen of those years with CBS in New York and abroad. Hatch believes most people today get their news and form their opinions from the electronic media, especially television. His efforts at ARCO reflect that conviction.

Hatch originated "Energy Update," a visual magazine for television. It is not simply an ARCO propaganda outlet. As a newsman, Hatch knew he would have to create a thoughtful, objective, and professionally produced vehicle to earn the attention of skeptical editors and producers. Many media people, he knew, consider any former newsman employed by industry to have "gone to the other side" or even "sold out." The burden on men like Hatch is therefore doubled. And when his efforts are respected by the news media and his materials are used, it is a tribute to his professionalism and his newsman's dedication to objectivity, whatever "side" he may be on.

Success for Hatch is measured by the number of stations using his program — from 20 to 140 in short order. Men like John Naisbitt, publisher of the *Trend Report,* are interviewed on camera by Hatch. They provide a national focus and often challenge ARCO's positions.

Thirty cable outlets take Hatch's program, some of them using the full half-hour he provides. There are "strictly ARCO" stories, of course, but always with a public thrust.

For example, Bill Duke, ARCO's manager of federal programs and former vice president of the Corporation for Public Broadcasting, is the creator of ARCO's driver conservation program: saving energy through sensible driving. ARCO also sponsors an auto maintenance program to save car-owners time and money, improve mileage and save energy. Hatch invited Duke to discuss his project on "Energy Update" for broadcast across the country.

"There is a lot of spin-off and feedback," Hatch reports with satisfaction. "One station manager in Dallas liked the Naisbitt interview so much he flew to Washington and interviewed John for his own local energy program."

Hatch doesn't crowd his guests: "We let them talk; we don't push on to the next question if the speaker is still responding in some detail to a previous question. And if the guest takes off on something we didn't anticipate, but it's interesting, we don't cut it off. As a result, we produce in-depth, conversational pieces. And the response suggests there is a need and desire for this kind of unhurried, descriptive dialogue."

While most subjects have some relationship to ARCO's fortunes, many do not. They are simply items Hatch thinks will be of interest to the diverse national audience. For example, he did a story on heat obtained from cow's milk in the milking process which is used to heat the water on a large dairy farm. The water is used to wash down the barns and to provide all the farm's hot water requirements. "It was an unusual heat transfer to energy story," says Hatch, "and I thought people should know about it. American ingenuity has pulled our country out of trouble in the past. It will again."

The imagination and care Hatch puts into his efforts have stimulated more imaginative reporting elsewhere on energy conservation, Hatch believes. ARCO is receiving good press for its efforts — directly through the broadcast of the series and in news reports and word of mouth about the series.

Hatch looks and talks like a newsman. Intense, serious-minded, and direct, he is quick to assure visitors that he maintains a newsman's objectivity in carrying out his activities for ARCO.

Born in New York, raised in Chicago, schooled in Connecticut and New York, Hatch was editor of the weekly newspaper and news director of the campus radio station at Hobart College.

He was a copy boy for NBC Radio News before joining the Associated Press at the United Nations. Later, he worked as a newspaper reporter and then rejoined AP in Albany, New York.

After a stint in the army, Hatch joined CBS in 1961 and wrote for Douglas Edwards, Roger Mudd, and Harry Reasoner.

Hatch has reported from the Middle East, trained Arab and Israeli journalists in broadcast news production, covered the flight of Apollo 13, and received two Emmy Awards — and numerous other awards — for his documentaries and special programs.

As manager of media relations for the corporation, he teaches company personnel how to use media tools and directs the company's media relations activities.

Why did ARCO hire Hatch and embark on an aggressive media program? Because ARCO, like other big oil companies, didn't like the way it was depicted in the news media, and especially on television. ARCO determined to tell the story itself as it thought it should be told.

"Energy Update" is distributed free to 140 domestic and foreign stations once a month.

"We're trying to send out timely, authoritative, and objective feature stories about a major subject that television ignores for the most part," Hatch claims. Most television editors agree that the material they receive from Hatch is professionally produced, balanced news.

Not surprisingly, the show also has its critics.

Most stations lack both the resources and inclination to examine energy issues in depth. If they use the ARCO material, they are likely to use it without adding local comment. ARCO's analyses are thus accepted at face value. Hatch points out that as a professional television journalist, he refuses to send out material he would not have welcomed while at CBS. He prides himself on producing balanced programs. But he has not convinced everybody of his virtue.

"I'm suspicious of any kind of vested interest," says Rabun Mathews, news director of KITV in St. Louis. He rescinded the decision of his predecessor and asked ARCO not to send the tapes. "I automatically reject any material prepared by outsiders," he states. It was unclear, however, whether Mathews also rejected all government statements and releases.

Hatch presses the point. "Stations receive free footage provided by sports leagues, movie studios, Detroit [automobiles], and government agencies."

Hatch also points out that his show is identified at the beginning and end of each segment as a service of the Atlantic Richfield Company.

Critics complain, however, that the show is indistinguishable from other news shows. Hatch is the moderator, because, he says, his annual budget of $160,000 does not permit him to hire outside talent.

Many of the shows do not even mention ARCO. But they face up to all the tough questions posed to the industry. "If we slip up just once by avoiding a tough question or ignoring the other side, then we rightfully deserve to be ignored. Credibility is the issue," he emphasizes.

In a segment devoted to Alaskan lands legislation, Hatch included spokespersons from the Audubon Society and other groups opposed to industry's efforts to open millions of acres to exploration.

"We get some ideas handed down," Hatch admits, "but there is no pressure [by top management] to do or avoid doing any specific stories."

All the stations that receive the show have expressly agreed to receive it. Most stations say they use the material for background information and story ideas. Some stations run the shows in their entirety or use "snippets."

Paul Dicker, program manager at WOWK in Huntington, West Virginia, sums up the feeling of most users: "As long as I can pick and choose what I want from it, I'm happy."

The lesson for all of industry is to produce useful, professional materials in the public interest. The company's self-interest is served by addressing the general interest first, and by sprinkling the programs with material that is simply fun or unique. In short, company-based producers should learn to think and act like newsmen. Or hire a Tony Hatch.

Hatch believes attitudes toward the news media at ARCO have changed even since his arrival in 1977: "When I came here most of the executives were still jumpy about public criticism leveled at the oil industry relating to the Arab embargo of 1973 and 1974. I found most of them suspicious of both print and electronic media. But they knew they had to deal with the media. My employment was one evidence of that."

Hatch worked hard at telling his peers that the media were not "out to get ARCO" but simply were not well-informed about the industry. He stressed that the burden for closing the gap was on the company.

"There are few energy specialists in television," says Hatch. "On the local stations, especially, a reporter is assigned to an abortion story in the morning, a big fire at noon, and a meeting on energy in the afternoon. Reporters are versatile, intelligent people, or they couldn't stay in the game. But you can't expect any reporter to be at ease in a conference room full of energy experts, or medical experts, or aviation experts, and the like, and be able to fully analyze what is said.

"Industry people are put off by naive questions and offended by superficial stories. The challenge is to provide reporters with information in a way and in a setting that is not compromising and that protects their integrity and ours."

One of the things Hatch has done is take a group of executives "on the road" to meet with reporters and editors in on-the-record informal discussion: "These are shirt-sleeve working sessions. Nothing pretentious. We usually meet in a private room at a hotel, order sandwiches, and talk. We meet in small groups, eight or ten men and women, including our own executives. We try to include ARCO's president or chairman whenever we can. We've held a number of these sessions and they've all been helpful."

Other companies, Aetna Life & Casualty and General Motors among them, have provided similar forums for informal exchange, and all report helpful results in terms of improving media understanding and advancing the education of company executives.

"I think we've blunted suspicions. Just the fact that high-ranking executives are willing to meet with the media on these terms proves they know how important it is to turn things around. It's not a show. There are no cameras or lights. The discussions are tough. Our people are tested. Everything is on the record, but we're not selling. That is, we have no special idea to promote, no story to tell other than the philosophy and policies and goals of our company and the industry, as we see them."

Hatch believes the meetings have accomplished one principal objective: "Oil people are no longer a faceless bunch of manipulators to the media. They are people with ideas and concerns and an abiding regard for the health of this nation. Through direct conversation, the media have challenged oil people and gotten to know them as individuals."

Through personal contact, Hatch at ARCO, and his counterparts at General Motors, Aetna, and other forward-looking companies, have "defanged" media relations in the "paper and electronic war." The informal meetings have served as a Neutral Zone for the candid exchange of ideas, the cooling of tempers, and the resolution of basic misunderstandings.

The manner in which it has been done also matters. No plush clubs, lush dinners, and long cigars. Just plain talk in plain surroundings. "These are cold-cuts-and-salad sessions; no big deals," says Hatch.

"During the Iranian revolution, there were rumors that ARCO and other oil companies had tankers sitting offshore loaded with oil, purposely delayed to maintain shortages and high prices. It was absolute nonsense, but public indignation was so high and media attitudes so skeptical that the rumors persisted.

"Our small private meetings with key players from industry and the media did much to put an end to that erroneous public speculation," Hatch recalls.

Hatch is of the school that firmly believes the job of the internal media specialist or public affairs executive is to prepare his management people to "meet the press" and "address public issues" as an essential and vitally important part of their responsibilities. He adamantly opposes the notion that public affairs people should be the "mouthpieces" for management.

"When I was a journalist, I did not want to speak with a public affairs representative," says Hatch with some heat. "I wanted access to the top management people. The public affairs executives I most respected were those who served as a conduit to top management, and were themselves considered part of the top management team. One of the jobs of public affairs is to prepare executives to deal effectively and forthrightly with the media. Our job is not to speak for management. We should not be the people in the public eye. That only compounds the problem."

When management speaks up is also of critical importance. It is not sufficient for a company to do the right thing; it must also convince the media and the public that it is acting wisely and responsibly. When a company fails to speak up at the right moment, its motives are automatically suspect.

If a company is in the right, why does it refuse to speak? The media concludes it must be hiding something, and digs for negatives that perhaps aren't there. The public, reading and hearing that company spokespersons have resorted to "no comment," also senses that "there must be something to the allegations; they're not talking."

When the Kepone produced by a plant of Allied Chemicals polluted the beautiful James River in Virginia, denials of wrong-doing filled the pages of area and national papers, but not until after a damaging period of "no comment" by company officials which gave rise to a spate of increasingly inflammatory rumors. The story and its ramifications stayed on the front pages of major newspapers and on network broadcasts for many weeks, and continued to surface whenever a new accusation or claim was leveled at the company.

What few remember is that another major spill occurred not far from Hopewell, Virginia, the site of the Allied plant, during the height of the controversy about Kepone.

A Du Pont Company plant was responsible, and its management people quickly gathered the facts and hurried to the newspapers and broadcast stations to say what had happened, why it had happened, and what the company had done to make sure it wouldn't happen again. The story appeared once on the front page of Washington newspapers, and about a week later, the *Washington Post* editorially praised the forthright action and the public statements of the Du Pont Company, a reaction quite different from the protracted criticism leveled at Allied Chemicals.

The role of communication is critical in building public trust and maintaining public confidence through the media when things go wrong. And things go wrong from time to time in everyone's business.

Hopefully, environmental tragedies of the seventies have convinced management that business is functioning very much in the public arena, under the constant scrutiny of a distrustful public and a jaundiced press corps, and that its first priority, if it wishes to maintain its integrity and a measure of its cherished independence, is to get its communication machinery into high gear.

MEDIA NEED TO DEFINE NEWS

Hatch and other former newsmen and newswomen working in the corporate ranks. as well as many working journalists, believe that the electronic media have confused news reporting and entertainment. And they believe it is a grievous disservice to journalism and the public.

"Shows like 'Real People' and '20/20' cross over the line from news to entertainment," Hatch contends. "They are show business personalities putting on a show. They aren't trained to deal with hard news or public issues. But the public, turning the dial from one station to another, going from straight news to one of the new entertainment-news formats, doesn't stop to differentiate. It's a sorry development. I recall one show on which oil representatives were present but could not be heard. The organizers of the show had intentionally riled up the audience against them. When they tried to speak they were hooted down. If that's news dissemination and objective exposition of issues, then I work for a dairy company."

Fair treatment or not, Hatch agrees that the profiteering label attached to the oil industry won't be erased overnight by thoughtful communication or any combination of efforts.

Corporate reputation is a fragile asset, subject to the whims of public opinion; vulnerable to the public attacks of special interest groups, the news media, and government officials; and reflective of the words and actions of management people.

The oil industry has been tagged as the villain, the bad guy, the rip-off artist. Its handsome profits are an embarrassment to some industry leaders, while others are defiant when challenged.

Even the remarkable social leadership of ARCO's Thornton Bradshaw and Robert Anderson — while setting ARCO above the pack and drawing generous praise from every segment of American society, including the news media — has not made a dent in the public's general perception of the oil industry as a whole.

Interviewed by Hatch for one of ARCO's television programs, Anderson scoffed at the notion of taking a government appointment when he retires from the company. "It's not that I wouldn't be interested," Anderson explained. "I just wouldn't be asked. I'm one of the guys wearing a black hat. It wouldn't be politically wise to ask me."

It would be unfortunate for the nation if a man of Anderson's depth and stature, marvelous record of public service, and concern for the national welfare were denied an invitation to serve his government because he had directed the fortunes of a major oil company.

"Will oil executives ever be trusted?" Hatch asked Anderson in the television interview. "Not in my lifetime," he replied sadly.

Where does the circle begin: with the press or with the industry practices? The media would say, with justification, that the industry has left too many questions unanswered for too long a time.

Journalists report the news. They ask questions and probe behind the facades thrown up by defensive industry spokesmen. They do their job, and if the oil industry made mistakes in the past, and is paying for those mistakes today, that's just the way it is.

The industry would admit imperfection. But it blames the news media for exaggeration, for newsmaking rather than news reporting, for inaccuracies and incompetence in reporting industry affairs, and for reporting rumor with fact.

In the face of this recent hostility, it is no small feat for Hatch to rally his industry executives around a table with editors from the print and electronic media with no holds barred and everything on the record. And it is no small thing that Hatch and media experts like him are bridging the gap between industry and the media, and in doing so, helping to close the communication gap between business and government.

Hatch has shown his colleagues in other companies that it can be done, if not precisely in his way, then by their own designs. He has identified a piece of the Neutral Zone, a way to heal wounds and solve problems, given time and persistent attention.

Hatch and other public affairs and media personnel are worried, however, that a new generation of top managers may not continue the social programs introduced by men like Anderson, Bradshaw, Filer, and Marusi. What happens when these men retire? Has the concept of corporate social responsibility, open communication, and public accountability really been institutionalized in American industry? Or is it still vulnerable to management shifts, the fickle attitudes of the public, the score cards compiled by pollsters, and changing conditions in the marketplace?

Hatch and his fellow workers at ARCO believe that no company can return to the isolation of the past. They believe, or profess to believe, that the successors to Anderson and Bradshaw will automatically and necessarily carry on in the same tradition. But there is nagging doubt and general acknowledgment among the troops that things could change.

If the social light does dim in ARCO, it is likely to dim in hundreds of other companies across the nation for, as Hatch knows, ARCO is held up as the shining example to support countless other proposals: "Look, this is what ARCO did, and this is what ARCO management supported, and it helped. We ought to do something like that."

But Hatch worries more about the ineptness of reporting about the oil industry than the wavering commitment of oil company executives. The news-entertainment business has got to be stopped, he says. Self-policing by those responsible for news gathering and reporting in the electronic media is essential, he believes. Industry's complaints may appear to be self-serving. But if the public is fed a mixture of entertainment and news, speculation and fact, all under the label of news and investigative reporting, it will only confuse issues, not clarify them, accelerate the paper and electronic war, and make the Neutral Zone a distant dream.

Chapter Sixteen

Policing the Media

The public views both industry and the media with suspicion.

Industry is seen as a violator of the environment. The media are accused of sensationalizing stories, poor reporting, and questionable involvements with news sources. The latter include buying stories from unsavory characters and thereby, critics say, rewarding crime and glorifying negative behavior.

Reporters are also alleged to have stooged for the Central Intelligence Agency, an action which, it is observed, not only soiled the integrity of all other journalists but also endangered their lives and limited their access to news sources.

One of the principal roles of the media is to scrutinize big institutions, public and private. If a reporter is receiving money or favors from those institutions, it is virtually impossible to maintain objectivity. But collusion is limited and surely the least expressed of the complaints against the media.

In the eighties, industry's unhappiness with the news media is shared by almost every segment of society — the public relations craft largely excluded.

Businessmen may believe they are singled out by hostile reporters and made to bear the brunt of unfavorable reporting. But their complaints are matched by officials in other walks of life.

Supreme Court Justice William J. Brennan, one of the nation's strongest defenders of the freedom of the press, had harsh words for the country's journalists in October 1979, publicly charging the press with engaging in unnecessarily vehement, unreasonable, and unintelligent attacks on, of course, the Supreme Court. By doing so, he said, the press was destroying its credibility on issues vital to its future welfare and to the proper functioning of free government.

Brennan's hard words sent a shock wave through newspaper and broadcasting offices in all parts of the nation, for Brennan was no disappointed politician or irate business executive venting his displeasure over some alleged hurt, but a member of the highest court in the land and a recognized champion of the press.

Justice Brennan's chief point was that the press had been clinging to an old and revered concept of the First Amendment that prohibits interference with freedom of expression. He argued that the amendment also protects the structure of the whole process through which citizens may express their wishes. The Supreme Court, Brennan said, must balance the rights claimed by journalists against other compelling social interests, without endangering the right of free expression.

The *Washington Post* commented editorially on Justice Brennan's position: "Unlike most criticisms of the press, it provides a theory whose wisdom the press and the judges can debate without engaging in outrageous rhetoric . . . when a balancing process occurs, as it does under this theory, in matters like libel and the shielding of confidential information, other interests can outweigh the claims of journalists."

The unusual editorial comment concluded by saying, "Because sound commentary on the court's work has always had an important place in its future decisions, his [Brennan's] suggestion raises the possibility that the press is systematically eliminating itself from a role it has long held. That is a possibility not to be dismissed lightly."

Brennan's comments sparked other judicial responses. The chief judge of Maryland's highest court called on the state bar association to form a committee that would act as a "truth squad" in defending Maryland judges against unjust media criticism.

When one is stung in public, he or she not only wants to soothe the sting but also kill the bee. But attack and counterattack only protract issues and make solutions more elusive.

Panels, private meetings, one-on-one luncheon discussions, and other informal exchanges might better help clarify many of the issues debated in the press.

The job of the media is to report the news, good or bad, and to expose wrong-doing and corruption. But things are not always what they appear to be, and the reporting of assumption and conjecture, when issues are clouded and facts are few, is not helpful. The candid exchange of information could avoid legal hassles, reduce acrimony and unnecessary debate, and improve media reporting.

The late Bert Goss, former president of the international public relations firm of Hill & Knowlton, in a speech before the Antitrust Committee of the Chicago Bar Association in 1962, lamented the force of unproved accusations.

News stories may be discredited, he pointed out, but inaccuracies are repeated in speeches and in newspaper and magazine articles, based on the original news item. Goss forecast that the rising tide of antibusiness "propaganda," as he put it, would increase antibusiness regulation.

One might argue whether the rush of legislation that came down upon industry in the sixties and seventies was antibusiness or propublic, but his prediction was accurate.

In 1962, Goss urged business to understand that rebuttals to attacks upon industry had to be immediate if they were to be effective. "News is perishable," Goss said. "In most cases, the news media will publish rebuttal along with an attack — but they are much less likely to do so in a separate story which limps along 24 hours or so after the charge is made."

Despite counsel from men like Goss, and the trauma of the riots in the late sixties, business may not have learned many permanent lessons. While certain companies aggressively seek out press attention for their actions and opinions, most do not. Most companies seem not to have learned that "a hostile public is one step removed from hostile legislation," as Goss put it. Nor did all companies remember his final counsel: "The best public relations is compliance with the law."

What most business executives have come to realize is that legal debates may be won in the court of law and lost in the court of public opinion.

Other harsh words about print and electronic media were voiced by Hodding Carter III, a spokesman in the State Department during the long Iranian hostage crisis.

He participated in a symposium on press freedom and responsibility at the Lyndon Baines Johnson Library in Austin, Texas, in April 1981.

Calling the news media "big business" institutions run by "power people" divorced from the concerns and conditions of their readers and viewers, Carter noted that the news media haven't gotten ahead of a single wave over the past twenty years. "The press had to be kicked in the face by each of them," he said, referring to the civil rights, antiwar, and women's movements.

Sociologist Daniel Yankelovich discovered in a poll conducted in 1980 by his Public Agenda Foundation that citizens are sympathetic to the idea of having government require newspapers and broadcasting stations to present opposing views on important issues.

This view was expressed by a majority of the 1000 respondents to the study, who represented a cross-section of the citizenry.

Yankelovich also found misunderstanding among media owners and top executives, many of whom said that public cries for fairness were in fact demands for public representation and censorship.

"This misconception [by media management] has caused some leaders to discount public criticism of the media and to cast the public as an outsider with no legitimate stake in freedom of expression terms," Yankelovich wrote in the foreword to the report.

The study emphasizes that failure by news executives to acknowledge or respond to serious public concerns about lack of fairness in the media could erode public support for the First Amendment as we now know it. "At the very least, there is an obligation for leaders to explain to people why their position has been seriously considered and rejected," Yankelovich wrote.

Interviewed in 1981 by *U.S. News & World Report* on his retirement as anchorman for CBS News, Walter Cronkite lamented the superficiality of much of television reporting, especially at the local level.

"A lot of young people who in an earlier time might have gone on the stage or into the movies are now entering broadcasting. They are 'pretty people' who want to play the star roles. They're about as interested in journalism as most actors are. They're far more interested in money, personal aggrandizement, and a sense of fame," Cronkite observed.

The revered broadcasting personality also complained that the "pretty people" were going through communications schools and "learning Trench Coat I, Trench Coat II, and Makeup I, Makeup II."

Cronkite observed that television news is all hypercondensed, hyperdigested. He urged communications schools to stress print journalism as well as broadcasting. "Unless you learn how to organize a news story down to the 32nd paragraph, you can't really know what ought to be in the top two paragraphs, which is what we're delivering most of the time on television," Cronkite said.

The CBS newsman said flatly that television journalism "is never going to substitute for print in the total spectrum of communications. . . . It's [television] a great guide to the day's news, but we cannot cover in depth in a half-hour many of the stories required to get a good understanding of the world. We have to find a way in schools to teach people how to read the newspaper and how to watch television so that they will go from the television to print for further information and greater explanation."

A decade earlier, in 1970, on the eve of his retirement as executive editor of the *New York Times,* Turner Catledge commented that the American news media were in the grip of a "credibility crisis."

A year later, Newbold Noyes, a longtime editor of the now deceased *Washington Star* and former president of the American Society of Newspaper Editors, told that organization at an annual convention: "Our

readers' confidence in their newspaper press is at a low ebb these days."
He pointed out that reporters too often look for one startling or conten-
tious or silly statement, and make it their lead, then back it up with other
direct and indirect quotes to make a story.

Paul Forbes, a lanky, Brooklyn-born public relations executive in
Washington, D.C., wanted to study medicine but spent twenty years
relating social and economic goals with Joe Danzansky at the Giant Food
Chain. When Danzansky died, Forbes moved on to Drug Fair, where he
promptly initiated one of the nation's most successful anti-drug-abuse
campaigns.

An advocate of handgun control, Forbes joined with thousands of
Washingtonians in mourning the death of the noted author and car-
diologist, Michael J. Halberstam, who was shot down in his home by
"master" burglar Bernard Welsh.

Despite his wounds, Halberstam drove himself to the hospital. En
route, he spotted Welsh and ran him down with his car. Halberstam later
died in the hospital. Welsh recovered, stool trial, and was found guilty of
Halberstam's murder. He is serving a 143-year sentence in a maximum
security prison.

During the trial, millions of dollars worth of jewelry and art were
discovered in Welsh's home; his crime career had spanned several years.

Life magazine contracted with Welsh for photographs. Outraged that
Life had rewarded the criminal and ignored the victim's family, Paul
Forbes made a business decision: he banned the offending February 1981
issue of *Life* from all Drug Fair stores. "It was a voluntary boycott to protest *Life's* compensation of the murderer," Forbes explained.

It was, in fact, an extraordinary gesture of disapproval by one
business of another. Letters poured in supporting the decision. And letters
to the editors of Washington papers also applauded the action.

A spokesman for *Life* said 35,000 copies a month are normally sold on
Washington newsstands. In February 1981, sales were down 30 percent.
In addition, *Life* officials admitted the publication had suffered "a lot of
negative publicity.'

The incident prompted Nelson "Pete" Shields III, chairman of
Handgun Control, Inc., a Washington lobbying group, and a friend of the
slain Dr. Halberstam, to call for an "examination of the ethics of paying
criminals and accused criminals for their stories and photographs. The
victims of crime are ignored and the criminals are glorified by the media."

There is a new willingness to demand corrections and retractions by
the media, and less reticence about threatening and actually waging court
battles.

When ABC's news magazine program "20/20" accused Kaiser
Aluminium & Chemical Corporation of intentionally marketing unsafe

residential wiring and withholding information about the product's performance, Kaiser chairman Cornell C. Maier screamed, "The charges are blatantly wrong, and we will not let them go unchallenged."

In an unprecedented action, ABC agreed to air an unedited response by Kaiser during one of its "20/20" broadcasts. The agreement was initiated by the threat of a lawsuit against ABC by Kaiser.

Interestingly, Kaiser had been invited to be interviewed on the offending show, but had declined.

In addition to threatening a lawsuit and negotiating the right of public rebuttal on "20/20," Kaiser also appealed to Rep. Lionel Van Deerlin, chairman of the House Subcommittee on Communications, to hold congressional hearings on what the company called "trial by television." No hearings were scheduled.

ABC personnel shrugged and said, "We just wanted to be fair. This action [giving Kaiser rebuttal time] does not restrict us from updating the story."

But business was fighting back, challenging details, demanding the right of rebuttal, and bringing legal counsel to the front line. What it still failed to do, for the most part, was to cooperate fully with networks and newspapers when they were preparing stories in order to avoid the acrimony and legal debates after the fact.

The respected journalist Richard Reeves wrote in February 1981, "networks are constantly and deliberately blurring the lines between news and entertainment, breaking down the distinctions between fact and fiction." He criticized television programs like "Real People" and "That's Incredible" as being part of a game called "reality programming." Reeves claimed that such shows are "designed to look like a magazine show, but are not; that's why those shows have writers."

Reeves believes "we are in real trouble" in the media. He is bitterly critical of so-called "docu-dramas" about such serious subjects as the situation in Iran and the release of the American hostages. He was shocked that two of President Jimmy Carter's closest aides, Hamilton Jordan and Gerald Rafshoon, had contracted with CBS for more than $6 million to produce a story on the release of the hostages. "There will be commercials and CBS will make a lot of money because faked history is more interesting than 'Happy Days,'" Reeves wrote.

The truth would make us free, Reeves concluded, if we could only remember what it was.

The lower courts are getting after the media as well, spurred on by Justice Brennan and the complaints of business executives.

CBS was threatened with "a very large fine" by a Newark judge in March 1981 if it failed to turn over unused recordings of interviews by correspondent Mike Wallace for a segment on alleged food franchise fraud for the Sunday evening show "60 Minutes."

Although the show reported that the fraud was under investigation, the judge said it failed to say that the suspects were presumed innocent. "Much of the exculpatory evidence was left on the cutting room floor," the judge said.

The boom in libel cases and the increase in the number actually going to trial are a grave concern in the publishing and broadcasting industries.

Journalists are being asked to testify as expert witnesses, second-guessing the performance of their colleagues. Attorneys are making greater use of such witnesses to buttress their claims that news organizations are negligent.

Many editors fear intimidation and a form of censorship of the news. Critics tell editors to stop crying and clean up their act.

But fear of censorship seems well founded. Should freedom of the press be diminished in any way, every citizen would lose a precious right, including those citizens who now rail against alleged inaccuracies in print and on the air.

How is this right being threatened?

Fifteen days into the new decade of the eighties, nine reporters and television cameramen were convicted of trespass charges growing out of their coverage of an antinuclear protest at a power plant construction site in June 1979.

Charges against more than 300 other protesters at the Oklahoma demonstrations had been dismissed by the same district court judge who found the journalists guilty.

The case tested the First Amendment as to the right to gather news rather than disseminate news. Reporters escorted by plant personnel and confined to certain areas were not arrested. The nine reporters who walked with the protesters were arrested. All reporters were judged, then and later, to have been "peaceful and law-abiding."

In Dallas a few months later, a judge ordered the *Wall Street Journal* not to publish an article because it contained information from a report made by a law firm on the financial transactions of one of the firm's client companies. The company, through its counsel, told the judge that publication of that information would breach its confidential relationship with its lawyers and cause it "irreparable injury."

After being educated by attorneys for the *Wall Street Journal,* the judge rescinded his order. But, as the *Washington Post* editorialized, "the fact that he was willing to flirt, even ever so briefly, with plain old-fashioned censorship is a sign of how much has changed — for the worse — in the courts."

Judges have attempted to tell the free press in the United States how to report on national security matters, criminal trials, and, in the Dallas situation, even on corporate dealings.

"The genie named censorship is out of the bottle that held it for more than two centuries, and it is going to take much hard work, much 'educating' of lower court judges, and thousands of dollars in legal fees to bring it under control again," the *Post* said.

The press must correct its deficiencies from within. It can meet on middle ground with business and government without compromising an ounce of its independence or guaranteed rights.

The press must remain skeptical and aloof to do its job. But it will perform more effectively if it is less preconditioned and more understanding of the goals of jurists, business people, women, government officials, minority leaders and others whose statements and actions make news.

Justice Brennan has stated the case. Journalists will ignore its implications at their own peril and the jeopardy of a free press.

Chapter Seventeen

The Era of the Ombudsmen

The seventies became the era of the ombudsmen. Major newspapers assigned experienced editors the unhappy task of judging their peers in print. They were asked to respond to public criticisms of alleged unfair and inaccurate reporting by their colleagues. Moreover, they were expected to take their colleagues to task publicly if they agreed the reporters had been in error. The ombudsman's critique usually appears on the oped page.

Being an ombudsman is not a job for the timid, the thin skinned, or people who need constant praise.

On local radio and television, station managers also began to air editorial comment on community issues. And under the fairness clause, they welcomed and aired rebuttals.

Network television was more difficult to judge. There were docudramas, half truth and half drama; news magazines, part investigative reporting, part entertainment; and promos for the news, teasers at seven promising full details at eleven.

Commentators commented on almost every issue troubling the nation and the world, except, of course, with rare exceptions, one issue troubling business and institutions and government: the responsibilities of the news media.

Charles Seib of the *Washington Post* was king of the ombudsmen in the seventies. A wise, caring man, highly respected by his peers throughout the country, Seib set a standard that other ombudsmen gratefully followed.

On March 26, 1976, Seib wrote a column on "Business and the Media" in which he observed, "The adversarial relationship between press and government has a long and stormy history. It sometimes — too often — results in journalistic excesses and bureaucratic cover-ups, but generally it works in the public's interest. Now another adversary relationship is coming into full blossom: the one between the press and the business community."

Seib said worldwide bribery by American firms, illegal corporate contributions to our own politicians, problems behind banking's marble facades, and other indiscretions were focusing press attention on business and finance as never before.

"It is an area," wrote Seib, "in which the press has always been weak. Although what happens in corporate board rooms can have more impact on our lives than many official acts traditionally scrutinized by the press, business coverage, at least in the general circulation media, has been both inexpert and lackadaisical . . . all of which means that we can expect a growing intimacy between the press and business — and all the strains that go with an intimacy built on suspicion, distrust, and a communications gap as wide and deep as the Grand Canyon."

Seib credits business executive Donald MacNaughton for having "set the stage accurately" when he said, "I almost never read or hear an accurate media account of a business subject with which I am thoroughly familiar, but many business executives are excessively secretive and often inaccessible or prone to double-talk." MacNaughton was chairman of the Prudential Insurance Company of America for ten years before taking over the chairmanship of the Hospital Corporation of America in the midseventies.

Seib ended his column by noting that "paths of business and media must frequently cross. I would add that those crossings are increasingly likely to be marked by collisions."

The news media are paying more attention to business, thanks to Seib and MacNaughton and men like them. Special sections of major newspapers are devoted to business news. Business reporters, once a rarity in newsrooms, are more common. Business columnists are more highly regarded and more widely read. Business publications have increased their circulation and readership.

In the past decade, many major newspapers have doubled their coverage of business news: The *New York Times, Chicago Tribune, Chicago Sun-Times, Los Angeles Times,* and *Boston Globe* among them. Business magazines have also grown in stature: *Business Week, Fortune, Forbes,* and *U.S. News & World Report* top the list. *Forbes* — to the pleasure of 80 percent of American businesses, including those owned by minorities — continues to be the only national business publication that regularly places stories on small companies. *Black Enterprise,* under Earl Graves' dedicated management, has attracted a wide range of readers and advertisers. Regional business publications have also surfaced, notably *Crain's Chicago Business,* a weekly tabloid that probes behind the scenes and pulls no punches.

Donald MacNaughton is still critical of his colleagues as well as of the news media.

"Nothing haunts the business-media relationship more than the commonplace evidence that many writers, reporters, commentators often do not understand the meaning, uses, and benefits of profits," he says. He points to opinion polls that show a growing public ignorance about profits and profit margins, and he blames the public's lack of understanding "at least to some degree on the basis of media coverage [of business]."

Angered newsmen retort that it isn't understanding that men like MacNaughton seek, but agreement. "It isn't so much that the public doesn't know about profits," says Richard "Max" McCarthy, Washington bureau chief for the *Buffalo Evening News* and a former member of Congress, "but that many people think profits are sometimes excessive and benefit only a limited number of people."

MacNaughton agrees that industry must do a much better job of explaining itself. "Many business executives are excessively secretive. And business people are not noted for reducing complex matters into simple, understandable terms," he admits. "Business arouses hackles in newsrooms because so many companies press so hard for space or air time when they have good news, but remain underground when their fortunes are receding."

MacNaughton smiles when he reflects on the public image of the businessman. "A hallmark of American business is its willingness to keep up with the times — to innovate. Yet, before the press, radio and television, the businessman comes on like the original Neanderthal man, mouthing cliches that literally went out with the hoop skirts."

Summarizing his five years as ombudsman for the *Washington Post,* Seib wrote an essay in November 1979 titled "The Error of Our Ways." He said he had learned that readers are perceptive and caring about their newspapers. And he denied any deliberate slanting of the news.

"Readers are quick to notice the inevitable errors of commission and omission that occur in all newspapers," Seib wrote. "But...too often they mistakenly see those flaws as evidences of deliberate slanting of the news rather than what they almost always are — the products of poor judgment, deadline pressures, or simple stupidity. I blame the acceptance of this conspiracy theory of journalism on the aloofness of newspapers from their customers and the pose of infallibility the press tries to maintain."

Seib agrees with critics that newspapers are more tolerant of their flaws than they should be: "I have yet to see an editor pursue an allegation of error with the zeal he or she would show in pursuing a hot tip on a news story. Fast action on an error usually requires a lawyer's warning of a libel suit or a complaint from someone with access to the editor or publisher. Yet the error that is casually accepted or reluctantly investigated may be far more important to those affected than a news story that is much more aggressively pursued."

Retiring to write, teach, and lecture, Seib concluded his essay by stressing the need for "a much greater concern than now exists for the effects of errors and distortion, however innocently committed."

While business people cheer Seib's admonition to his journalistic colleagues, they also suffer from a certain arrogance, an intolerance for the errors of others, and a tendency to overreact to real and imagined journalistic injuries.

Picture, for example, the top managers of a Connecticut company gathered around a table in their executive dining room; they are grousing bitterly about a misleading headline that appeared in a Saturday edition of the local newspaper concerning the company's excellent quarterly earnings statement.

The story under the headline was totally accurate, perhaps relying too heavily on the company's own news release for interpretation. Accurate, positive stories had also appeared in the *New York Times* and the *Wall Street Journal.* But the inaccurate headline offended the company managers in their hometown. The more they groused, the more inexcusable the error became. Perhaps the goof was even intentional. By George, the editor was going to hear about it.

It would not be difficult to get the editor's ear; the company's chairman often played poker with him. The headline was not the company's only complaint, of course.

The relationship between a big hometown industry and a small hometown newspaper is almost always characterized by bickering and occasional hostility.

It need not be that way.

But the big company demands respect and praise. It doesn't expect the local paper to play hardball on allegations of unfair labor practices, or environmental spills, or other grievances lodged against the biggest employer, taxpayer, and contributor to local causes in the whole area. Whether the management of the company will admit it or not, it usually expects the local paper to be a sort of booster or cheering section, reminding the local population to be grateful for the jobs, purchasing power, and stability the company provides, and to be understanding of its occasional faults.

Yet, the company is rarely understanding of the newspaper's occasional foibles.

This is not to suggest that inaccuracies should be ignored or that damaging and erroneous statements in the press or on the air should not be challenged.

But there is still another avenue, a Neutral Zone for the honest and fair exchange of gripes and opinions between company and newspaper management, especially in smaller communities.

The company can arrange periodic briefings for newspaper staff, with everything on the record and no questions prohibited.

People change jobs in both industry and the news media with sometimes disturbing frequency (which is one of the problems editors have in assigning trained people to industry stories), so the briefings would have to be conducted once or twice yearly. If the company is really concerned about generating more accurate reporting of its activities, the briefings should not constitute an undue burden.

The briefings would be planned carefully, in collaboration with the editors, to erase any notion of "buying favors."

The briefings would not assure accurate headlines every time, or agreement on issues every time, or perfection in reporting the company's complicated earnings statement, or explaining its technical facilities to the company engineer's satisfaction. But they would help.

When a minor goof occurs, a friendly but pointed note or phone call should cool the temper of the company executive and serve to remind the editor that more surveillance is needed. If it should be a major goof, then the editor should be asked — and expected — to run a correction in as prominent a place in the paper — or time of day on the air — as was given the original story.

Feuds between industry and the media are not confined to small towns. In 1975, one of the giant companies headquartered in New York demanded that its public relations agency compile all the editorial comment published about the company by a prominent Long Island newspaper.

The company was convinced that the newspaper was not only inept in reporting on company and industry affairs, but that it sometimes wrote with malicious intent.

When I walked into the agency on Lexington Avenue one afternoon, temporary employees occupied several rooms filled with newspaper clippings which they were dutifully pasting in huge scrapbooks. The objective, I was told, was to prepare for a confrontation with the editors, at which time company officials would set forth the newspaper's doleful record.

I was never sure what the company really hoped to achieve or why the public relations firm didn't counsel against the silly exercise.

I believe the idea was abandoned later on. But the experience reflected industry's basic attitude toward the press and its penchant for striking out rather than finding common ground for discussion.

Why intelligent people in one of America's largest companies would let a problem fester for so long and not seek informal opportunities for candid, helpful dialogue is difficult to understand.

Several years later, a Connecticut company contemplated the same kind of "showdown" with its local newspaper. They prepared "their case" in like manner, filling clip books and writing analyses of alleged inaccuracies, and worse.

I called on Charles Seib in Washington to discuss the company's concerns, and he shared my recommendation that the company should pursue gentler and more productive avenues for discourse with the allegedly errant editorial staff. To my knowledge, no great confrontation took place, but several discussions were held.

The role of the media in society does not produce many lasting friendships among industry and media executives. The media are not cheerleaders. But neither should they strike a jingoistic pose toward business or disparage the contributions of business in a changing society. Neither business nor the media are served by didactic approaches to the other.

Most businessmen think journalists should take a basic course in economics. Most journalists think businessmen should consider the public interest even as they pursue their own legitimate goals.

The power of the dollar and the spirit of reprisal are dictating a hard-line and a hard-nosed business attack on the news media.

Business is taking the "offending" newspapers and broadcasting stations to court for alleged distortions. For example, Bristol Myers Company sued CBS for $25 million because one of its affiliate stations in New York questioned the company's advertising claims for two of its products. Later, the companies agreed to an amicable dismissal of the suit. CBS said it did not mean to attack the integrity of Bristol Myers, and managements of both corporations concluded that nothing could be gained by continuing the dispute.

Leonard S. Mathews, president of the Association of Advertising Agencies, warned that TV journalists cannot expect business to continue supporting a medium that stereotypes it as "greedy, insensitive, and anti-social."

His comment poses a dangerous challenge to journalistic freedom and journalistic responsibility. Freedom must be preserved, and no news editor is going to react kindly to economic threat (although station owners may indeed be vulnerable to certain intimidation). The best means to assure independence, it would appear, is the scrupulous gathering, verification, and dissemination of news. But no station should be cowed into softening the facts, nor should business apply such economic pressure.

All companies have the obligation to understand the role of the free press in America, to govern their own affairs accordingly, and to suffer the likelihood, in today's open society, of occasional embarrassments and unwanted public exposure.

The media, for their part, must increasingly become more sophisticated and self-challenging in their appraisal of other groups, including business, not out of fear of offending those who deserve the glare of public scrutiny, but rather for the preservation of a responsible free press in America, and assurance of simple justice for those whose activities are reported.

The issue is a serious one, and the public has a stake in the outcome. What citizens know and don't know, what they understand and misunderstand, can make a significant difference politically and attitudinally in America.

People act on the truth as they perceive the truth. And general perceptions are most often conveyed through the mass media. Public confidence in institutions can be dangerously undermined if those institutions are unfairly attacked. Conversely, the public may place false confidence in institutions if their ineptness and wrong-doings are inadequately reported. The challenge now, as it was at the beginning of the Republic, is to maintain balance and strive for fairness.

Attorney F. Peter Libassi, the former general counsel of Health, Education, and Welfare, who now works with big industry, says astute business leaders are giving more credit to the news media for their increasing fairness, competence, and sophistication. Moreover, says Libassi, industry can take some of the credit for this improved performance because it raised a little hell when it considered itself unfairly attacked.

For example, the *Los Angeles Times* is digging deep to answer the criticisms of industry about its reporting. Complaints are matched against the paper's performance, not only in the pages of the *Times* itself but also at the broadcast stations the paper owns and manages. The *Times* concludes that some of its business reporting has been "simplistic, careless, and cursory." But almost no cases have been documented suggesting that distortions have been deliberate. Like Charles Seib of the *Washington Post,* the *Times* concludes that errors, while not excusable, are not designed.

When industry has been under attack by government or special interest groups, the news media have not always been inclined to push hard for its response. Nor has industry always been eager or even prepared to offer comment. As a result, industry's replies are often published many days following the allegations.

Obviously, industry must be prepared to respond quickly or face the consequences. It cannot fall back on "no comment" to carry itself through a period of crisis or stress.

But the media must always try to solicit a response from industry — to any serious allegation — for inclusion in the original story.

Are business stories slanted to show the worst side of business practices?

Researchers at the University of Minnesota who studied business coverage in four Minneapolis and St. Paul newspapers for four months in 1979 found that 56 percent of the stories were neutral, 25 percent reflected favorably on business, and only 19 percent unfavorably.

Other surveys verify a correlation between current news developments and the public regard for business. Public opinion moves like a roller coaster on the basis of good news and bad. News of energy shortages, or payoffs to foreign governments, or a threatened disaster such as Three Mile Island will seriously influence public opinion in any survey taken at that time.

It is not always the editorial writer or the news writer or the television news personality who raises hairs on the back of the necks of business viewers. Often it is an unexpected event, such as a tank car derailment, a poll negative to industry, or even a cartoon.

Especially a cartoon.

A. Kent MacDougall, in a brilliant series of articles he prepared for the *Los Angeles Times* on media and business in the late seventies, cited the tragic case of the crash of the American Airlines DC-10 at Chicago's O'Hare Field in May 1979. The plane's builder, McDonnell Douglas, accused the press of "pillory" and was especially aggrieved at newspaper cartoons which showed DC-10 engine mounts falling apart at a single hammer blow, and the big jet compared to the ill-fated Edsel automobile. The cartoons struck McDonnell Douglas as cruel and crude.

McDougall concludes that business must resign itself to the same kind of probing and even impolite press that politicians have had to endure for decades. "With the business of America more than ever business," McDougall wrote, "it seems reasonable to hold the people who run industry and commerce as accountable as the people who run government. However," he continued, "journalists need to be sure that skepticism about business does not sour into cynicism."

CONCLUSIONS

The First Amendment to the Constitution signaled the first time in the history of the world that a nation guaranteed in writing that its press would be free of all constraint. The press in America functioned as the founding fathers determined it should for almost 200 years. Since the late sixties, however, numerous challenges have been raised, and conferences held, about the First Amendment rights of the news media.

As far back as 1957, an edition of CBS's "Face the Nation," featuring none other than Nikita Krushchev, the First Secretary of the Russian Communist Party, instilled fear in the broadcasting industry that the government would attempt to restrict television news programming.

It was on that program in May 1957 that, through the interpreter, Krushchev uttered his now famous warning to America, "We will bury you."

The quiet presidency of Dwight Eisenhower was displeased, especially Secretary of State John Foster Dulles, who expressed outrage that the network would have the effrontery to give the Russian leader the opportunity to spread his propaganda directly into America's living rooms.

Sig Mickelson, who was then in charge of CBS news, huddled for twenty-four hours with Frank Stanton and other top network officials following the Sunday program, debating the kind of statement they should issue in response to public and government attack. Even the licensing status of five CBS-owned television stations was thought to be in peril.

It was the late arrival of an outside public affairs counselor that set CBS on the offensive. He recommended that CBS express its pride in "Face the Nation" and note the contributions it had made toward better world understanding.

CBS presented that case in full-page ads in major newspapers on Wednesday, three days after the program. In the ad, CBS demanded the same full First Amendment protection for broadcasting media as that granted to the print media.

Mickelson, who later became a professor at the Medill School of Journalism at Northwestern University, believes the Krushchev caper was the springboard for subsequent defenses by broadcasters against all manner of criticism.

Why was the question raised at all? Would Secretary Dulles have objected so strenuously to an exclusive front-page interview with Krushchev in the *New York Times* or *Washington Post*? Did not the Federal Communications Act of 1934 assure the independence of broadcast program content, excepting the provision prohibiting "obscene, indecent, or profane language"?

But it is not so simple. The government, through the Federal Communications Commission, licenses broadcasting stations. And the "fairness clause" of 1959 was written into law (the previous "equal time" provision, while onerous to the electronic media, was a simple policy statement), increasing the complexity of implementation and interpretation.

Since 1949, local broadcasters have had the right to air editorials, providing they offer equal time for opposing views. Broadcasters did not immediately jump at the opportunity, however, and many stations to this day do not take advantage of the privilege because of the inherent political difficulties.

The licensing procedures are themselves complicated and vulnerable to a variety of abuses, Mickelson believes, since commissioners must rely on fallible and subjective human judgments in making decisions on competing applications.

Broadcasting media *are* different. Entertainment is sometimes confused with news reporting, as Tony Hatch of ARCO complains. And the fairness clause places unusual requirements on editors for balance and diversity of news and opinions.

The licensing provisions also put the government in a dual position of authority: granter of rights and monitor of performance.

Not all media leaders are passive and accepting of the fairness clause. Nor do they believe its constraints will indefinitely be confined to the broadcasting media alone.

In a speech to the 1979 Associated Press Broadcasters convention, CBS chairman William S. Paley said the fairness doctrine simply doesn't make sense, given the expansion of the broadcasting industry. "It is strange, to say the least," Paley told his audience, "that the medium on which the public places most reliance for news is the medium with the least First Amendment protection." Paley believes that television has attained the greatest degree of responsibility and objectivity in its long and colorful history, and finds it odd and disturbing that it is being given adverse treatment by the courts, government, and business.

Paley also presented an interesting caution to the print media. "It is already technically possible to bring newspapers and magazines into the home, both on television screen and by printout. Before long, all this will be delivered as easily as the television pictures now come to you." And when that happens, Paley asked, "What is to prevent the print media from being drawn into the same regulatory web?" Paley called for a declaration of war on the fairness doctrine by all media.

Mobil Oil's Herbert Schmertz might disagree. He and other industry spokesmen are fighting for "equal time" to present industry positions and to air "issue advertisements" on television. The first of such ads began on ABC in 1981 in the late evening hours.

The businessman's complaints cover all media, however, and are not unlike the protests of government officials: the media are prone to write about everything that goes wrong and nothing about the things that succeed; the media are too powerful and arrogant and self-righteous. Business can't get a fair deal with editors; editors are predisposed against free enterprise. Controversy sells papers; reporters mix fact and rumor, don't take time to understand the significance or background of what they write.

Editors and broadcasters counter by saying business executives create the problems for themselves by stonewalling the media much of the time; by seeking a sheltered life, as if business organizations are not socially responsible and (mostly) publicly owned institutions. Because business has such a profound role in society, media representatives think business leaders should be less defensive and less antagonistic, and more willing to accept the same scrutiny and accountability standards that are imposed on government.

The businessman resents the demands of the media partly because the media, protected by the First Amendment, are not bound by the same rules.

When Richard Nixon was nosed out by John F. Kennedy in their race for the presidency in November 1960, the announcement that the old *Detroit Times* was to be closed down came on election eve, with scant notice to its employees. Many reporters and clerical personnel received wires at 5 a.m. November 3, telling them to stay home, that the paper had been sold. All that day reporters and editors and secretaries commiserated over many drinks in the Detroit-Leland Hotel, then the home of the Detroit Press Club. They waved at Richard Nixon who paraded by on the last day of his campaign and later cheered and booed his image on the television screen; the Californian was then clearly tired and testy and annoyed with the interviewer. It was a sad day for Nixon and the employees of the *Times*.

"If an automobile company had closed shop on a few hours' notice and put its long-time employees out on the street, the Detroit newspapers and broadcast stations would have accused its management of every sin known to man, and rightly so," a business executive in Motor City told me at the time. "But the newspaper types live in their own world. The rules that apply to everybody else don't apply to them."

Things have changed in twenty years. The media, as well as business, are being challenged by the public. Both are responding constructively. Public interest in business affairs has grown steadily, and with it, the interest of the news media. The training of unemployables, equal job opportunity for minorities, development of minority-owned businesses, promotability of women, protection of the environment, safety in the work place, the alleged certitude of products, the accuracy of advertising claims, and other critical matters have put business front and center on the public stage.

In fall 1977, a remarkable seminar on media and business was held in Princeton, New Jersey, sponsored by the Ford Foundation and six major newspapers. The interrogatory, hypothetical case method was used that had been successfully employed in a previous seminar on media and the law.

Almost ninety conferees exchanged ideas for two days, prodded by four expert discussion leaders from Harvard and Columbia universities. The idea, as Fred W. Friendly, the host, later would write, was to examine "the important ambiguities of the business and media relationship which is certainly tangled and often hostile. Our objective is not to try to reach conclusions, but to bring the participants and observers into learning proximity to each other."

Representatives of business, the media, government regulatory agencies, and legal experts sat around a horseshoe table to discuss hypothetical cases that strongly resembled actual situations in which business and the media had been involved. There were also many observers at each session who were free to speak if they wished.

The skilled professors baited and goaded the participants into exploring the roots of antagonism among them.

"To be sure, minds and mind sets were not necessarily changed as a result of this brief learning clash," wrote Friendly, "That was not its purpose. Its purpose, rather, was to make journalists and business people more aware of the reasons for each other's conduct and behavior and to provide a sense of the institutional limitations facing each of these institutions."

Walter Wriston of Citibank wrote, "The accusatory has replaced the explanatory. Let one scientist resign and say that nuclear power is a lethal accident waiting to happen, and he is awarded the front page with pictures. . . . We see daily illustrated a point made by the jurist Oliver Wendell Holmes: 'When the ignorant are taught to doubt, they do not know what they safely may believe.' The media should beware of sowing the dragon's teeth of confusion."

Said media critic Herbert Schmertz of Mobil Oil, "The stories that don't make television news are those that are too complicated to adapt easily to network formulas, or are not controversial enough to draw national interest, lack requisite drama and activity for exciting footage, or are produced by non-network, free-lance producers."

The Princeton meeting was helpful. It might be seen as the model for the development of a kind of Neutral Zone for improving business-media relations. Similar, perhaps less formal and less intimidating sessions might be held in communities across the nation on a regular basis. It should not be difficult to do so, if schools of journalism and chambers of commerce are willing to cooperate. Regular exchanges between business and the media are to be encouraged.

One model would suffice: a series of informal exchanges in Buffalo or Hartford or Atlanta, cohosted by print and broadcast media and the local chamber of commerce. Participants would be local business leaders and representatives of area news media. The interrogatory approach might be waived, but a skilled discussion leader is essential. The seminars should be smaller, I think, and the cold-cuts-and-salad approach advocated by Tony Hatch at ARCO would seem just right.

Regular, informal contact between business executives, editors, and reporters is needed.

Chapter Eighteen

Riding the Schmertzmobil

In the early seventies, Yankelovich, Skelly & White surveyed the public response to company-sponsored advertisements on social issues. Mobil Oil Company was at the forefront of that activity then, as it is still. Survey findings showed that favorable response to the messages, in terms of credibility and believability, ran from 6 to 15 percent. Not only were the ads ineffective, they were clearly counterproductive by those measurements. Yet, Mobil Oil has persisted in the effort at tremendous expense and in the face of criticism within the oil industry.

Herbert Schmertz, Mobil's feisty and imaginative public affairs boss, has the ear and the confidence of Mobil's chairman, Rawleigh Warner. And Schmertz tells colleagues in his own company and in other oil companies that he doesn't care what surveys show, that he takes none himself, and that he is personally confident the messages are having a positive effect on public attitudes toward his company and the petroleum industry. Moreover, says Schmertz, the ads, appearing regularly on the op-ed pages of major newspapers, including the *New York Times* and the *Washington Post,* have earned the respect of government officials and put the news media on notice that the industry will not sit still for incompetent reporting. Not everyone agrees with Schmertz's self-analysis.

One high-ranking executive at ARCO told me in July 1980, "Herb Schmertz clearly has no equal in American industry, and most of us thank God for that."

Most oil industry representatives agree with most of what Schmertz has to say in the paid messages, however. Many of the men and women who now raise questions about the ads were once numbered among Schmertz's staunchest admirers. Even now, some of the oil companies, such as Union Carbide, occasionally run versions of the Mobil ads on similar subjects: oil industry profits, oil exploration, energy conservation, nuclear power, and government regulation.

Observers claim, however, that the ads serve more to make the sponsoring companies feel good about themselves and to draw praise from other oil companies (who are not paying the costs for the space) than to win public support.

What has sometimes troubled Schmertz's oil industry colleagues is the strident tone of many of Mobil's messages, and the tendency to take on the White House, the Congress, and the regulatory agencies with whom the industry seeks access and understanding.

The consequences of the fast-moving "Schmertzmobil" are debatable, but most oil industry people are climbing off and wishing Herb would put his ad machine in the garage. It would save money, they say, and a lot of anguish. They could do without the stridency and the name-calling and what many consider to be a certain didactic arrogance that rubs off on all other oil companies.

Schmertz is not impressed by the criticisms, which actually seem to firm his resolve. But neither is he a single-minded zealot. The same Schmertz is also responsible for Mobil's extensive sponsorship of public television programming (with IBM, ARCO, and other corporate giants), extraordinary community relations projects, and unquestioned public affairs leadership.

In 1979, Schmertz astounded friends and critics alike by finding time to write a book with a colleague: a fictional version of oil company maneuverings, replete with government intrigue and sexual exploits. Later, he joined the campaign of Democratic presidential hopeful Edward Kennedy as a media adviser in the senator's unsuccessful primary battle with incumbent Jimmy Carter.

Herbert Schmertz is no common man. His critics might well be advised to leave him alone. He just might decide to dismantle his Schmertzmobil if he thought no one cared.

The Mobil advertising messages often call for debate but seldom suggest compromise. They take on the news media as well as the White House and the environmentalists.

Although Schmertz claims not to care a wink about survey results regarding his advocacy advertising campaign, he cited surveys and took umbrage when the *PR Reporter* in 1977 said that Mobil's ads were ineffective, based on a study conducted by Yankelovich, Skelly & White. Schmertz complained in letters to Dan Yankelovich and the editors of the newsletter.

Then *Dun's Review* published an article based on the same study, further infuriating Schmertz. The *Journal of Commerce* and other papers also picked up the story.

Schmertz wrote, "Our ads deal with substantive issues that impact on Mobil, the industry, and the nation. We have reliable data to indicate that we have been successful in this effort."

Schmertz called attention to independent studies taken by Opinion Research Corporation and the Louis Harris organization in 1976 and 1977 which, he said, showed Mobil was "clearly the oil industry leader." He wrote, "Editors of major newspapers, magazines, wire services and radio and TV regarded Mobil more favorably than other oil companies."

Schmertz spelled out his philosophy on advocacy issue advertising: "A properly executed [advocacy] program can do a number of things for a company. First, it cautions aggressive opposition that they do not have the information arena to themselves. If they swing, somebody is going to swing back. This does not stop an opponent, but it makes him careful about making sure of his facts. Second, it can show supporters that you have the courage to fight for what you and they believe in. If Mobil isn't going to defend Mobil, then who is? Third, if you keep providing the facts, and if you are right, eventually you stand a good chance of winning. Finally, corporate management has a responsibility to protect the investment of its shareowners. The day may come when management is judged by how well it discharges this responsibility through communicating its views to certain key publics, including government, the media, and other opinion leaders."

Mobil's ads have been constructive as well as strident. Many are persuasively appealing and impressively researched in support of national goals: energy conservation, mass transit, and use of profits.

I thought the best ad in the long series — and I'll wager one of the most read — appeared in the *New York Times* on January 17, 1974. In big type and few words, the message read in part: "In 1972 we made $574 million, but our average profit was slightly more than a cent and a half a gallon . . . that's not much when you consider how much we invest, the risks we take, and the products and services we provide."

In May 1976, Schmertz acknowledged the mixed reaction his ads were receiving when he titled one message, "The Soapbox Is a Lonely Place." He bemoaned the lack of broad-based complaints against some 500 bills then before Congress to restrict the oil industry.

Mobil's ads championed decontrol of the industry, criticized television programming, fought for nuclear power, railed against economic stagnation, lamented the time constraints of broadcasting, defended its profits (often), called ABC's news-entertainment show "20/20" irresponsible, led the fight against government regulation, defended the industry against charges of "rip-off," took on the President of the United States when he chided Mobil for using its profits to buy new companies (Montgomery Ward) rather than explore for oil, and appealed to the Congress for more incentives. Some of its earlier ads were reprinted to show that the company had been anticipating trouble (even if most people hadn't been reading its op-ed page ads. Ads lectured the organizers of a "Big Oil Protest Day," attacked the windfall profits tax, again told the President he was misled (in charging that Mobil had violated price guidelines), and labeled a 1970 amendment to the Clean Air Act requiring strict auto emission standards "a $66 billion mistake."

"We are selling ideas," Schmertz says. "And the principal idea is that big business — oil companies in our case — are not a danger to society as they are portrayed by politicians, the press, educators, and others," he told a Florida audience of institutional investors in 1976.

Most observers support his intent and even admire the thrust of his advertisements, but still reject his style and believe that many of his personal statements are as exaggerated as the alleged media distortions he criticizes.

Agree with him, or disagree with him, Herb Schmertz is a hard man to ignore.

Ted Koppel was the first broadcaster to offer network time to industry for issue advertising. He broke the news, appropriately enough, during a segment of ABC's "Nightline" on March 3, 1981 while interviewing Herb Schmertz and Newton Minnow, former chairman of the Federal Communications Commission.

Koppel had invited Schmertz and Minnow to discuss what he termed "The growing inclination of business and industry to challenge the fairness and the accuracy of media reporting."

The *Wall Street Journal* (WSJ) responded by saying that electronic issue advertising would open a Pandora's box of problems. "Until now," said the *WSJ,* "networks have considered controversial issues the domain of their news divisions and have treated them so, much to the consternation of such companies as Mobil Corporation, which have paid for print ads to get their views across but have been unable to buy air time."

ABC said its "experiment" represented an effort to address the issue of advertiser access to the airwaves. Messages with contrasting viewpoints to those already aired, said ABC, "may be provided on a paid basis by other advertisers or groups, or if a paid response is unavailable, it is planned that constrasting views will be presented in ABC's late night programming, where required."

ABC began to air one-minute paid commentaries in tightly controlled late-night entertainment time slots in July 1981. The network was careful not to schedule such messages close to its news programs. And it permitted only one such message each night.

Schmertz urged wide experimentation of the sort ABC had initiated. "In newspapers, we have letters to the editors; we have op-ed articles by independent people; we have free-lance journalism. We don't find any of that in television," he complained.

Schmertz objected to the late-night restriction for paid commentaries and asked Koppel for an explanation.

Responding like a true businessman, Koppel said, "Probably because it's cheaper."

In one of the more interesting exchanges of that evening, Koppel agreed with Schmertz that television commentators had become "more conscious of the need to be as objective as possible," and Schmertz agreed with Koppel that "oil executives were caught very unaware of the need to communicate. They weren't trained for it. They didn't feel comfortable with it. It had never been really a part of their job, and they clearly were not ready. I think over the past seven years [since 1973], we've seen an enormous change on their part."

Newton Minnow, who once described television as a "vast wasteland," told Koppel that "business people were afraid of a television camera and a television journalist." Minnow added, "In today's world, they're really in politics, and they've got to be out there talking to the press and not being afraid of it."

A. R. "Lew" Angelos is a different kind of corporate advertising man, with his Hollywood smile, acquaintanceships with the greats and near greats in the movie capital, and a devotion to his company, Atlantic Richfield, and its management that borders on religious faith.

As manager of corporate advertising, he looks after television ads on the networks, print ads in the major magazines, and an energy conservation series of ads and promotions utilizing all kinds of media.

"People want to know what they can do, now, today, themselves to conserve energy," says Angelos. He is animated, enthusiastic in his speech. He smiles often. A visitor is immediately made comfortable.

"I try to display issues as simply but as dramatically as I can," he explains. "For example, in the argument about the environment and coal, one might ask, is coal dirtier than freezing?"

Angelos believes ARCO sets the advertising pace in the oil industry. "There is a certain mind set about the oil industry, but ARCO has established its own position, a little removed, and quite a bit above the fray," says Angelos. His belief is based on his conviction that ARCO's leaders, Thornton Bradshaw (now chairman of RCA) and Robert Anderson, have set standards for social involvement much higher than is common in most of American industry: "They set the tone for all of us. Their policies are adopted by management throughout the organization."

Could things change when Anderson leaves? Yes, Angelos admits, shaking his head. The smile disappears. "It's hard to institutionalize a man's philosophy after he's left. All of us have taken pride in the social leadership demonstrated by both Anderson and Bradshaw. Their personal reputations have helped to make ARCO's reputation. But what we're doing here today could change. I don't think it will change, but it could."

Angelos says Milton Friedman's philosophy that business has no obligation other than to make a profit isn't accepted at ARCO and "never will be."

Before Anderson and Bradshaw came to ARCO, says Angelos, there was no discussion about what a corporation owed to society. Friedman would have been welcomed then, says the personable advertising executive. "Not today," he emphasizes. "If economists were such pundits we wouldn't be in such an economic mess."

Angelos has handled everything from tree plantings in China, with top officials of that nation, to special events at Lincoln Center on a mere few days' notice. He works closely with Bill Duke, ARCO's highly respected manager of national programs, in carrying out the "Drive for Conservation" program, and also arranges noon concerts on top of the nearby Bonaventure Hotel for the citizens of Los Angeles. Angelos operates smoothly, pleasantly. He is an idea man but also a team player. When the phone rings — and it rings constantly in his office — it may be a famous movie star wanting to talk about his or her favorite charitable activity or community project, or a member of top management seeking counsel.

"I don't like abrasiveness," says Angelos. "It's counterproductive. Abrasive advertising is not good advertising. I have had plenty of evidence of that in the past 20 years."

When Herb Schmertz of Mobil started his issue advertising campaign, Angelos admits that almost every ARCO manager below Anderson and Bradshaw urged him to follow Mobil's example. "Why aren't you doing what Schmertz is doing?" Angelos repeats the question slowly. "That's what I used to hear. But Mr. Anderson backed me up when I refused. Sure, a lot of what Herb publishes is on the money. The content is right. But I am uncomfortable with unnecessary confrontation. It doesn't do the job."

Despite the weak showing of corporate-sponsored public issue advertising in the polls, the Senate Subcommittee on Administrative Practice and Procedure in 1978 subpoenaed materials from four oil companies and their advertising agencies related to ads the companies had run explaining their generous profits and contributions to society.

Barron's, the financial and business weekly publication, wrote of the action in April of that year, "the subcommittee is only a part of a growing and multifaceted federal attack on advertising, one which bodes ill for future freedom of expression. It also seems to run counter to several recent U.S. Supreme Court decisions that 'Speech does not lose its First Amendment protection because money is spent to project it, as in paid advertisement.' Heating up to the argument, *Barron's* added, "the federal attacks on advertising strike some observers as an attempt to undermine the financial foundations of the free press [by limiting advertising]."

In the House of Representatives, staffers compiled figures showing that corporations were spending $1 billion or more a year on advertising and mass mailings aimed at influencing public opinion on legislative matters. The argument was over the legality of deducting issue and image advertising as a cost of doing business.

Former Internal Revenue Commissioner Jerome Kurtz had already written the General Accounting Office, in December 1977, that the IRS would audit half the returns filed by trade associations to see if they were in violation of Section 162 of the IRS code which deals with the thorny issues of defining indirect lobbying, educational materials, and free speech.

Since the "public interest" is often in the eye of the beholder, the congressional challenge was seen as a punitive action against the oil companies rather than a legitimate concern for free speech. The Constitution, after all, does not guarantee free speech only to those promoting the public interest, whatever that interest may be perceived to be.

The obvious lesson for the oil companies — or any company entertaining the notion of sponsoring public issue advertisements — is to address broad issues in which the public clearly has a stake and identify company interests within that framework as supporting the national welfare.

Advocacy issue advertisements fail not so much because they are mushy, or strident, or too wordy, but because they are too self-centered. Too defensive. Too explanatory. The company usually promotes its own activities, saying how much it is spending for this and investing for that, and suggesting somehow that the public really ought to be a little grateful and appreciative and stop carping.

A simple statement about the need for harmonizing the divisions in society and what the company is doing to help would seem to suffice. The public is not impressed by self-promotion, however disguised, or how much a company is spending to cure a problem that clearly isn't being cured and can't be cured by the flow of dollars alone.

Business's complaints about government and the news media usually aren't very persuasive. The citizen has his own set of problems with government, and he may not be all that happy with the media either. He would be comforted to know of business's willingness to work with government and the media to solve some of *his* problems — and also some of the big problems that neither business nor government alone can solve. The citizen would find that approach very refreshing.

Finally, industry might be pleasantly shocked to find that its unapologetic commitment to voluntary public accountability would speed the demise of unwanted government regulation and earn the respect of the citizenry.

Editors and publishers and broadcasters are making renewed efforts to bolster business reporting and maintain the highest degree of accuracy.

Now business can cool the rhetoric, ease tensions, find common ground, and search for the Neutral Zone within which men and women of good intentions and high intelligence can fashion a better and more enduring working relationship.

Chapter Nineteen

Telling Stories out of School

Companies have used corporate advertising to convey many different stories for a very long time. In some instances, the ads focused on issues of equal importance to company and community.

In 1960, when business was moving away from downriver Detroit and the Greater Wyandotte Chamber of Commerce was searching for ways to fill the vacant stores that dotted Biddle Avenue along the Detroit River, Wyandotte Chemicals Corporation sponsored a study by Opinion Research Corporation to ascertain citizen attitudes about their community and the company.

Founded by John Baptiste Ford, the old chemical company had been the town's mainstay of employment for a half-century. The Ford family had built the marina and the hospital and a park for community activities. When young Robert Semple took over the reins at the age of 39, fresh from his research role at Monsanto Chemicals, he picked up the Ford family tradition of relating to community needs.

A skilled musician and president of the Detroit Symphony for many years, Bob Semple often played clarinet with the local band at summer concerts in the park, sponsored by Wyandotte Chemicals. He was good enough to sit in with the Detroit Symphony from time to time. And when he sought a moment of relief in the executive suite, he could be heard playing Artie Shaw arrangements of popular tunes.

Corporate social responsibility had not yet been defined when John F. Kennedy defeated Richard Nixon for the presidency in 1960. Traditional ways of contributing to community needs prevailed then: the summer concerts and fastball leagues to entertain the town folk in the lighted ballpark next to the employees recreation center.

Retirees congregated there for the annual old-timers picnic, and citizens enjoyed the bowling alleys and used the gym for all kinds of community events.

Once a year the company held its twenty-five-year award dinner there, catered by a local firm. Big-time entertainers such as the late Frankie Fontaine knew that gym, having wowed the employees of Wyandotte Chemicals and their spouses at the big annual event.

Wyandotte was a company town. Fifty-five percent of the company's employees lived in Wyandotte, and most of the others lived in nearby Trenton and over the privately owned bridge in Grosse Ile, the narrow island in the Detroit River, with a small naval air station at its southern tip.

So it was significant that Wyandotte Chemicals sponsored a study to identify the causes of economic stress downriver, and to learn the attitudes of the citizens about their changing community and the old company. It was even more significant that the company, in announcing the study, promised to report all the findings in a series of paid advertisements on the op-ed page of the local newspaper.

Hugh Hoffmann of Opinion Research was in charge of the project. George Baker, the former football great from Stanford who played against the "four horsemen" in the Rose Bowl game of 1925, was vice president of employee and public relations for the company, and coordinated the project.

Not all the findings pleased Wyandotte Chemicals' officials. Some respondents criticized the company for fouling the air and water. Some said the Ford family had been more paternalistic than involved. As a result, not all the executives were comfortable in keeping the promise of full disclosure.

But Semple insisted, and Baker approved a series of explanatory ads that spelled out what Opinion Research had determined through personal interviews and questionnaire replies.

The town was dying, the report said, and people were leaving to find jobs elsewhere. It would require an infusion of capital, plant expansion, and new service industries to turn things around.

The ads drew immediate editorial comment from the local newspaper in which they appeared, and from the public, in letters to the editor. Semple and his colleagues also received letters at the red brick headquarters in front of the antiquated chemical complex on Biddle Avenue, just north of the Wabeek Tea Room where Semple and his top staff met daily for lunch, and a stone's throw from the empty stores that verified the hard times that had fallen on the river city.

Jim Irwin, the company's Chicago-based public relations counselor who had known Semple at Monsanto and continued to serve him in Michigan, was in and out of the city during the reporting period, offering advice, kibitzing the ads, but supporting the program all the way.

Irwin and Baker and Semple knew that the effort was bringing real benefits to the company in terms of its credibility, its concern for the citizenry, and its abiding regard for the future of the downriver economy.

It was a solid example of business taking action in its own interest, and in the community's interest. And it set forth an effective role for the media, through paid advertisements, unsolicited editorials, and news stories, in reporting the results of a community study conducted objectively by one of the nation's most respected social research organizations.

There was no manipulation of the media here. On the contrary, the company had promised in advance of knowing the findings that it would report fully and fairly on all that the study revealed.

It kept its word. And the paper responded editorially, not to any special appeal the company made, for it made none at all, but rather to the usefulness and helpfulness of the study and its meaning for the current life of the city and its future.

Industry is not unique in its efforts to use advertising space to win the hearts and minds of thought leaders and the citizenry.

Many labor unions have turned to the media to tell their stories. The use of advertising by labor groups has more than doubled in recent years. The trend is still on the rise, and the number of unions buying advertising space and time may increase tenfold in the eighties.

A spokesman for the United Brotherhood of Carpenters and Joiners of America says his organization turned to advertising because "the general public has a confused attitude about labor. They see mostly television stories about strikes and dissension." The union has run a television spot showing a carpenter cutting out the union emblem with a jigsaw and placing it on a wooden map of North America. The message: "We're Building the 20th Century."

The International Ladies' Garment Workers' Union, which during the thirties produced a prounion musical hit on Broadway, sponsored the first national union advertising campaign in 1975. To encourage shoppers to buy products made in the United States, the union commercial asked viewers to "look for the union label."

Most ad-minded unions can't afford national advertising, so they concentrate on local newspapers and broadcasting stations. Sometimes groups of union organizations will buy space and time. In Buffalo, New York, for example, twenty building trade unions used radio to "tell people about the social things we do, like charitable work," a spokesman said. Now the group also uses television.

Even those unions that do not advertise are keeping watch to make sure that unions are not characterized negatively in soap operas, evening entertainment shows, and in advertising paid for by business interests.

Unions are also considering sponsorship of national cable television programs on such topics as taxes, the economy, and collective bargaining.

The late Allen Zack, assistant director of information for the AFL-CIO, said, "The attitude around here used to be, 'Who cares what the public thinks?' But now we've got a much better understanding of how public attitudes are formed — through education and television, and we're learning more about it all the time."

There was a time when "telling stories out of school" was a no-no.

Today, all kinds of organizations and institutions are telling all kinds of stories "out of school," recruiting workers, expressing opinions, talking back, selling ideas, reducing medical costs, preaching conservation, trying to reduce crime, and more.

Here are a few samples:

"Competition makes for better health care. It's just that simple" was the headline of an ad run by the Hospital Corporation of America (HCA) to promote privately owned and managed hospitals. "The result," said the ad, "is quality community health care — in an environment of cost-consciousness."

HCA operates 180 hospitals in the United States and abroad. HCA chairman Donald S. MacNaughton, former chairman of Prudential Life Insurance of America, believes that competition has always made people strive for improvement.

In the advertisement which bears his picture, he adds, "It shouldn't come as a surprise that this is true in today's hospital industry." The ad ran in the *Wall Street Journal,* other major newspapers, and periodicals. The point: America does not have to put up with volunteer, nonprofit, less efficient hospitals. The private enterprise system works in hospital management too. [I did not poll the reaction of not-for-profit hospitals, but one can surmise it.]

Another health ad was run by, no, not the American Medical Association, but by General Motors: "How to Help Get Health Care Where It's Needed Most." The giant automaker told the story of Meharry Medical College, supported by GM, which, as the nation's only privately supported, predominantly black, four-year medical school, has been training economically disadvantaged persons to serve their communities' health needs for more than a hundred years.

Calling Meharry "a vital national resource," GM reported in the ad that it has been providing money and technical support to the Nashville institution for many years and has set up two scholarship funds. The advertisement went on to say that GM also supports other colleges and universities to the tune of $27 million annually, and conducts its own fully accredited undergraduate engineering and industrial administration college in Flint, Michigan. The closing message: Before any business can do good it must do well.

The ad addressed a national issue, reported support for a black educational institution, and made the case for profits. Not bad.

W. R. Grace ran an ad in the *Washington Post* saying that the *Post's* editorial writers were "confused" about President Ronald Reagan's tax proposals. Grace argued that the Reagan cuts favored the lower-income taxpayer and thought it proved its point with numbers. The *Post* ran an editorial "Clearing up the Confusion" in which it pointed out why it thought Grace was wrong. Grace rolled up its sleeves, took out its pocket-bood, and wrote another ad, this time placing the offending *Post* editorial smack in the middle of it. Using margin notes, with lines and circles, Grace proceeded to wage its argument anew.

It was an effective format, taking the argument point by point as a teacher might grade a paper. It also ran its original ad under the marked-up editorial. The headline? "We say Reagan's tax cuts *don't* favor the rich. The *Washington Post* says we're wrong. You be the judge." Good show. Let the reader decide.

The Chevrolet Division of General Motors came under heavy criticism at the end of 1980 for allegedly using gore to sell "safer" cars. To push sales of their American-made Chevette subcompacts, a group of New York metropolitan-area Chevrolet dealers placed ads picturing an accident scene in which medics are heaving stretchered victims into an ambulance. Alongside is a mangled foreign car and two obviously shocked spectators. "But it got 43 mpg!" the bold headline declares. The copy asks: "In what are your children driving tonight? Is it a car which passed the latest U.S. safety tests? Chevette did . . . Toyota, Datsun, Volkswagen, Honda, and Subaru didn't."

The ad drew fire from Washington to California. "A cheap shot and a travesty in advertising," said an official of Nissan Motor Corporation. "Reprehensible," said the director of the International Automobile Dealers. And said GM, "We're not terribly proud . . . nobody liked it." GM disavowed all responsibility for the dealers' initiative.

Defenders of the ad said it presented a real reason for consumers to purchase as American-made car. But critics pointed out that the tests are highly controversial and that a serious accident could occur in any make of automobile. It is doubtful that this ad sold cars, but it did get a lot of attention.

Du Pont ran an ad promoting the popular Junior Achievement program that emphasized Du Pont's involvement in it. The ad told of a merger between Du Pont and the Images Company that "didn't light up Wall Street as much as it did the faces of eleven high school students from Wilmington, Delaware. They belong to Junior Achievement. And in order to get their small company off the ground, they needed the help of a big company. That's where Du Pont came in." Softly, the ad shows Du Pont's confidence in youth, the private enterprise system, and the future of America. The tag line reads, "A little pride will go a long, long way." Can't miss.

Atlantic Richfield ran a series of ads whose theme was "It's time we all went on an energy diet," in which it promoted its nationwide "Drive for Conservation Caravan." The idea: "Find out why a lot of drivers eat up more gas than their cars do." The ads support the actual "hands-on program" which teaches drivers to drive efficiently as well as safely. ARCO demonstrates that the average driver, by making simple changes in his driving habits, can get as much as 30 percent more miles per gallon from his car. It was a practical ad, designed to save the customer money. It spelled out where the caravan would be stopping across the country. A good program. A successful ad.

The chemical industry mounted a multimillion-dollar ad campaign in 1980 in an attempt to offset an increasing spate of news stories about the industry's failures: reports of improper disposal of hazardous wastes, the toxic effects of some chemicals, the pollution of air and waterways, and more. The new "image" campaign focuses on advertising, but also uses films, newsletters, and speakers.

The industry resolved to do something when an Opinion Research poll ranked the chemical industry sixteenth in a field of twenty industries in terms of public favor. The industry not only feared loss of public acceptance, but an increase in government regulation. Recruiters also said they were having trouble attracting the best people to the industry because of its unfavorable rating and the constant flow of negative news stories.

Not everyone agrees with the industry's ad approach, believing that the money would be better spent getting information directly into the hands of educators, students, opinion molders, and the news media.

Hercules, for one, is developing a program designed to assist business journalists.

Outside the industry the criticism of the ads is even stiffer. "I'd feel better if the companies put a little more money into testing chemicals for toxic effects and less into advertising themselves as Mr. Clean," says Jacqueline Warren, an attorney with the Environmental Defense Fund.

But Dow Chemicals has embarked on a $2 million ad program in its plant communities, believing, as does Stauffer Chemical, that the chemical industry is getting a bad press and must tell its own story. In this arena, ads alone obviously aren't going to make the critical difference. The public must believe that the ads reflect reality. And a recent study by Yankelovich, Skelly & White indicated that 64 percent of the general public thinks chemical wastes pose grave health problems, compared with 62 percent in a 1979 poll. Among government officials, the concern rose from 79 percent to 91 percent. Ads can help. But one Love Canal or Kepone spill in the James River, and it is all for naught.

SmithKline Corporation took an ad to "take off" after the news media, titled "Bad News, America." In a full-page ad with photographs, the copy ran four columns wide and lambasted the news media for its poor judgment, poor reporting, distortion, questionable values, bias against business, and gross irresponsibility. The ad cited specifics and spoke hopefully of the revolution in cable and satellite technology that will "vastly expand the possibilities for competition and diversity."

Quoting philosopher David Kelley throughout, the ad began with this commentary: "Why do American TV viewers see a dangerously distorted picture of industry and commerce? Philosopher David Kelley looks at media bias."

The ad presented a thoughtful, detailed and powerful case. It was also harsh and one-sided in its criticisms. Unlike Donald MacNaughton of Hospital Corporation of America, the SmithKline ad made no suggestion that business was in any way responsible for the condition of its press relations.

In the ad, Kelley urges the decontrol of the airwaves to "encourage the underlying commitment to objectivity that most reporters have." A threat and faint praise in the same sentence. No doubt the ad pleased industry and delighted SmithKline.

One wonders, however, if any attempt to talk with publishers and broadcasters had preceded the placement of the ad. Perhaps the editors weren't interested in talking.

Industry should keep in mind that advertisements are more suspect than news stories. Messages must be fair and balanced, even understated. The temptation to throw punches ought to be curbed.

PART FOUR

Business and the Environment

Chapter Twenty

Three Mile Island and Other Alarms

Of all the problems facing industry, none has presented a challenge equal to protection of the environment, presented a larger paradox, nor drawn sharper criticism from the public and legislators.

In the late fifties and early sixties, industry resisted government's insistence that it clean up waterways and skies near its manufacturing and processing facilities.

Industry was more inclined to point to waste discharges from municipalities along rivers and streams and identify other villains rather than spend money for filters and dust collectors. Industry's stated — and more often unstated — message to employees and community was that jobs and buying power were provided by the employers and that the price for economic stability was a little dirt in the air and water.

Pesticides and herbicides, hailed by farmers, were challenged by environmentalists who wanted more proof that new chemicals would not be harmful to the environment.

Industry was inclined to defend products and deride critics with equal enthusiasm. Charges of profiteering at the expense of human suffering and ecological damage were voiced by industry critics.

On the Detroit River early one spring morning in 1961, a husky former football great climbed into a blue and white helicopter with a cameraman and pilot to record the rainbow of colors downriver from the Motor City. The films, he would report, showed that the municipalities were the chief culprits. The government really ought to get after the mayors and county officials, he said, not the steel mills and chemical plants that provided jobs and security for the whole area.

There was scant talk in boardrooms along the river in those days about the effect of air and water pollution upon employees who lived and worked there. "Listen, Carl, when the mills install dust collectors, then we'll install dust collectors. You're talking about a lot of money. Why should we invest now?"

The basic argument that the installation of controls was inevitable and necessary did not prevail at that time. The notion that it would cost more to add the devices later — that public opinion of business would decrease and the governments insistence for controls would increase — also was shrugged off.

"We'll see. It's a matter of economics, and we're not ready to agree that we're all that responsible. The pressures may ease up. Give it time."

When industry did begin its expensive cleanup, following the enactment of government regulations in the sixties and seventies [which it might have had a stronger hand in writing], the public did not applaud. Compliance with the law was no cause for celebration; it was expected and required.

Nor did industry's advertisements and press releases describing its efforts to curb air and water pollution — detailing how much it was spending to do the job — attract many cheerleaders in the public domain.

Industry and government were adversaries; dialogue was limited and guarded. One does not put all one's cards on the table with an adversary.

The adversarial bickering continued, and the nation came to know much more about pollution across the land.

Headlines in newspapers and items on the seven and eleven o'clock news broadcasts about pollution and toxic wastes upset the citizenry.

Hazardous wastes were detected in wells near St. Paul, Minnesota; traces of benzene and toluene caused some private wells to be closed. State officials said the chemicals were believed to have seeped into the groundwater from a nearby disposal site. Because of shoddy record keeping, authorities could not determine what chemicals had been dumped there, or even the names of the companies that had used the location to dispose of wastes.

Chemicals dumped near Puerto Rico allegedly caused two deaths in the Dominican Republic and poisoned millions of fish in one of the world's richest fishing grounds. Dominican officials said they found several unmarked 55-gallon barrels with liquids containing mercury, chlorine, sulphur, and phosphates which they believed had been dumped intentionally. Vast blankets of dead fish appeared on the eastern tip of the island and two citizens died, it was claimed, as a result of eating poisoned fish.

Fishing also was halted in parts of Puerto Rican waters.

New laws restricting the dumping of waste products in 1980 allegedly spurred a rash of dumpings on the eve of their enactment. The *New York Times* reported on November 16, 1980, that thousands of hazardous and toxic wastes had been hurriedly dumped into the city sewer systems, spilled from moving trucks onto busy interstate highways, and abandoned in shopping center parking lots in a last minute rush to dispose of wastes before the federal "cradle-to-grave" waste-monitoring system began across the nation.

Industry had time to prepare; the system was actually mandated by Congress in 1976 but was debated for another four years before being enacted. Its purpose is to channel all of the 40 million tons of dangerous chemical wastes produced in the United States each year into approved treatment and storage facilities.

Proper disposal techniques are expensive: they can cost as much as $10,000 per tank car. The farther the dumping location from the manufacturing site, the more the cost of disposal affects the competitiveness of the producer in the marketplace.

As a result, it was alleged that cut-rate, "no questions asked" disposal services sprang up — some suspected of having ties with organized crime — that would remove wastes for a tenth of the cost of the disposal methods required under federal standards.

All kinds of games were said to be played: shipments of wastes by railroad car to fictitious addresses hundreds of miles away; the renting of warehouses by disposal companies that later disappeared and could not be traced, leaving hundreds of barrels behind; trucks dumping wastes into streams, swamps, fields, and landfills that could later work their way into groundwater supplies.

People were already angry and afraid when the nuclear accident occurred in Pennsylvania.

THREE MILE ISLAND

The famous Three Mile Island nuclear accident in 1979 continued to cause an uproar into the eighties when the cost of cleaning up radioactive debris accelerated like a chain reaction, with estimates approaching $1 billion. Struggling to avoid bankruptcy, the owner of the shutdown facility, General Public Utilities Corporation, argued that Uncle Sam — the United States taxpayers — should pay for the cleanup. (The companies that fight for independence from government regulation often are the most insistent on government help when things go wrong.)

It will take at least five years to clean up the contaminated mess, and perhaps longer. Inflation increases the costs as time goes along, and the nuclear plant hasn't produced any electricity since the reactor core of its Number Two Unit partially melted on March 28, 1979.

Three Mile Island became synonymous with public concern for industry's performance in controlling pollution and protecting the public safety and general welfare.

On the second anniversary of the accident at Three Mile Island, 7000 protestors marched through the streets of the state capital, Harrisburg, in opposition to nuclear energy. Organized labor joined in the march of mostly young people, many carrying placards depicting tranquil pastoral scenes.

In 1980, an executive of a major trade association in Washington admitted to me that many nuclear facilities still lacked disaster plans and had made no organized provision for evacuating nearby communities should another, perhaps even more serious, mishap occur. When I expressed shock, he said, "Look, this is a conservative industry. It moves slowly. We urge all of the utilities to design and rehearse such plans. But we can't make them do it."

Perhaps the plants will wait until the government requires them to produce proof that such arrangements have been made. Then, of course, we shall hear more cries against government intrusion.

Wrote Congressman Edward J. Markey of Massachusetts in the *Boston Globe* on March 28, 1980: "Evacuation plans are crucial buffers against death and injury. If half the Strontium 90, Cesium 137, and other radioactive isotopes in an average reactor were scattered by the wind, a lethal dose of radiation could be delivered within four hours to everyone inside an area six miles long and one mile wide. That area could double within 24 hours and eventually increase to more than 50 miles downwind. Unless evacuation were begun in advance . . . people would receive lethal doses of radiation."

Public opinion was also influenced by the Three Mile Island Legal Fund in Harrisburg whose mailings and press notices said the nuclear industry was "covering up" and that the United States government had not "told the whole story about this [accident] and other major accidents at nuclear installations."

The public remained upset and confused, and unhappy with industry in general. Unhappy with government. Unhappy with the news media. Unhappy with the Nuclear Regulatory Commission for its refusal to consider psychological stress and community fears in deciding whether to restart the undamaged Unit One reactor at Three Mile Island.

Said Commissioner Joseph Hendrie, "The actual level of risk is essentially irrelevant to the psychological stress claimed to be suffered. . . . There is no way to allay that fear except not to build or operate the reactor."

Said nuclear critics, right on Mr. Commisioner!

GROWING FEARS

Fear feeds on fear. In July 1980, 7500 men, women, and children, including soldiers from Fort Knox, were evacuated when 10 derailed tanks cars of toxic chemicals exploded. The train crew was hospitalized. And a cloud of thick, black smoke spread out 3000 feet high and 10 miles wide over the little town of Muldraugh and the surrounding countryside. The cloud contained vinyl chloride, chlorine, acryinitrile, toluene, and propane.

In Louisville, Kentucky, on February 13, 1981, a series of sewer explosions caused millions of dollars of damage in a section of Old Louisville, triggered, it was reported, by an accumulation of flammable industrial solvent from a nearby mill. A twenty-block industrial area and four schools were evacuated. National Guard units were called in to help local police. The explosions involved some 200 gallons of hexane, a volatile liquid hydrocarbon, but no one could say for sure how the chemical had gotten into the sewer system.

In Millfield, Ohio, on January 13, 1981, 750 persons were evacuated when a tanker car derailed, spilling the flammable toxic chemical toluene into a creek. The water systems of nearby Athens and Chauncey were shut down for many hours.

Industry alone is not the culprit. The United States military services have stockpiles of poison chemical weapons that will cost some $3.7 billion to dispose of safely. The figure was estimated by President Ronald Reagan's transition team and made public in March 1981.

The transition team's report warned that "the obsolete and deteriorating stockpile requires a comprehensive plan" for detoxifying chemical weapons stored around the United States, on Johnson Island in the Pacific, and in West Germany. The transition team said some of the stored munitions "have been identified as 'leakers.'" Before releasing the previously classified document, the Pentagon censored just how many weapons actually are known to be leaking.

On January 25, 1980, four tank cars carrying flammable gases and liquids derailed in the early morning near Acworth, Georgia, forcing the evacuation of 700 people from their homes. The cars carried butadiene, a flammable gas, and styrene, a flammable liquid.

Flames engulfed a 30,000-gallon propane gas storage tank hit by a derailed coal train at Sledge, Mississippi, on February 13, 1980, and authorities emptied the town of its 600 residents.

In Casper, Virginia, in February 1981, a dairy farmer finally figured out the cause of the mysterious deaths of his cattle: commonwealth water authorities learned that a wood-preserving operation 3 miles from the farm had allowed more than 200,000 gallons of the highly toxic liquid chemical chromium-arsenic to enter a stream several days earlier. On its way through peaceful dairy pastures, the chemical had killed cattle, fish, and poultry.

TO PUT IT KINDLY, A MESS

The effort to control hazardous chemical wastes began belatedly and tentatively, prompted by critical public opinion and aggressive government regulation.

Whether the effort will change the business mind set about anticipating as well as responding to environmental needs is not yet clear.

But it seems doubtful that the chemical industry's public affairs executives would ever again sit around a conference table in Washington, poring over the galley proofs of a book written by a renowned environmentalist, and then say rather piously some weeks later, when *Silent Spring* appeared in bookstores across the nation and received respectful reviews, that "the industry is not yet familiar with Miss Carson's opinions, but from what we have heard, her criticisms of the chemical industry are exaggerated and unfair."

Almost twenty years after her book was published, Rachel Carson was posthumously awarded the Medal of Freedom, the nation's highest civilian award. It was presented on June 9, 1980, by President Jimmy Carter, who praised Carson for creating "a tide of environmental consciousness that has not ebbed."

No one expected the chemical industry to cheer Carson's book in the early sixties. Neither was it expected — or wise — for the industry to strike out at so respected a conservationist with blind certitude in defense of products whose properties were in question. Nor was it honest to pretend ignorance of her positions when every word she wrote had been read and digested and discussed weeks before her book appeared in print.

The old tactics — defend, attack, ridicule — dictated their response. Industry might have taken a more statesmanlike position and expressed its deep concern for the health and welfare of all citizens, and indicated respect for Rachel Carson as a person, even as it strongly challenged her conclusions. It might have found things on which to agree with the author. Privately, many chemical industry executives did agree. Publicly, they tried to discredit her.

In the following years, America's chemical genius created as many as 1000 new compounds each year. Nearly 50,000 chemical products are on the market. Many of them have extended man's life, improved his health, prevented disease, preserved food supplies, purified water, produced new and useful products, created jobs, and boosted the nation's economy.

But some 35,000 of those chemicals are classified by the Environmental Protection Agency (EPA) as being either definitely or potentially hazardous to human health. The cause-and-effect relationships are difficult and sometimes impossible to establish, however, and that is where the arguments stall.

Former Surgeon General of the United States Julius Richmond cautioned in 1980 that the nation was confronting "a series of environmental emergencies" posed by toxic chemicals that "are adding to the disease burden in a significant, although as yet not precisely defined way." His report to the Senate said, "The public health risk associated with toxic chemicals is increasing, and will continue to do so until we are successful in identifying chemicals which are highly toxic and controlling the introduction of these chemicals into our environment."

His report was supported by a study of thirty-two major chemical-contamination incidents that was conducted by the Library of Congress. The library's survey said these cases "represent the tip of the iceberg of truly unknown dimensions" and concluded that toxic chemicals "are so long lasting and pervasive in the environment that virtually the entire population of the nation, and indeed the world, carries some body burden of one or several of them."

Ronald A. Roland, president of the Chemical Manufacturers Association, attacked the surgeon general's report for exaggerating the threat of toxic wastes. But EPA administrator Douglas M. Costle added, "We didn't understand that every barrel [of chemicals] stuck into the ground was a ticking time bomb, primed to go off." And Dr. Irving Selikoff, director of the Environmental Sciences Laboratory of New York City's Mount Sinai Medical School, said, "Toxic waste will be the major environmental and public health problem facing the United States in the eighties."

EPA claimed that 77 billion pounds of hazardous chemical wastes were being produced every year and that only 10 percent was handled in a safe manner.

The greatest fear in many parts of the country is that toxic wastes have infiltrated groundwater systems.

ILLEGAL DUMPERS

The federal government and most states are cracking down. Under a 1979 New Jersey statute, offenders can be fined up to $50,000 a day for every day they leave wastes unprotected and may get jail sentences of up to ten years. Yet, the undercover operators flout the law and find plenty of businesses to serve. Of the 50,000 dump sites identified by the EPA, the government believes 2000 pose serious health hazards.

The chemical industry supports the federal regulations requiring the tracking of all toxic chemicals to the point of final disposal. Violators can be fined up to $25,000 a day and jailed for a year for a first offense. Roland says this is "a perfectly reasonable thing for the federal government to do. We don't want irresponsible disposal."

But chemical companies are fearful that EPA standards will approve an insufficient number of sites, giving companies only two options: close down, because they have no place to dump wastes, or break the law. The chemical industry established a hazardous-waste response center on its own in Washington to advise state and local officials about waste-disposal procedures and ways to improve old dump sites.

Irving Shapiro, retired chairman of Du Pont, cautioned business and industry in 1980 to "work together rather than get emotional. Let's start today," he said, "and not worry about who did what in the past. We've got to get going rather than sitting around trying to figure out who's wearing the black hat and who's wearing the white hat."

How much damage is irreparable? No one knows. But Shapiro offers the only sensible answer: stop fighting, start working together, keep working together. Seek answers, not villains.

Easy said. When legal action results, the lawyers properly take command. Dialogue is lost, except for the formal exchanges in courtrooms and documents.

Dialogue must precede and minimize legal action. The whole idea is to create a Neutral Zone in which free exchange is not only encouraged, but expected. The idea is to follow Shapiro's advice, and John Gardner's counsel, and accepted common sense: reduce friction, bring people together in common cause, solve the problems.

Chapter Twenty-one

The Unlovely Love Canal and Midnight Dumpers

Right up there with Three Mile Island on the list of environmental award winners sits Love Canal, near Niagara Falls, New York. Not only is Love Canal the world's best-known dump site, it is probably the most misunderstood pollution crisis as well.

Len Delmar, now an editor with the *Buffalo Courier Express,* was a reporter for the *Niagara Falls Gazette* in 1952 when Hooker Chemical Company warned the board of education that the land it wished to use for the construction of a school contained dangerous chemicals. It warned the board at meetings. It warned the board in writing. The board persisted, and got the land.

In 1957, Hooker's chief legal counsel, Arthur Chambers, appeared before the board on two occasions to caution its members not to sell off some of the land, as the board proposed to do, for the building of houses. Hooker had said that the land could be used for a school building, if no basement were dug, and for a playing field, since the dumped chemicals below ground in barrels would be covered by 4 feet of hard clay.

Delmar recalled these facts when questioned by Ted Koppel on ABC's popular late-evening news show "Nightline" on May 21, 1981.

"The newspapers in western New York covered the situation accurately and throughly," Delmar said. "But few people paid any serious attention outside of western New York." Delmar said it was not until the late seventies, when Love Canal became an "ecological explosion" and forced city officials to evacuate 700 persons that national media converged upon Niagara Falls and asked questions.

Somehow the Hooker warnings were disregarded. And, as time passed, company spokespersons became more ambivalent about the record.

Why? Because in 1952 the company clearly was warning residents about the dangers of the chemicals buried at Love Canal. In the seventies, Donald Baeder and his fellow executives at Hooker were claiming that the chemicals had not been proven to hold any danger to human health.. The fuzzy battle lines were drawn.

It was a classic example of a company having done the right thing initially, following through responsibly, and then losing control of the situation because of legal considerations and poor communication.

Later, when seepage of chemicals caused the evacuation of families and drew critical comment in the media and from the President of the United States, Hooker tried to redefine its role and avoid legal responsibility.

Hooker officials held a news conference in 1978. Baeder, now an official of Hooker's parent company, Occidental Chemicals, in California, recalls media interest was so low that the company "took out an ad" to tell its story.

A visitor to Love Canal today sees boarded-up homes, a wire fence surrounding the area, and the famous school in a state of serious deterioration. Company executive Bruce Davis says Hooker "has no legal liability" because the record is clear that the company warned the board of education publicly and forthrightly to use the site for certain restricted purposes, and the board ignored the warning.

Critics point out that Hooker eventually gave in to the pleadings of the board of education, rather than persisting in its cautions and taking out advertisements then to warn the public.

The board did send Hooker a letter, acknowledging its awareness of the buried chemicals, but avoiding specific mention of how the board intended to use the land.

Later, the school was built and some of the land was sold off to a housing developer.

Several years later, Eric Zeusse of *Reason* magazine in California would do a comprehensive article on Love Canal in which he concluded that the company had taken every reasonable action. He said the general news media had been surprisingly lax in reviewing records and challenging community and school board officials.

Hooker had set forth the record in the 1978 news conference, Zeusse emphasized. The media practically ignored the record. Only when Love Canal became as famous as nearby Niagara Falls did the national media swarm into the city, set up cameras, interview officials and citizens on the street, and follow the story to Washington where both the White House and the EPA would offer critical comment.

Reflecting on all the events leading up to Love Canal in his television broadcast of May 21, 1981, Ted Koppel asked Donald Baeder how he could account for Hooker's "poor public relations" performance. He pointed out that Hooker had declared the chemicals dangerous in the fifties and benign in the eighties. How could that be?

Baeder replied that Love Canal was never a dump site, as such; that even in the fifties, many homes had been built in the area. He said neither the scientists nor the public knew very much about toxicity in those years, and that new information revealed during the sixties and seventies raised public concern and motivated governmental action.

Baeder and Davis sometimes infuriate the local citizenry, and others, by their repeated statements that Hooker has no legal liability and that there is "not a shred of evidence" that chemicals stored underground at Love Canal have in fact caused human illness. According to Baeder, no real health study has been conducted, and an environmental commission appointed by the governor of New York said no illnesses could be attributed to the underground wastes.

Writer Michael Brown strongly disagrees with those conclusions in his book *The Poisoning of America* and has challenged the current position of Hooker officials publicly and privately. Brown appeared with Baeder and Delmar on Koppel's program and reported that the miscarriage rate among women in the Love Canal area was 3.5 percent above "normal" in the late seventies, and contended that the company is now exaggerating the warnings it gave to city officials in the fifties.

A HAPPIER HISTORY AT NIAGARA

Given the recent events at Lovel Canal, it is interesting to review the alliance between the city officials of Niagara Falls and local industry that existed in the past. Principally old-line chemical companies settled along the mighty river to benefit from the water supply and power source. The Niagara frontier has long been recognized as one of America's major chemical complexes. The sights and smells of chemical processes are quite familiar to residents in the Niagara frontier.

William H. Wendell, president for many years of the Carborundum Company at Niagara Falls, studied the interactions of business and society long before the notion became fashionable among social scientists and academics. He was concerned about the rising cost of government at all levels and the diversion of investment capital — through taxation — into what he considered to be poorly run, inefficient local government services.

About the same time, the famed Committee on Economic Development (CED) in Washington was articulating similar views. Wendell spoke his mind along the Niagara frontier, and elsewhere, calling for tax reduction to encourage more capital investment, thus strengthening industry and increasing employment — not only in Niagara Falls, but in cities across the country.

Wendell founded the Society for the Promotion, Unification and Redevelopment of Niagara, Inc. (SPUR). He became its first president and driving force. C. Y. Cain of Hooker Chemicals served on the board along with top-level representatives of Union Carbide, Bethlehem Steel, Du Pont, and General Motors. Public board members included representatives of housing, education, tourism, local government, urban renewal, citizen action groups, area development, and even an institute for international study, concerned principally about relations with Canada across the river. But public members served ex officio. They could counsel but had no vote.

The alliance did not save the city from financial stress. By 1976, Niagara Falls, New York, faced bankruptcy — along with many other municipalities in America, including the Big Apple, New York City, at the other end of the state. Labor costs were higher in the Honeymoon City than almost anywhere else in the nation other than San Francisco and Oakland.

By May 1976, SPUR, in cooperation with the chamber of commerce, recruited a top-flight management team to help restore financial stability in the area. The area companies provided top-level management people to work with the group at no charge. Local banks bought $7.5 million in city notes. Citizens subscribed $1.2 millon in response to a public campaign to save the area. Two New York City financial houses bought $11.4 million of the city's notes because, they said, they were impressed by local resolve and unified action.

Other action was taken: deferral of $500,000 in payments to the state urban renewal authority, and the granting of short-term loans of $2.5 million from local banks to improve cash flow and head off operating problems.

By 1977, the city had an operating surplus, had wiped out its debt, and regained its pride. The mayor estimated that the management team would have cost the city $400,000 in fees alone. SPUR, the chamber, local industry, and the citizens had paid the bill.

This was Love Canal territory. Hardly a hostile climate for business. Surely not a record of indifference here to social needs by the business community.

Hooker officials definitely do not see themselves as bad guys wearing black hats. When the storm broke over Love Canal and the news media descended upon the city of 80,000 people at the edge of the famous falls, Hooker wasn't at all happy with the trend of reporting and took out a series of paid advertisements to say its piece.

One of those ads read: "Try Telling Bruce Davis that Hooker Doesn't Care about Niagara Falls." Davis, a bespectacled, serious-faced Hooker executive, was pictured in the ad, coffee cup in hand, telephone at his ear. The copy explained that Davis was in charge of Hooker's industrial chemical group and that "Bruce knows that Hooker's action is speaking a lot louder than words [the media's] on the subject of chemical waste."

The company's ads telling the citizenry how much it had spent for pollution-control equipment to "meet and surpass" environmental requirements ($12 million), and its ads describing the thousands of manhours and the skills of its forty environmental specialists, may have been therapeutic for company officials. But at that late stage in the development of events, they failed to win the hearts and minds of the people living in the Niagara frontier. Hooker's frustration was understandable. It had shared information with the board of education, but no one had paid serious attention. Life went on. A school was built. Homes were constructed. The original cautions were forgotten.

Then new technologies were developed. Public awareness of the dangers of toxic chemicals increased. And, finally, as Len Delmar described it, Love Canal became an "ecological explosion" on the American scene.

Then people asked questions. There had to be a villain in the play. The dumper, of course!

What is this stuff about Hooker's early warnings? Cover-up talk, of course. Legal defense talk, of course.

Yet, the record was there in newspaper files for all to see. But the media at first ignored the data, then attacked. The company defended. There was no reasonable exchange.

The lawyers were there to make open dialogue difficult if not impossible. The company was angry, confused, under stress. The media were determined, competitive, skeptical and public attitudes toward business in general were at low tide. Old, familiar sides were drawn.

But no one was to blame, really; everybody was at fault. It will take several more years for the facts to sort out and the full story to be told.

Communication under stress is subject to many interpretations. That is why constant dialogue is important. Dialogue tends to prevent problems from developing, and when problems do develop, to speed the decision-making process in a less hostile climate.

But one cannot begin a dialogue in the middle of a crisis.

How did the Love Canal become an "ecological explosion"? Why did New York State health officials declare an "emergency situation" in 1978?

After all, it was in 1958, twenty years earlier, that children were reportedly burned at the site. Hooker inspected the property then and found some barrels exposed because, company officials contended, housing contractors had lifted the thick clay cover.

Hooker solved the problem in 1958 by refilling the site with clay. Not until 1976 did more serious problems become known.

Residents complained of odors in the basements of their homes. It seemed clear that chemicals were leaking from the disposal area. Water seeped in, carrying wastes. Some of those wastes contained dioxin residues from Hooker's trichlorophenol production.

Repairs had to be made. Hooker agreed to pay one-third of the costs based on moral rather than legal considerations. The city and the board of education were to raise the other two-thirds, but could not.

Thus, for three years, work was delayed. The sum needed? Only $830,000. Critics of the Love Canal phenomena jump on this point. If Hooker agreed that it had a moral responsibility to help and the city and board could not come up with the balance, why didn't the company extend its "moral" responsibility, at least in the form of a loan to be repaid, so that repairs could be made promptly? What sort of moral responsibility prevailed, critics wonder, when the problem was allowed to fester?

Work was finally begun in 1979, including the installation of a new clay cap and a 3-foot-wide drainage ditch around the canal perimeter. The flow of the canal was reduced from 30,000 gallons a day to less than 8000 gallons a day, and Hooker contended that the abandoned houses could safely be reoccupied.

By the end of 1979, Davis was to say, "Our credibility is open to question at Hooker. It's going to take a little while before we convince them, [media, government, public], but what we're doing is correct, the right thing to do."

The "right thing to do" at Hooker included a $250 million five-year program to demolish old structures and processes, and modernize, beautify, and clean up its chemical works.

It was no small thing. When I was a boy growing up in Kenmore, New York, the road to Niagara Falls was known as "stink alley" and punctuated all visits to my relatives north of the chemical complexes.

Driving along Robert Moses Parkway by the Niagara River in 1981, I was pleasantly surprised to see that the ugly brown fences that formerly hid chemical works from view have been replaced in part by shrubbery and landscaped lawns.

Only the superstructures of chemical installations are now visible at some points, and many surface buildings are painted in primary colors. Attractive signs identify the companies, and there is a whole new look to go with the improvements in chemical processing.

In the sixties, it was clear that chemicals could harbor insidious dangers as well as new blessings for mankind. Rachel Carson's *Silent Spring* alerted a generation to the new perils of abundant pesticides. Later, localized accidents molded public opinion: persistent toxics polluted Lake Michigan, Lake Erie, and the Hudson River.

In the seventies, the pesticide Kepone not only poisoned workers at a Virginia plant but also fouled the beautiful James River for years to come. Moreover, the list of chemicals alleged to cause cancer grew by the month. Then came Love Canal.

The Congress responded in 1976 with the Toxic Substances Control Act, to prevent the most dangerous new chemicals from ever reaching the market and, ultimately, to remove from the market the most dangerous known chemicals in circulation. In addition, a key section of the Resource Conservation and Recovery Act was revised to increase safeguards for the disposal of hazardous wastes. But passing laws and enforcing them are two different things.

DEPENDENCY ON CHEMICALS

Almost every item of commerce is based on a chemical substance. As Monsanto Chemicals is fond of repeating in its advertisements: "No chemical can be safe all of the time in every circumstance." But the industry bears a special and heavy responsibility for the safety of its products and the conditions under which they can safely be used, long before they enter the marketplace or are incorporated into the fabric of other products.

It costs industry at least $250,000 to determine if a chemical substance might be a cancer-causing agent. Long-term animal tests can add another $500,000 per substance. A lot of money. Yet, the terrible price for not taking these expensive precautions is apparent.

People will willingly take risks over which they believe they exercise some personal control: smoking cigarettes, scuba diving, flying a plane. But they resent and reject unknown, uncontrollable risks presented in the food they eat, the water they drink, the air they breathe, and the clothes they wear. Chemicals permeate their lives — automobiles, electronic appliances, paints, paper, rubber products, textiles, steel — if not in the finished items, then certainly in the processes used to produce them. More personally, chemicals are present in mouth washes, perfumes, shampoos, soaps, and ingredients used in food and food processing. It is a chemical world.

Allied Chemicals calculated a few years ago that it had spent more than $1 million to computerize data on its 13,000 products, detailing how and where they are made and what is known about their toxicity and other health effects.

Shell Chemicals in 1979 spent about $2 million for these purposes; substantial costs, but hardly significant sums for multibillion dollar corporations to invest in product safety.

Small chemical companies can't always afford to do it; often innovative chemical specialty companies are forced into mergers with the big companies in order to meet the testing requirements and survive.

These are serious disruptions in the free enterprise system; the burdens of compliance present truly formidable challenges to small firms. But the protection of human life and the public welfare are of paramount importance. Providing that protection is the chemical industry's first priority. If the industry fails in that fundamental task, it cannot succeed in any other.

There is a critical need to establish a Neutral Zone for dispassionate, product-by-product review. Government could speed up and improve the approval process without violating patent rights or disclosing confidential information.

In the past, industry has often been "put off" by constantly changing rules and regulations. If the rules are to work, industry must join with government in preparing them. Gathering data on all the properties of all the chemical products is an expensive, time-consuming process. Cooperation between government and industry can speed the process and assure a better result.

Union Carbide collected data division by division not so long ago, only to learn belatedly that the EPA wanted the information collected plant by plant. It had already spent $1 million to comply with the regulations as its executives understood them.

One might speculate that a freer, less restricted information exchange — at the front end — might have resolved the misunderstanding and saved money, irritation, and precious time.

A company can lose even when it wins an argument in the environmental theatre.

Monsanto Chemicals produced a plastic soft drink bottle made of styreneacrylonitrile copolymer. It hoped to produce 4 billion units by 1982 and become a leader in the field. By 1976, Monsanto was selling the bottle in twelve states. Then the Food and Drug Administration banned it, saying unpolymerized acrylonitrile remaining in plastic might cause cancer and birth defects.

Monsanto wrote off $20 million and may end up writing off $100 million. The company contends the product is safe and is fighting the ban through the courts — adding legal expenses to its losses. But even if Monsanto should win its arguments later on, negative publicity may prove an insurmountable market liability. If Monsanto wins, it could lose.

Had Monsanto done all the testing it should have done? Was it fearful of going to government before it embarked on its investment? Sheldon D. Murphy, former Harvard University toxicologist, who reviewed Monsanto's health-effects literature in 1973, later said it might have been "prudent" for the company to be sure it had done all conceivable testing and all reasonable safety evaluations before entering the market.

The trick is to obtain speedy approval from the government on innovative items that merit approval so as not to lose market advantage. Why create and invest, if the competition can move faster and put a similar product on the market while government types are leisurely thumbing through approval documents. Business and government must work together or the process will not work at all.

Speed and protection of confidentiality are the key issues. Polaroid once sued the EPA for its poor administration because the EPA had permitted unauthorized persons to see the company's confidential data. EPA revised its procedures to tighten requirements on access to its computer in Virginia. Employees mishandling information now are subject to a $5000 fine and a year in jail. But says Lowell F. Ludford at the 3M Company, "the penalty does not equal the harm that can be done."

"The government will always bring out a sledgehammer to hit a mouse," complains John R. Yost, president of Muskegon Chemicals in Michigan. "I don't think society realizes the price it will pay for this [testing] approach."

But Congressman Robert Echardt of Texas says premarket testing is the only sensible answer: "It is better to spend money to be sure a chemical is safe before it is made than after it is distributed."

OLD MIND SET HARD TO CHANGE

In the old days (before EPA) a plant manager was thought to be doing his job when he told his boss, "Don't worry about that waste problem. I took care of it." Few bosses asked how or when or where the plant manager took care of it — at least not until a neighbor filed suit to recover damages for lost trees, or animals, or smelling up a waterway.

If the manager "took care" of the problem at 3 a.m. by flushing wastes into a stream or at 4 a.m. by emitting gases into the air, he wasn't questioned.

The manager who didn't trouble his superiors with pollution problems, but took care of them, was rewarded. That was the way it was. If a nearby farmer agreed, for a sum of money, to make part of his land a fill for waste materials, it was a simple business transaction, confirmed with a handshake.

Thousands of unidentified dumping grounds were created in that fashion.

Today, the reverse is true. It is almost impossible to get approval to create a landfill site. The thousands of sites already in existence are scrutinized and closed when found in shoddy condition. The public, aroused and frightened, doesn't want a new landfill within sight or sound.

Very often it is the public, not the EPA, that is responsible for closing landfills and even shutting down manufacturing and processing facilities. An Indianapolis plant was shut down at a cost of $500,000 because of an odor problem. A Wilsonville, Illinois, judge closed a 130-acre showcase landfill with nearly impermeable 40-feet-thick clay walls because the public considered it a nuisance. The EPA argued to keep it open. There was no valid technical reason to close it.

The irony is that America is pockmarked with the crude results of the midnight dumpers while scientifically sound landfills are being rejected. The dangers to human health arise in old dumps, particularly, because no one can predict the synergistic effects of newspapers, batteries, drugs, discarded refrigerators, old paint, and more, as they degrade and mix.

Inherently hazardous wastes come from many segments of society, not just chemical plants: hospitals, farms, government installations, and laboratories.

Wastes are yesterday's problems come back to haunt us.

Our collective sin is that we have imagined that the problems would go away or that someone else would solve them. Each company has argued that it wasn't its fault.

Like the companies along the Detroit River in the late fifties and early sixties, it seemed more important to stall for time, place the blame on municipalities, than to plan for the inevitable cleanup and give consideration to employees and community residents who suffered from the pollution.

It seemed then more of an economic than an ecological problem. Government snoopers were looking for trouble, people groused. But what could they do about such a diverse collection of industries along a river? Humor them. Take them on a tour. Show them the problems of pollution control in old plants. Walk them through half-deserted towns on the river with their stores closed along Main Street. How could any government snooper think of adding more cost burdens to the company, the town employer, the biggest taxpayer? Show them the film taken from the helicopter with the raw sewage pouring out of downriver towns. The mayors were responsible for those fish kills and that water pollution. Show the snoops the film.

How do places like Love Canal come to be?

William T. Love proposed in 1892 to build a power canal between the upper and lower Niagara Rivers, utilizing the 300-foot drop in water level to generate electricity. In 1894, work started — but stopped when an economic depression cooled the investment.

For thirty years the site was abandoned. In 1942, Hooker obtained approval to use the site for disposing of residues.

The canal is a trench, 3000 feet long, 10 feet deep, and 60 feet wide. Hooker acquired a strip of land 200 feet wide with the canal approximately in the center. Dumping began in 1942, in the northern section, and continued into 1946, in the southern section. It was then covered with clay, compacted, and closed.

In 1952, the school board made its request to use the land for the construction of a school.

The remaining question is old and tired: Must we have a crisis before the technical genius of American industry can be rallied to do what it has always been capable of doing — provide safe, clean working areas and a healthy environment?

It is not a simple challenge today. Nor an inexpensive one. Twenty years ago, contaminants were measured in parts per million. Today, substances are measured in parts per billion, and, in some cases, in parts per trillion.

One part per trillion is 1 drop in every 2000 tank cars.

One part per billion is 1 drop of vermouth in two 36,000-gallon tank cars of gin. That would be a very dry martini by any standard.

America has learned not to do a great many things it had been doing.

X-ray units, commonly used in shoe stores, were taken away.

Dentists now use x-rays with greater caution. But in those two instances, citizens did not tend to berate the shoe store owner or the dentist for excessive use of x-rays in the past. They seemed to realize that the shoe store owner and the dentist had heard about the alleged dangers of x-rays about the same time as everyone else. The past was the past. No one was to blame.

But the citizenry did not view industry in the same light. They began to hear stories of callous dumping of chemicals in years gone by that killed fish and contaminated waters. They heard about detergents bubbling up in creeks downstream from chemical plants; home exteriors pitted by residue floating in the air from plants nearby. People began to read about the caustic effects of some chemicals, ingested through the air they breathed and digested in the food they ate.

Horror stories multiplied by word of mouth and in the news media.

Jack Anderson, the muckraking columnist, wrote on June 14, 1980, that "Love Canal is just the tip of the iceberg — chemical wastes from 30,000 dumpsites are poisoning the ground on which thousands —

perhaps millions — of Americans have built their homes, schools, and churches."

Allied Chemicals agreed to an out-of-court settlement with more than 230 individuals and firms whose livelihoods were adversely affected by Kepone contamination in the James River. In October 1976, Allied was fined more than $13 million for contaminating the river and entered a no contest plea in response to 940 counts of pollution. Later, the fine was reduced to $5 million after the company set up the Virginia Environmental Endowment with a donation of $8 million.

The action reminded me of a popular television commercial for an automotive part: "You can pay me now [for installing the part] or pay me later [a larger amount for failing to install the part]."

Allied set up a handsome endowment rather than pay a fine. Earlier, when the Kepone tragedy was revealed, the company spent its time denying allegations, protracting the negative story, and infuriating a citizenry already enraged that the beautiful James River had been violated.

Will there come a day when industry acts first to protect the environment and to develop public support, rather than after a crisis has occurred? The information on which to act is almost always available. It simply is not heeded.

Arthur White, the vice-chairman of Yankelovich, Skelly & White, the international social research and marketing organization, often comments that both the news media and polling organizations are accused of creating bad news. "If polling firms wouldn't ask all those questions, and if newspapers and radio stations and television stations didn't report the answers, the problems would somehow all go away," he laughs. "We are the bearers of bad news."

But the problems are terribly real. And the people know they are real.

Products long thought to be safe are discovered, through modern methods of testing, to cause cancer or lung disease. It is frightening. And in the wave of concern, many false allegations also are made — and repeated, over and over — causing businesses to fail and workers to be unemployed. Separating fact from fiction is sometimes impossible.

When a crisis such as Love Canal occurs, who has the authority to act? The state or the federal government? In what way? Said the *Washington Post* editorially: "The government's long delay in testing the residents of Love Canal is questionable on more grounds than human compassion. The problem seems to have been that the agency in charge — EPA — was not equipped with either the Congressionally defined mission or the necessary money to do the basic scientific research . . . the fundamentally flawed chromosome research project that caused this...uproar [alleged harm to humans without substantive scientific foundation] is a perfect example of the kind of problem such conflicts create."

The *Post* speculated that such flawed research would not have been undertaken by the National Institute for Environmental Health Sciences, the Center for Disease Control, or any one of several agencies explicitly responsible for scientific and medical studies in the aftermath of hazardous waste accidents.

It was, in fact, the federal chromosome studies and their premature announcement that prompted the evacuation of 239 Love Canal families.

Legislators were as troubled as the citizenry. Said Sen. Daniel Moynihan: "This is the most serious development we have yet had at Love Canal. Everything the government can do must be done."

Rep. John J. LaFalce, who represents the Love Canal area, admitted the study results were "troubling and ominous." The Love Canal residents were understandably outraged and fearful, but they may in fact have been evacuated on the basis of faulty scientific data — on fear, not fact. And that is bad precedent, to say the least.

In an editorial comment on May 24, 1980, the *Washington Star* called the EPA and its deputy director "inept or insensitive in the way they feverishly announced in a special press conference . . . that preliminary results of a genetic study were 'so alarming' that it might be necessary to evacuate more than 700 families . . . even though there had been no review of the study by a panel of geneticists." Said the *Star*: "That is an incredible way to handle raw scientific data, leaks or no leaks."

In its rush to get before the television cameras, EPA had failed to notify Love Canal residents privately, in advance. Some of the residents received word as the broadcast was being aired. Others knew only what they saw and heard in the media.

Said the *Star*: "If that was not calculated to unduly alarm, indeed terrify, those residents who already have been through a nightmare of uncertainty, we can't imagine a better way to do so."

Neutral Zone? Not even basic communication and common sense were applied in this case. No one even had clear authority to act. No bona fide study was conducted by an appropriate research unit. An ecological crisis was compounded by a crisis in communication, crass and insensitive handling, and, at times, inexcusable behavior.

President Jimmy Carter declared Love Canal a disaster area. Indeed, Washington shared in the disaster and contributed to it.

Neither business nor government can begin a dialogue in the middle of a crisis. Industry and government people know this. Yet, few seek the safety of a Neutral Zone in debating issues as they emerge — long before they become legislative or legal battles. It is never enough to do the right thing; industry must also convince others whose support and understanding it needs that it is, in fact, doing the right thing.

WILL REAGAN COOL THE ARDOR FOR REFORM?

Ronald Reagan had hardly warmed the seat of the high-backed chair in the Oval Office when he made clear his intention to scale back federal efforts aimed at cleaning up hazardous wastes.

The President said he wanted to give more power to the states to decide the kinds of pollution-control and waste-disposal procedures they wish to adopt, and to diminish the role of the EPA. But Capitol Hill promised to wage a strong and continuing fight for adequate protection against pollutants and toxic wastes.

One reason the battle lines are drawn is that the so-called "superfund" bill enacted in the final days of the Carter administration did not prescribe such a strong role for the states. The bulk of the money for cleanup was intended to come from new taxes on chemical and related companies with the federal government contributing about 12 percent of the $1.6 billion fund.

There were other signs that the Reagan administration would seek to relax air pollution regulations and make it easier for oil refiners, steel producers, and other basic industries to expand and modernize their plants.

An industrial plant would not have to meet pollution-control requirements on new furnaces, mills, or other installations if the pollution from the new installation was balanced by reduced emissions elsewhere in the same plant.

In short, if the industry didn't make things worse, even if it didn't make things better, everything would be all right. The policy is in fact an extension of a late Carter initiative, called the bubble policy. The policy imagines that a plant is covered by a "bubble." The company can modernize or revise processes under the bubble as long as overall emissions decline or remain the same.

Public attitudes aren't likely to change regarding waste disposal sites, however, and the pressures from localities are certain to fuel the debate on Capitol Hill.

TAKING THE INITIATIVE

The director of occupational and environmental protection at Atlantic Richfield Company, William A. Ridpath, is convinced that industry must take the initiative in controlling pollution and have more tolerance for necessary government regulation to protect the environment. He also believes industry should persist in its efforts to eliminate unnecessary and impractical regulations.

"Some regulation is necessary," he emphasizes. "No one really knows how many Love Canals and other outrageous messes are out there waiting to be discovered. Business and government must work together to clean up the errors of the past and to develop safe and efficient waste disposal methods for the future."

Ridpath believes the so-called superfund will enable business and government to work together on the cleanup. When offending companies can be identified, Ridpath thinks they should pay the costs. The same should hold true, he thinks, when a group of companies in a common geographical area can be identified. But when the cause-effect relationship is fuzzy, he agrees that general funds should be applied.

"It's a political and technical and health problem all in one. We've got to work together it we expect to get the job done. Passions run high in places like Love Canal. That will continue. We've got to combine legal, technical, and public affairs expertise to solve today's problems and get out front of emerging problems. At ARCO, management is committed to a cooperative, results-oriented effort with government and all of industry. There is a high degree of sensitivity at ARCO, and we've organized team visits to all our operating units. No military-type, surprise white-glove inspection tactics," he emphasized. "A local manager has time to get his house in order. The team of experts from various disciplines makes a thorough review of all health and safety procedures and equipment, and analyzes how well employees are trained in their use."

Ridpath stresses that ARCO does not conduct an OSHA-type review, counting fire extinguishers and measuring the size of toilet seats. "We deal with the basic problems and human attitudes. We want to know if the facility is really prepared for a disaster. We want to see that people are well-trained; that back-up systems are working. We're concerned that managers and employees recognize potential hazards and minimize them."

The ARCO review is thorough. The team stays ten days, reports to local management orally, then prepares a written report. "There is no wish to embarrass, only to improve performance. Sure, facility managers have the normal apprehensions about a ten-day visit by a group of experts looking for ways to upgrade performance regarding safety and the environment. But they also know the team is there to help more than to judge," Ridpath said.

Every ARCO manufacturing and processing unit is reviewed every three years. Team members include representatives of personnel, legal counsel, technical services, planning, administration, safety, and other company units.

An ARCO team was in Alaska in advance of pipeline construction in an effort to anticipate and prevent problems, and to share its findings with other companies and government personnel on the scene.

"When the reports are in, the plant manager makes his or her own decisions about how the recommendations should be implemented," Ridpath emphasizes.

Ridpath reflects a more understanding and tolerant view of the government regulators than is common among industry executives. "EPA and OSHA have a terrible job," he believes. "Someone is going to raise hell with them no matter what they do. Fuzzy regulations hurt them as much as industry. They have a thankless job. Sure, we at ARCO raise hell with them, too, when we think foolish things are happening that ought to be stopped. But our job is to work with them, to cooperate with them, to stay in accord where we can, and to debate only when we must. We do that.

"The nation won't tolerate any backing off in environmental protection. No President can relax the rules. The Congress won't either. The public wants protection. No more Love Canals! They want the machinery for protection locked into the system of producing and marketing products and making the work place secure."

ARCO acts through preparedness to avoid disasters, says Ridpath and he is confident that most companies are taking similar measures.

Industry can lead. It can take the initiative. It does not need government prodding to produce quality products or design life-saving and health-saving equipment for products and plants.

But in order to take a different view of the bottom line, industry must reflect upon the reasons for the intrusion of government into the marketplace and the work place during the past twenty years.

Chapter Twenty-two

Critics in the Marketplace

Once upon a time an avid group of consumer protection advocates asked the Congress and the President of the United States to create an Agency for Consumer Protection to safeguard the buyer from fraud, faulty products — and himself.

The President — Jimmy Carter — supported the idea. He had publicly expressed his support in 1977 when he said, "Individually, the business leaders of our country are fair; they want to be sure that their own customers are protected. Unfortunately, when business leaders organize and hire lobbyists, they lose that individual commitment to their customers."

The proposed agency would have taken an initial $15 million from the taxpayers every year to protect the consumer from the shoddy performance of some businesses. The agency would have had the right to intervene in the actions of almost all other federal agencies and compel businesses to answer written interrogatories.

The character and scope of the proposed legislation, and the President's expressed notion that business executives should not organize themselves to fight proposals they considered unfair and unwise, helped to assure defeat of the proposed Agency for Consumer Protection.

Business executives were enraged by the proposal and determined to fight. They rallied their resources and won.

Astute executives then began to ask why such legislation had developed in the first place, why buyers were so unhappy with the products and services available in the marketplace.

Some of them recalled a study by Opinion Research Corporation in 1969 which showed that 7 out of 10 Americans believed that federal legislation affecting consumer products was inadequate to protect public health and safety. And 55 percent of the respondents said new laws were needed to assure consumers of full value for their money.

Twenty pieces of consumer legislation had been enacted in the late sixties. Nearly 100 bills were in the legislative hopper in 1969. Eleven House committees and nine Senate committees were then dealing with consumer bills.

It wasn't that industry didn't know about consumer unrest — nor were the warnings obscure. Industry simply failed to act in time.

If there was a single tip revealing the public mood, it was Richard Nixon's attempted appointment of a part-time White House consultant on consumer affairs. The outcry from the Hill and elsewhere was sufficiently impressive to persuade a probusiness administration to change course abruptly and appoint instead a full-time special assistant for consumer affairs — and one with a record of aggressive public leadership at the state level, Virginia Knauer of Pennsylvania. Knauer has returned to government in the Reagan administration.

The Consumer Federation of America boasted 112 consumer organizations even then and was also supported by an increasing vocal body of public concern for the safety and performance of all kinds of products.

Industry responded to some extent.

The Whirlpool Corporation devised a simpler warranty document and publicly acknowledged what consumers had long known: warranties had too often been confusing and unclear.

Federated Department Stores began to experiment with a new way to provide basic comparative information through the development of "info-tags" on appliances.

Congress acted too.

When the late Senator Philip Hart of Michigan introduced the original truth-in-packaging legislation in 1961, the posture of business was, in the words of *Fortune* magazine, "to adopt an attitude of intransigent opposition. The companies concerned denied any need for the bill, challenged the right of the federal government to interfere and attempted to kill the legislation."

This blind opposition and the harsh feelings it generated helped to keep the bill alive for six years and, as *Fortune* commented, lost for industry "a number of opportunities to come to terms with Congress on an easy compromise."

Looking back, one wonders what the fuss was all about. The bill was passed in 1966, and business and government have since cooperated in developing packaging standards for thousands of products.

At that time, business executives also began to feel the wrath of minority citizens who had been living and working outside the mainstream of opportunity, education, and affluence. They were the most likely victims of fraud, deception, and deliberate exploitation that existed on the margins of business practice.

The public did not make fine distinctions when a segment of industry misbehaved. Public outrage among both minority and majority citizens was not confined neatly to the shady or marginal operator; it lapped over onto business in general, and it fueled public willingness to accept government regulation. The shady practices of a few operators became the problem of all businesses.

Business was not organized to deal with consumer issues across the board. A. R. "Gus" Marusi, then Borden's chief executive officer, advocated the formation of a Business-Government Council, which would include members of consumer-oriented organizations, to provide continuing guidance for consumer education and information programs.

Marusi envisioned that the council could also help set priorities for voluntary action on a whole range of consumer-related problems and practices.

The council was never formed, but the White House conference on food, nutrition, and health in the late sixties did take up many of the issues Marusi had identified. Marusi served as co-chairman of a major conference body, the committee on food packaging and labeling.

Part of the unhappy change in buyer attitudes in the sixties was caused by the impersonalization of the modern marketing system. Customers missed the friendly shopkeeper who formerly greeted them by name. There was nostalgia for the psychic rewards of a personal market. Being a shopper simply wasn't the social experience it had been. There was an important loss of personal rapport, of human contact.

There was also a concomitant loss of contact for business. In the old, personal market, there was built-in feedback. The customer told the shopkeeper what he or she thought of his merchandise. The shopkeeper conveyed the force of his customer's opinion on to the salesman or jobber when he came around.

When the marketplace grew more complex and became less personal, there was often no person, no responsible human being, for a customer to talk to. Organized consumer groups stepped into the vacuum. Business rejected them although they represented business's best chance to learn what buyers were thinking so they might take voluntary action to ward off government mandates.

Consumer groups were seen as the enemy. It would take several years for business to learn to work with consumer groups and to use their resources to solve mutual problems in the marketplace.

The Grocery Manufacturers of America arranged a number of briefings on consumer complaints in cooperation with Virginia Knauer's office and consumer groups.

The National Automobile Dealers Association and the Association of Home Appliance Manufacturers also opened lines of communication with Knauer.

The National Association of Food Chains responded to the boycotting of supermarkets in 1966 by holding a series of·"consumer dialogues" nationwide to bring supermarket owners and managers into closer contact with the consuming public.

All businesses learned that complaint letters, properly handled, could be of tremendous help in alerting managers to problems with warranties, products, and services. Letters provided the best direct intelligence on what bothered customers.

Within corporate structures, a new position was born: vice president for consumer affairs. The officer would represent the voice of the buyer in the corporate decision-making process and maintain dialogue with organized consumer groups.

The consumer chief was also asked to monitor the performance of managers throughout the enterprise: the handling and evaluation of complaints, the management of services, the quality of product information and packaging.

Understandably, the new officer was not always popular, but gradually the function became an integral part of corporate life. Business was reminded that the customer makes the final judgments, that the customer controls the bottom line. And the customer began to raise the bottom line in the sixties because business was producing products previously unheard of with materials and processes that hadn't even been invented in the fifties.

More than half the products in use in 1970 were either not invented at the end of World War II or were made with entirely new materials and technologies. Technology accelerated even more in the seventies, and American industry began changing the human environment on a scale without precedent.

Business, consumer groups, government agencies, and universities are discovering that the full effects of technological change are difficult to know or predict.

Business needs to work closely with government and consumer groups to protect the marketplace and the free market system, because industry has seen seemingly benign products turn out to have dangerous side effects.

Progress is complex: the benefits of pesticides are offset by serious liabilities; the benefits of nuclear energy are offset by real dangers.

America is working at the limits of human experience in a time when no one can be absolutely sure of the consequences of new technologies and new products. An extraordinary degree of cooperation between business and government is required to keep common knowledge apace with technology.

The world is over a billion years old, and it still doesn't know how to feed itself. Technology, transportation, and communication have not yet erased pockets of poverty, starvation, and malnutrition in many parts of the world — including parts of the United States.

Man is still the victim of his own hostility, greed, and violence. World leaders are even now debating the extension of the weapons race into space. Man's humanity has not begun to keep pace with man's technological achievement, nor has man learned to apply technical progress toward peace.

Leaders in business and government, in science, and education, here and around the globe, ought to resolve, in the name of mutual self-protection and survival [if not noble purpose] to channel technology toward peaceful goals: food supplies and distribution systems, health care, the abolishment of weapons. If man tries, he may achieve these goals in another thousand years. If man fails to try, he will surely destroy himself, and on some distant day, a primitive creature will reinvent the wheel and begin the cycle all over again.

Robert B. Reich, former director of policy planning for the Federal Trade Commission, believes that American business executives had better address the immediate problems even as they ponder future goals.

The here-and-now problems, Reich contends, include the demise of the free enterprise system, because of the poor performance of American industry.

Consumers are unhappy, Reich says, because U.S. manufacturers have let them down. The rise of consumerism, he believes, is based on American industry's failure to invest properly in its own future, to reach an accommodation with government — as industry has done in Japan, Sweden, and other parts of the world.

Consumer protection is really the positive side of marketing, he says, and other nations have recognized this fact before we did.

Efforts to establish a Neutral Zone in the United State for discussion of consumer affairs have usually been initiated by government personnel and have almost always failed.

When I worked for John Gardner at the Department of Health, Education, and Welfare, he approved a recommendation that the Food & Drug Administration (FDA), an agency of HEW, invite affected industries to issue joint statements when the recall of their products was required. Should a joint statement be inappropriate, the industries would be given the opportunity to offer comment in the original story given to the news media.

No recall was to be announced until this had been done, and until the stock market had closed for the day. The arrangement was approved by the late Manuel Cohen, then chairman of the Securities and Exchange Commission, and blessed by Gardner and Dr. James Goddard, then commissioner of the FDA.

Theodore Cron, Goddard's able public affairs chief, found few takers among public relations people in industry. Implementation was weak because industry was not in the habit of heading off problems through non-legal action.

Reich reported the same problems of implementing cooperative dialogue a dozen years later. In 1979, he said the Federal Trade Commission (FTC) received a barrage of complaints from consumers concerning products produced in one particular industry. Before the FTC even launched its formal investigation, Reich sought information about industry's current measures to correct the problem and its plans for the future. "Perhaps," imagined Reich, "we could work together on a solution. I telephoned several industry executives and invited them to meet with us. Each expressed enthusiasm. But within a week, each phoned to apologize. They had talked it over with their attorneys, who advised against such exploratory meetings."

Reich asks, "How can we hope to overcome suspicion and distrust unless we are willing to talk?"

Indeed, industry can always turn to its lawyers and fight the battle in the news media. Why not establish a clear record of having tried to resolve a sticky issue through commonsense discussion before pulling out the legal-size yellow pads?

On Big Business Day in 1980, James Farmer, his resonant voice booming at a rally on Capitol Hill, called for congressional enactment of legislation that would open corporate boards to public membership and change the rules under which large corporations operate.

"For the first time in my memory," the civil rights leader said, "the consumer movement, the labor movement, and the progressive movement have come together for this day."

The day was filled with attacks on corporate activities, such as the alleged poisoning of lands surrounding Love Canal and charges that corporations, not the people, dictate national policy.

Business groups countered with their own Growth Day, issued complaints about excessive government regulations, and presented their views on the contributions of industry to society.

Ralph Nader, an organizer of Big Business Day, admonished big business to obey the laws of the land and raise its horizons. Former congresswoman and social activist Patsy Mink set up a "Corporate Hall of Shame" and exhibited complaints against eleven companies.

Big Business Day and Growth Day: well-intentioned groups of people, each talking over the shoulder of the other; neither listening very much to the other. Each feeling good about telling its own story. Each story having truth and merit. But little being done to pull the groups together for no-nonsense discussion in a quiet Neutral Zone void of media posturing and constituency politics.

When Big Business Day and Growth Day help to bring people together, they will serve a real purpose. If they simply polarize opinion for and against industry and consumer groups, they will widen the breach and perpetuate the problems in America.

The sooner the shouting stops and discussion begins, the better off we will be. Excesses on both sides make dialogue difficult.

The insurance industry came under attack by the Federal Trade Commission in the late seventies, and major carriers stopped being ambivalent about whether the federal government or the states should regulate their activities. The states got all the votes.

Partly because the attack by the FTC was heavy-handed and unfriendly, and partly because the insurance industry was self-righteous, tremendously affluent, and powerful, the issue commanded headlines for many months. The industry, in fact, speculated that a massive conspiracy to discredit state regulators might be under way to bring about public demand for federal regulation of the insurance industry.

The industry had itself complained about the problems it encountered in having to deal with myriad and conflicting regulations among the fifty states. Various consumer groups were critical of state insurance departments for not publishing detailed cost comparisons of various types of insurance: life, homeowner, automobile policies. Consumer groups said insurance carriers were not responsive to consumer expectations, had failed to strengthen state regulation, and thus had brought the federal control problem on themselves.

The industry reacted with indignation to the FTC's criticisms — and to its recommendations, supported by a few powerful members of Congress, that the federal government should regulate its activities.

Testifying on October 17, 1979, before the Senate Committee on Commerce, Science, and Transportation, Aetna's chairman John H. Filer said, "It . . . comes as somewhat of a shock to find it necessary to have to appear here today to defend this industry's record and to refute the charges recently made to this committee that we are employing deceptive practices to sell shoddy merchandise."

Filer told the committee that the business of life insurance had played an important role in the social and economic growth of the nation for more than one hundred years and had served millions of families by providing financial security. He said the industry had provided long-term financing for business and industry, and earned for itself a reputation for integrity.

He expressed grave concern that because of the FTC's attacks, policyholders might be misled into lapsing or replacing their policies.

The FTC report had said that whole life insurance is a hybrid combination of term insurance and personal savings. The FTC argued that "savings" under insurance policies yielded a "rate of return" of only 1.3 percent (in 1977) and alleged that policyholders were losing billions of dollars annually because they were uninformed. It recommended new cost disclosure requirements for the industry and sought to investigate insurance activities from top to bottom.

Calling the FTC report a "reckless misrepresentation of our business" and claiming that the FTC staff had begun its work with "fixed opinions about the nature and value of 'whole' life insurance and a determination to show that 'term' life insurance was a better buy for most people," Filer accused the FTC of having a hidden agenda to "show that the states were not properly regulating the important matter of cost disclosure and . . . to demonstrate the need for federal intervention."

His face flushed, and anger in his voice, the tall, white-haired executive told the committee that it was simple to summarize the insurance industry's position on cost disclosure: "We are in favor of it. We have supported it for more than 10 years. We have worked diligently to support state regulation to help bring it about on a more uniform basis throughout the country."

Filer explained that whole life is not partially insurance and partially savings. It is wholly insurance. "It is not designed to provide for the possibility of economic gain in return for a risked sum of money. That's an investment," he said.

"Nor is it designed to accumulate deposits of money building toward an individual or family goal so long as the depositor remains alive to make the deposits. That's a savings account.

"It is designed to provide guaranteed benefit at death, whenever death occurs, in return for a price which is expressed as a fixed periodic premium. That is what whole life is; that is what it does."

The FTC barely survived the counterattack by the insurance industry and other industries who believed that the agency had exceeded its authority and should be curtailed.

But what has been learned?

Even before the dust had settled on the FTC matter, I was engaged in a discussion with government relations people in the insurance industry about upgrading state surveillance and anticipating other attacks the industry might face in the years ahead.

The industry — and the individual carriers — analayzed all the information on hand on legislative proposals, public opinion about the industry, and emerging issues that might cause consumer concern, and began to develop new strategies.

The industry began to evaluate its communications to help prevent future unfair attacks.

The industry considered less adversarial means for relating to consumer groups and government agencies.

The industry began to reflect upon its public posture, its size and power and influence, its alleged arrogance.

But there is no hard evidence that the industry is taking a middle road, looking for Neutral Zones to nip problems in the bud and avoid legal debates.

The FTC attack has simply made some industry executives more willing and eager to fight.

But issues aren't solved by shouting. Why permit another FTC-like attack to develop? Why not engage in a continuing dialogue, even as the attorneys run up to the Hill and the regulatory agencies and report their "inside information" to hushed audiences of industry executives at trade association briefings?

The industry has everything to gain.

DEMOCRAPHICS ALTER MARKETS

The consumer issues facing all industry are broad and deep. Demographics are changing. The northeast corridor is declining; the sun belt is booming. The buying power of the post-World War II baby boom is being felt in the eighties, but the population growth has slowed to less than 1 percent per year, and the birthrate is expected to continue at a very low level.

Some 400,000 immigrants will account for almost one-fifth of the population growth in the eighties.

Illegal aliens living and working in the United States may total another 5 million persons, or more. It is impossible to know. Illegal immigration could possibly equal half the total U.S. population increase in this decade.

The median age of the countable population is rising — to thirty years of age. Census officials say it will be thirty-two years of age by 1990. The teenage population will decrease. Middle-aged and older citizens will dominate the scene, causing severe changes in marketing patterns and consumer expectations.

Two-income families, with fewer children, now represent the biggest block of buying power. Inflation is taking its toll, however, and the full impact of the Reagan cutbacks is only now being felt among the population as a whole.

What is even more difficult to calculate is the impact of high unemployment and human frustration among the least affluent members of U.S. society in the years ahead. Government support for social programs is vanishing. Industry support for social causes is limited to begin with, and its willingness to do more as the price for getting government "off its back" has not yet been tested.

Industry's view of society and consumer needs must be more sensitive to the effects of public issues and expectations on the marketplace.

Yet, industry and Washington are full of "hard noses" who would pull down almost every consumer-oriented agency built up in the sixties and seventies — the Consumer Product Safety Commission, the Federal Trade Commission, and the Office of Consumer Affairs chief among them. The Reagan thrust encourages the rollback of the Kennedy, Johnson, and Carter initiatives. One might add the Nixon initiatives as well, for the Commerce Department's Office of Minority Business Enterprise was formed under the Nixon administration (now called the Minority Business Development Agency) and is also subject to possible extinction by the Reagan budget cutters.

Says Neil Offen, president of the Direct Selling Association, "Business would be foolish if it doesn't try to work with consumers. The consumer of the eighties will be the most sophisticated ever. So marketing techniques and other dealings should be in line with this high level of sophistication."

John Robbert of the Louisiana Consumer's League says "Consumers may feel that business exaggerates the cost of legislation, and businesses may feel that consumer groups exaggerate its benefits."

Ohio State University professor Jean S. Bowers does not believe that consumers and business are going to "get married and live happily ever after." What is required, she believes, is "honesty and respect and willingness to listen" on both sides.

Consumers still want to interact with corporate decision makers, hopefully by placing consumer representatives on corporate boards. They want complaint-handling improved. They want to retain consumer legislation unless industry is willing to make public agreements assuring the same considerations to buyers. If industry meets consumer groups halfway, it may achieve more cooperation and credibility on its own, with lessening government constraints, than it has known in twenty years. If industry assumes a tough stance, it will suffer the stings of consumer anger in the eighties and hurry the return of government mandates.

Retired Prudential executive Floyd Bragg believes industry may be more defensive than cooperative in this decade. "But industry has assumed a broader perspective of its day-to-day function in society," he counsels. "The FTC attack on the insurance industry, for example, was very upsetting. It helped insurance industry leaders to perceive the way many people viewed them, and it hurt. At Prudential, and I think in most companies today, there is a social awareness factor in every decision that is made."

Bragg thinks that industry does best when it responds to local, visible problems and does something about them that people can see and relate to. "Put white lines on the streets where they are needed, provide garbage containers, paint houses — and employ local people to do the painting. We've got to take care of the problems on the street, right now, even as we do a better job of making massive social investments. We've got to personalize consumer and social action as much as possible."

Chapter Twenty-three

Finding Common Ground

In some instances, industry is demonstrating its willingness to find common ground in dealing with controversial issues.

When the private utility industry was accused of creating "acid rain" that killed lakes and caused an international confrontation with Canada, it did not churn out defensive statements. Conversely, it sent its representatives to Ottawa to gain an agreement with Canadian environmental officials to appear on public forums in the United States to discuss the phenomena with scientists and U.S. industry and government people. The Canadians agreed.

The first of these forums was held at Glens Falls, New York, on January 22, 1981, cosponsored by the Adirondack Association and the Adirondack Community College. Other key participants were the Edison Electric Institute (EEI), the association representing the private utility companies, and one of EEI's members in New York State, the Niagara Mohawk Power Corporation (NMP). NMP's community relations manager in Albany, Richard Swantek, working with the EEI and its consultants in Washington, organized the one-day workshop at the college, which is situated in the heart of the area affected by the acid rain problem.

Business and resort owners, educators, students, publishers, broadcasters, conservationists, environmentalists, scientists, government officials, and utility executives were invited. EEI paid the bills.

Including 20 students, who returned from holiday to participate, almost 200 persons attended the forum.

Niagara Mohawk videotaped the proceedings and edited the six hours of conversation and debate into a thirty-five minute presentation for showings to employees, service clubs, conservation groups, and also made a short version for local television stations.

The forum brought together Martin Rivers, director general of the Canadian Environmental Service; Kenneth Hood, an official of the Environmental Protection Agency in Washington; Vincent Schafer, an independent atmospheric scientist from Albany; and Al Courtney, an executive of Consolidated Edison in Chicago. The moderator was Harold Hughes, a semiretired professor of science from upstate New York. News media representatives from Albany, Syracuse, and Watertown attended. Every effort was made to present all sides of the controversy about the causes and effects of acid rain, a phenomena allegedly produced by natural acidity in the environment, compounded by sulphuric emissions from coal and oil-fired power plants. Especially vulnerable to criticism are those plants with tall stacks in the Ohio Valley, some of which rise 1000 feet above sea level.

The theory of acid rain is that sulphuric emissions from tall stacks are carried high into the atmosphere, moved aloft on prevailing winds for hundred of miles, and dropped as acid rain in distant places, killing lakes and fish and vegetation. Acid rain is accused by some observers as the cause of forest retardation.

Lack of definitive data at the forum did not comfort Martin Rivers, who cried for immediate action. But many of the news representatives were impressed that while a course of action was not yet clear, the industry was willing to join in public discussion with its adversaries. Indeed, industry was willing to convene the forum.

Industry's openness dispelled growing criticism that the utilities were ducking their responsibility and covering up. The news media were better informed to report on the phenomena; new research projects were initiated; current projects were expedited.

Niagara Mohawk used the video it had made as the basis for a statewide public information program, telling citizens about the problem and what NMP was doing to minimize its impact.

"We will abide by the results of collective research findings," said Jack Young, senior vice president of the Edison Electric Institute. "But we think it is only responsible and fair to all concerned that we have a clear picture of cause and effect before we modify plants and burden users with substantial rate increases."

The EEI premise did not satisfy all critics, nor did it convince skeptical media representatives. But it did serve to stabilize the situation and bring about more balanced reporting of the acid rain phenomena.

By taking the initiative, telling what it knew, reporting what it was doing, emphasizing what had to be learned, the EEI earned a measure of credibility and improved its media relations. The EEI also proved an old truth: when one seeks honest answers on public platforms, debate takes on a more civil face and manner. Answers can be found, given time.

Chapter Twenty-four

Business: Social Leader

For the first time since the Great Depression of the thirties, business — not government — is being asked to solve America's problems.

Will business accept this role? Will it succeed?

The answer to the first question is that it has little choice. Government is pulling back from the social arena as business insisted it should. Regulations restricting business practices are being relaxed. The burden is on business to perform voluntarily and effectively in meeting public needs and expectations.

The answer to the second question is, Yes, probably, but certainly not alone. To succeed, business must form strong alliances with government at all levels, with minority groups, conservationists, environmentalists, here and abroad. And it must create Neutral Zones with those groups to encourage the free exchange of ideas in advance of formal proceedings.

It can be done.

In the world arena, business must appreciate the cautions expressed by disparate men, such as Arnold Toynbee and Pope John Paul II that science and technology are dubious blessings when they fail to bring about moral resolve and public enlightenment about peaceful, harmonious ways to solve man's most basic aspirations: enough to eat, adequate shelter, and tranquility among men and women of all nations.

Business must seek to raise the level of human conduct and apply the magic of modern technology toward that purpose.

Business must accept the fact that it can make money — profits — working at peace, and producing products for peace, and promoting peace. The business of war and the materials of war assure man's self-destruction, given time. And time grows shorter with the development of each new weapon and insidious chemical.

To say that the arms race is out of control and unstoppable is to condemn the world to destruction. Is that the best man can do? Is that the best answer that technology can produce? The arms race is madness on a global scale. It proves that technology has not made us a civilized society, but simply increased our disposition for hostility and made barbarism all the more terrible.

Application of new technologies in medicine, food preservation, global communication and transportation proves conclusively that man can and does use science and technology for the betterment of mankind. But must these innovations be developed chiefly by patching up bodies torn by war and transporting and feeding troops fighting dubious battles thousands of miles from their home country?

Business has a social and moral role to conduct in world affairs.

Here in the United States, business must drop the short-range and expedient view and consider, at every turn, the long-range consequences of its plans and actions.

Policy must not be formed on the accumulation of small decisions that bubble up from a thousand special interest groups, but through the mobilization of resources in common cause.

Business has every right and reason to pursue its own narrow goals, but it must do so within the larger framework of public concerns. Business is now a social leader. It must act like one.

How does business go about being a social leader?

First, by giving much more formal attention to the design of information systems within its own structures and among its diverse constituencies focused on socioeconomic issues. Information is both a product and a function of business: gathering information is the first challenge. Interpreting information is the second. Applying and sharing that information is the third (and usually least achieved).

In planning for change — constant, rapid change — information flow becomes management's most critical responsibility in the eighties. Facing up to the consequences of what is known and forecast is the greatest need.

Given today's computerized, instrumented society, management spends a great deal of money obtaining information from myriad sources: research laboratories; pollsters; studies commissioned and observed; content analyses of newspapers; and in-depth interviews with decision makers. Information is available — so much information that its volume often tends to overwhelm and immobilize corporate personnel. Decisions are delayed, not expedited, when too much data and too little reason converge.

Management must therefore set its priorities in context with national and international conditions. Goals must be broad and clear and articulated up and down and across the corporate body. Information can then be used more effectively in channeling specific resources toward the accomplishment of those goals.

In a speech delivered November 28, 1979, ARCO's Thornton F. Bradshaw (now president of RCA) asked, "What will the corporation of the eighties look like?"

He answered, "Its foundation will remain rooted in business economics because the corporation must remain effective in an economic sense or it can be nothing at all."

Bradshaw said more: "Milton Friedman may gag on the idea, but it seems clear to me that social awareness has become a mandatory element of business conduct, one that will be increasingly visible in the corporate evolution of the eighties. . . . Second only to its economic function . . . is the role of the corporation as the source of new ideas and ways to apply them in society."

There is much that business can do voluntarily, cooperatively, effectively, and more imaginatively than any government bureau could ever conceive, much less carry out. If it does, the private enterprise system will be preserved and strengthened, and our nation will maintain its leadership. It may not have a second chance. Government will rapidly move back into the socioeconomic arena, taking over more firmly than before.

The trauma generated by the street riots of the sixties continued to traumatize industry throughout the seventies: excessive government regulation, lack of confidence in the private enterprise system, lack of respect by the public.

Government passed the laws; business carried them out.

Government was the good guy, business the bad guy.

Events, starting with Watergate, put black hats on everybody. Elections were won and lost on the basis of who was more unhappy with whom, rather than on clearly defined policies and personal preferences.

Now we passing over center ground, moving rapidly from left to right. The new President, Ronald Reagan, is seen as a friend of business. [But then, so was Dwight D. Eisenhower, under whose administration restrictive laws were passed, limiting corporate activity.]

In the eighties, industry has a marvelous opportunity to demonstrate its statesmanship and move into the social arena with the kind of enthusiasm Bill Norris, of Control Data Corporation in Minnesota, has always displayed. Norris, from the start, viewed the social needs of the nation as marketing opportunities for business and moved aggressively to solve those problems in that fashion.

No one is asking business to change its stripes and become something it is not, but only to recognize that it has become something quite different from what it was. The changes in society in less than twenty years have profoundly altered the corporate function in society.

Today, industry has the information and the technology to join with government in leading the nation — and the world — out of its pressing social and economic dilemma.

The question remains: Does it have the will and the wisdom?

Index